SOUTH APPROACH

IN THE EV-'NING BY THE

SING

COLUMBIA

94 RIVER

herman

MISSOURI

JEFFERSON CITY

ST. GEORGE'S

PREPARED
BY THE
Brush & Palette
Club
HERMANN, MO.

GENTNER HOUSE

A. HESSE

STONE HILL FARMS

94
MISSOURI RIVER
MARTHASVILLE
100
NEW HAVEN
O DUTZOW
WASHINGTON
UNION
50

ROTUNDA

AMERICANA GERMANICA

THE GERMAN SETTLEMENT SOCIETY

OF PHILADELPHIA

AND ITS COLONY

HERMANN, MISSOURI

WILLIAM G. BEK

Harrison Fellow in Germanics, University of Pennsylvania

1905-7

TRANSLATION OF GERMAN PARTS OF
THE GERMAN SETTLEMENT SOCIETY OF
PHILADELPHIA AND ITS COLONY,
HERMANN, MISSOURI

Elmer Danuser, Translator

Dorothy Heckmann Shrader, Editor

American Press, Inc.
1984

Dorothy Heckmann Shrader

vi

DEDICATION

The translation of the German sections of the Bek book and the reprinting of the entire book, is a Sesquicentennial project of Historic Hermann, Inc. It is a project of appreciation and respect for the ideals so ably laid down by our forefathers and a recognition of the service Bek made to his community when he researched the development of this unique settlement for presentation as his Doctor of Philosophy thesis in 1907.

The translator, Elmer Danuser, is a direct descendant of Daniel Oelschlaeger, who arrived at the site of the future town of Hermann, along with wife and child, on the last steamboat of the season in December, 1837.

The editor, Dorothy Heckmann Shrader, is a direct descendant of John Henry Heckmann, who, with wife and three small children, arrived at the site on the first steamboat of the following spring, 1838.

Both Danuser and Shrader were born and raised in Hermann and German was their first language.

Historic Hermann, Inc. acknowledges the significant contributions made by Kathryn Klinge, manuscript typist and Laura Graf, business manager; also Hermann artists, Alice Jacobson, Mary Streck and Anna Hesse.

Gennie Tesson, President, Historic Hermann, Inc.
Arthur Schweighauser, President, Sesquicentennial Committee
William D. Shrader, Project Chairman
Elmer Danuser, Translator
Dorothy Heckmann Shrader, Editor

WHARF STREET, 1907

PREFACE.

Interest in this subject was first excited in the writer while he was preparing a paper on the Germans in Missouri for the Germanic Association of the University of Pennsylvania in 1903-1904. Investigations at Hermann uncovered a great amount of manuscript matter there pertaining to the Settlement Society. Certain missing papers were later found in the Library of the German Society in Philadelphia. It is the purpose of this work to give as complete a picture of this rather unique undertaking of certain German Americans as the sources now extant permit.

In the preparation of this account the author has made use of the following sources:

1. The manuscript records of the society, preserved in part at Hermann, Mo., and in part at Philadelphia.

2. Correspondences between the officers of the society and its agents.

3. Communications concerning the society, written in Germany and America, preserved in *Alte und Neue Welt,* the official organ of the society.

4. The minutes of the Board of Trustees of Hermann, which body performed the functions of a city council until 1905.

5. The records of various social and educational organizations at Hermann and certain data published in the Hermann newspapers.

6. Old deeds and government certificates.

7. Personal observation of existing conditions in and around Hermann during years of residence at the place itself.

The writer wishes to express his gratitude to Professor M. D. Learned for the encouragement and most valuable assistance rendered by him in this work; to Mr. H. A. Rattermann, of Cincinnati, Ohio, for indispensable aids from his private library; to Mr. J. C. Danuser, County Surveyor of Gasconade County, Mo., and Mr. E. B. Smith, of Drexel Institute, for kind assistance in making the charts; to the town officers of Hermann, and to Miss Herzog, of the German Library of Philadelphia, for courteous treatment extended in giving free use of the Hermann manuscripts in their respective archives; to my many kind friends who in a great or small measure have promoted the progress of this work.

WILLIAM G. BEK.

Columbia, Mo., June 21, 1906.

TABLE OF CONTENTS

The German Settlement Society of Philadelphia and its Colony,
Hermann, Missouri

ILLUSTRATIONS

INTRODUCTION.

Since the beginning of the nineteenth century, there have been mighty stirrings among the Germans of the New World. The thoughtful observer will ask at once, Why did this activity not come at an earlier period? Before we enter into the treatment of our theme proper, which deals primarily and distinctively with a chapter of German progress on this continent, it will be pardonable to give, in a word, a few facts and reasons in answer to this question and thus furnish a setting, a background for our story.

It is true that as early as October 16, 1683, the "Concord," which Dr. Learned, in the work cited below, calls "the Pennsylvania German 'Mayflower'," landed the first colonists from Germany on our shore.[1] It is true that this colony found sure footing, and under the wise leadership of the renowned pioneer Franz Daniel Pastorius, soon flourished on Pennsylvania soil. It is true that thousands of Germans followed in the wake of the "Concord" during the century following this beginning.[2] It is estimated that in the year 1800 Pennsylvania alone contained 150,000 Germans.[3] It is true that from these colonies there came a people of brain and brawn, who willingly spoke and fought, lived and died for their new fatherland.

But still the query remains, Why did they not come even earlier, and why not in still greater numbers? Why were these people, who always yearn for the blue hills of the far-away, not in the van of the bold discoverers? Why did they not vie with

---

[1] cf. *The Pennsylvania German Dialect,* p. 6, M. D. Learned.

[2] *Ibid,* pp. 6-17.

[3] *Ibid,* p. 17.

other Europeans in laying claim to unknown stretches of land? If we but recall the conditions prevailing in Germany at that time, if we remember the conflict between Jesuit and Protestant fanaticism in the sixteenth century, which gradually led to the gruesome Thirty Years' War, we shall know the answer in part. Moreover, when Germany had, in a measure, recovered from these stunning blows, and was ready to play her rôle on this continent, our own country was involved in its War of Independence. Scarcely had our war come to a successful close, when Germany was forced to face the dread Corsican. Wars and unsettled political, social and religious conditions barred a large number of Germans, therefore, so long from our shores.

The Germans who had come early to this country and had participated in our Revolution were far less numerous than the representatives of some of the other European nations. When, for reasons above enumerated, immigration from Germany was checked, quite naturally amalgamation, more or less complete, took place with the nationalities more numerously represented.

The ground which Germany had lost in the eager race for American possession she could not regain. Nevertheless numerous attempts were made by certain of her princes and by various societies to establish German colonies here, even as late as the middle of the nineteenth century. Some fostered the absurd hope of founding a German state within the limits of the Union. Notable among these was the Giessner Gesellschaft, organized in 1833 at Giessen, Hessen-Darmstadt, by Friedrich Münch and Paul Follenius. In a pamphlet which these two men published, entitled: *"Aufforderung und Erklärung in Betreff einer Auswanderung im Grossen aus Deutschland in die nordamerikanischen Freistaaten,"*[4][*] they set forth the purpose of the society:

---

[*]*Invitation and Explanation in Regard to an Extensive Immigration from Germany to the North American free states.*

---

[4]*Gesammelte Schriften von Fr. Münch;"* Verlag von C. Witter, **St.** Louis, Mo., 1902, page 99.

"Die Bildung eines deutschen Staates, der natürlich ein Glied der Vereinigten Staaten werden müsste, doch mit Aufrechterhaltung einer Staatsform, welche das Fortbestehen deutscher Gesittung, deutscher Sprache sichert und ein ächtes, freies und volksthümliches Leben schafft."[5]* Unfortunately this society did not have an opportunity to carry out its well-wrought-out plans. Its history would form a curious chapter in the annals of the Germans in America. But even before they reached the land of their choice beyond the Mississippi, cholera snatched away many of them, while other disasters and discontent scattered the survivors, and defeated the purpose of their coming. We can but conjecture as to the result of such an undertaking. Its plans were well laid, and that its leaders were high-minded, trustworthy and capable men is indisputable. The names of Friedrich Münch and Paul Follenius will always sound well to a German American.

Many other societies grew up. Some had less lofty, less visionary, but more rational motives. Some came here and, for a while, existed, more or less successfully, under the rigid rules of communism. But most of them were ill-fated. The time had passed when isolated nationalities could prosper here. The American people had become too cosmopolitan in character. Such organizations were soon swallowed up and made to blend, as well as might be, with their surroundings.

The formation of a German state, which, of course, would necessarily have to be a part of the United States, but with maintenance of a political system which guarantees the perpetuation of German customs, assures the German language and creates a genuine free and national mode of living.

---

[5] *Das deutsche Element in den Ver. Staaten von Nord-Amerika.* Gustav Körner. Cincinnati, 1880. Page 300.

CHAPTER I.

A German-American Settlement Society.

1. Its Organization.

Only three years after the organization of the Giessner Gesellschaft, above mentioned, a settlement society was organized in this country, which for loftiness of aspirations and soundness of business principles stands second to none. It had its home in Philadelphia—the cradle of the German colonization in America. If such a society could be made successful, it was but fitting that it should emanate from the Pennsylvanians. Its founders were not of the old stock of Germans who had come during the seventeenth and eighteenth centuries. They were, for the most part, newcomers who still believed in "Deutschland, Deutschland über alles." The "Deutsche Gesellschaft" had existed in Philadelphia since December 26, 1764.[6] But its purpose was to aid and protect German immigrants. The organization, which we purpose to deal with, had nothing whatsoever to do with the "Deutsche Gesellschaft." It was formally organized at Philadelphia, August 27, 1836, as the "Deutsche Ansiedlungs-Gesellschaft zu Philadelphia." Its avowed purpose was to carry out those plans which the foreign societies had failed to promote, namely, the establishment of a colony in some portion of the United States, preferably in the "Far West," a colony which should be characteristically German in every particular. The promoters were prompted by several reasons. They were enthusiastic enough about their new surroundings and appreciative of its possibilities, but they missed so keenly those things so dear to the native Ger-

---

[6] *Das deutsche Element in den Ver. Staaten,* Körner, p. 23.

man. They believed that in partial isolation they could enjoy both the advantages of America and the pleasures of the Fatherland. Their kinsmen, whom they found here, they saw strangely changed, very much Americanized, and the language which some of the latter spoke was almost as unintelligible to the newcomer as the English itself. They realized that in their Americanized kinsmen they saw the future of their own children, should they remain in the same environments. To avoid this, and to find homes for themselves, at moderate cost, as well as to encourage the promotion of a laudable attempt to keep alive things German, they resolved upon the organization. They believed that, being somewhat familiar with American laws, customs and conditions, they could accomplish what others had failed to bring about.

The first written account obtainable concerning this society is recorded in an old German newspaper, *Alte und Neue Welt*—published in Philadelphia—under the date of May 7, 1836. This paper, upon resolution of the board of managers of the society, passed September 28, 1836, became the official organ of the society, and its statements may be taken as authentic. It was edited, during the period that concerns us, by J. G. Wesselhoeft, who was entrusted with offices of honor and trust by the society—secretary, and later treasurer—and of whom Gustav Körner says: "Sein ganzes Bestreben war, die Deutschen zu einigen, sie an die Erhaltung ihrer Muttersprache zu mahnen, sie politisch geachtet und stark zu machen."[7]

"All his endeavors were directed towards the unification of the Germans, to admonish them to the maintenance of their mother tongue, to make them strong and recognized in the political sphere."

---

[7] Gustav Körner, *Das deutsche Element*, p. 36.
[8] *Ibid*, p. 35.

The paper existed from 1834 to 1843. Its editors, after J. G. Wesselhoeft, were E. L. Walz, Samuel Ludvigh, and Scheele de Vere.[8] No history of the subject under discussion can be complete without the aid of this paper; its information is positively indispensable. Furthermore it is a most valuable aid in a study of German progress in general in America during the decade in which it was published. Körner comments on it as follows:[9]

"Das Erscheinen der *Alten und Neuen Welt* am 4. Januar 1834, kann als der Anfang einer neuen Zeit für die Deutschen in den Vereinigten Staaten bezeichnet werden. Das Blatt, in Royal Format, schon im zweiten Jahre in gross Royal Format, war auf gutem weissen Papier, mit vielfach geschmackvollen Lettern gedruckt, und enthielt mehr Lesestoff in seiner Wochennummer, als die zur selben Zeit in Deutschland erscheinenden Tageblätter, die Augsburger *Allgemeine Zeitung* etwa ausgenommen, in einer Woche enthielten."

"The appearance of the 'Alte und Neue Welt' on Jan. 4, 1834, may be regarded as the beginning of a new epoch for the Germans in the United States. The newspaper, already in large royal format the second year, was printed on good white paper with many artistic characters, and contained more reading material in its weekly issue than the contemporaneous daily newspapers in Germany contained in a week, with possible exception of the Augsburg 'Allgemeine Zeitung.' "

Wilhelm Weber, a contemporary of Wesselhoeft, editor of the *Anzeiger des Westens,* of St. Louis, has this to say of the *Alte und Neue Welt*:

"Sie unterstützt in Amerika, ohne grossen Unterschied Alles, was deutsch heisst, und darf sich als Patronin vieler deutscher Unternehmungen betrachten."[10]

---

[9] *Das deutsche Element,* p. 38.

[10] *Ibid,* p. 39.

"It supports in America, without much partiality, everything which is called German, and can claim credit as being the patron of many German undertakings."

The complete file of this valuable old paper, *Die Alte und Neue Welt*, exists now, so far as we have been able to ascertain, only in one collection, and this is owned by the well-known German writer, H. A. Rattermann, of Cincinnati, Ohio, to whose kindness I am indebted for the valuable information recorded there concerning my theme.

Under the date above quoted, May 7, 1836, appears this notice, which is the first reference to the society or rather a call for its organization:

"Schon seit einiger Zeit haben sich in mehreren Orten der Vereinigten Staaten Gesellschaften gebildet, um sich über die Gründung einer deutschen Stadt, welche der Mittelpunkt einer deutschen Ansiedlung in einer der westlichen Gegenden dieses Landes seyn soll, zu berathen. Eine solche Niederlassung, im Falle dieselbe von edelgesinnten, verständigen und fleissigen Menschen geschähe, würde gewiss für deutsche Sprache und Sitten, deutsche Kunst und Wissenschaft ein grosser Gewinn seyn, und würde Tausenden, welche gern das alte Vaterland verlassen wollten, wenn sie nur im fremden Lande dem schönen, gemüthlichen, deutschen Volksleben nicht entsagen müssten, einen willkommenen Zufluchtsort, eine neue Heimath darbieten. Es ist daher der Wunsch mehrerer Einwohner dieser Stadt, auch eine solche Gesellschaft zu errichten und dieselbe, wo möglich, mit den Andern zu einem grossen Ganzen zu verbinden. Es wird zu diesem Endzweck Samstag, den 21. Mai, Abends um 8 Uhr, in der "Northern Exchange in der dritten Strasse der nördlichen Freiheiten der Commissioners Hall gegenüber", eine Versammlung gehalten werden, wozu nicht allein Solche, welche geneigt sind, sich nach dem fernen Westen zu begeben, sondern Alle, welche die Aufrechthaltung und Verbreitung deutschen Volksthums wünschen freundlich eingeladen sind. Es wäre zu wünschen, dass sich Einige zu einer dem Gegenstand angemessenen Rede vorbereiten möchten."

(Signed)   „*Ein Deutscher.*"

"For some time past at various localities in the United States societies have been organized in order to discuss the founding of a German city which should be the center of a German settlement in one of the western territories of this country. Such a settlement, in the case that it were to be realized by sincere, intelligent and industrious people, would certainly be a great gain for German language and customs, for German art and science, and would offer a welcome refuge, a new home to thousands who would gladly leave the old Fatherland if only they would not have to renounce the fine comfortable German national traits in the foreign land. It is therefore the wish of some inhabitants of this city to also organize such a society and, if possible, to unite it with the others into one large unit. For this purpose there will be held a meeting on May 21, at 8:00 P.M. in the Northern Exchange on Third Street opposite the northern lot of the Commissioner's Hall, to which are invited not only those who have intentions of migrating to the distant west, but also all those who desire the maintenance and dissemination of German culture. It would be desirable that several would prepare discourses appropriate to the occasion."

(Signed) "A German"

This meeting could not be held for the reason that, as a notice of May 28th announces, the hall was, by some misunderstanding, pre-empted by another club. The second notice calls for a meeting on June 3d, to be held in the Commissioners' Hall, on North Third Street.

Just what was accomplished at this first meeting is not chronicled. From what followed soon after we may safely infer that from the very beginning the project was favorably received.

The next record which we have is dated June 10th, and consists of the minutes of a committee which evidently was appointed at the meeting on June the 3d. This committee met at the Penn Hotel, which was located in Laetetia Court, south side of Market Street, between Second and Front Streets. The hotel was owned by G. Zimmermann. All the meetings of the society were held here, and many of the committees met here. The minutes in question are prefaced thus: "Erste Sitzung des Aus-schusses, welcher sich zu Folge allgemeiner Abstimmung, zum Besuche der umfassenderen Beleuchtung des Projectes eine neue deutsche Stadt zu gründen, heute versammelte."* The committee consisted of six members: Anton Dunkelberg, Pfarrer Heinr. Ginal, Ferdinand Starck, G. Conradt, Dr. Wm. Schmoele, Xaver Jenderich. There were also two "berathende Glieder";*Ludwig Friedaus and Wilhelm Mohl.

Pfarrer Ginal was chosen as chairman, and Wilhelm Mohl as temporary secretary. The first item of business of this com-mittee appears to have been the consideration of a proposition by one Thomas Padaraque, "der Texas zur Erreichung des vor-habenden Zweckes im Vergleich der anderen vorgeschlagenen Ländern in günstiges Licht zu stellen sucht."* From this we are led to infer that as early as the meeting of June the third, or even previously, certain portions of America had been proposed as desirable for this settlement. Padaraque's proposition was set aside on the ground that Texas was politically too unsettled. (Texas had gained her independence in 1835 and was not yet a part of the United States.) Padaraque seems to have partici-pated in these early meetings for selfish ends only. In the city

---

"First session of the committee which assembled today in consequence of a general vote for the investigation of a more comprehensive illumination of the project for the founding of a new German city."

Pfarrer Heinr. Ginal "Pastor Heinr. Ginal."

"berathende Glieder" "advisory members."

Who strives to portray Texas in a favorable light towards the attainment of the proposed project as compared to other suggested territories.

directory of that time we find no such name. It is very probable that he was the representative of some land agents, who foresaw some rich profits from transactions with a society none too familiar with American ways. He appears only a few times in the records. After proposing and recommending the purchase of 104,000 acres of land in Jefferson County (the State is not given, it is to be inferred that Texas is meant), on June 20th, he is not again mentioned.

The Texas proposition by Padaraque provoked a good deal of comment. In one of these replies made by Jenderich, on June 15th, additional light is thrown on the condition as well as the aspirations of the Germans. We therefore quote a part of it here:

"Lange schon lag es in den Wünschen und in den Plänen von uns Deutschen, uns in den grossen Vereingten Staaten ein neues Deutschland, ein neues Vaterland, ein sicheres Asyl für uns, unsere Kinder und Nachkommen zu gründen und in dem Kreise unserer Familien ruhig und unabhängig, noch mehr wie wir es gewohnt waren, gesellschaftlich leben zu können.

Diese Wünsche blieben seither aus eigener Schuld unerfüllt, indem die zu diesem Behufe schon in unserem Vaterlande und hier sich schon oft und viel gebildeten Vereine sich stets wieder trennten, auseinanderliefen und sich bald da bald dort im Lande herumstreuten. Es fehlte stets an zwei wichtigen Erfordernissen: an Eintracht und — dem wichtigsten — den Mitteln. Nun scheint aber ein neuer Stern aufzugehen."

"For a long time the wishes and the plans of us Germans concerned themselves with the founding of a new Germany, a new Fatherland, a secure refuge for us, our children and their descendants in the vast United States, so that we might live peacefully and independently within the circles of our families to an even greater extent than we have been accustomed in the past.

"Up to the present these aspirations have remained unfulfilled due to our own fault. As already in our fatherland, and also here, numerous and accomplished organizations devoted to this purpose have always separated and dissolved and dispersed themselves here and there throughout the land. Two essential requirements were always lacking: harmony, and the most important one of all—the means. But now a new star appears to have risen."

Among the papers of the society is found: "Ein Entwurf zur Bildung einer Actien-Gesellschaft."* It bears no signature. From the tone that prevails in it, which sometimes savors strongly of communism, it may be safe to surmise that Pfarrer Ginal, who was mentioned above, was its author. That Ginal was, at a later period, engaged in a communistic venture is well known. It might also be mentioned that after the society had decided to pursue a non-communistic policy, Ginal entirely disappears from view.

Some things which the writer says in his "Entwurf" give us clues to certain views regarding the society.

The principal part of the paper begins with this sane statement: "Soll der Wohlstand des Ganzen dauernd begründet werden so müssen Ackerbau und Manufacturen Hand in Hand gehen."* Later the writer seeks to stimulate interest and arouse the pride of his countrymen:

"Wenn unser Zweck, ein neues teutsches Vaterland zu gründen, durch Einigkeit und brüderliche gegenseitige Unterstützung erreicht worden ist, so dürfen wir uns der tröstlichen Hoffnung überlassen, dass der Teutsche noch mit allen jenen Tugenden begabt sein mögte, wodurch unser Volk unter den andern Völkern der Welt dasteht, wie die kräftige, ehrwürdige Eiche unter den Bäumen des

---

"A plan for the formation of a share-holding society."

"If the prosperity of the entire project is to be built on a permanent basis then agriculture and manufacturing must go hand in hand."

Waldes; dass in ihrer Reinheit erhalten werden mögten jene un-
eigennützige Wohlthätigkeit, jene warme, treue Anhänglichkeit an
seine Landsleute, jene gerade Ehrlichkeit, jene Gastfreundlichkeit,
jener ausdauernde Fleiss, jene feurige Vaterlandsliebe unserer Väter
und jener begeisterte Freiheits-Sinn endlich, der in der Stunde der
Prüfung noch eben so lauter, wie vor Jahrhunderten sich bewahrend
einen ehrenvollen Antheil an dem Kampfe dieser Kolonien gegen
ihre Unterdrücker nahm."

"When our goal of founding a new German Fatherland has
been attained through harmony and mutual brotherly support,
then we may rely on the comforting hope, that the German will
still be endowed with all those virtues through which our people
stand out among all other nations of the world, like a rugged,
venerable oak among the trees of the forest; that in their purity
there may be preserved that unselfish generosity, that warm
faithful attachment to its own people, that upright honesty, that
hospitality, that persistent industriousness, that fervent love of
the Fatherland and our ancestors, and finally that inspired sense
of freedom which in the hour of trial is still as genuine as it
maintained itself centuries ago and when it played an honorable
role in the struggle of these colonies against their oppressors."

In the following we have an outcropping of the communistic
ideas above mentioned:

"Wenn einst Vernunft und Humanität und allgemeines Wohl-
wollen herschen werden, dass das Wohl jedes Einzelnen von der
Wohlfahrt Aller abhängt, und Jeder überzeugt sein wird, dass er
an seinem eigenen Glück arbeitet, indem er die Wünsche des Anderen befördert, dann wird kein politischer Fanatismus, kein After-
priester der Gerechtigkeit ihren seligen Frieden stören und Zwie-
tracht nie ihren stillen Wohnungen sich nahen."

"When once reason and humanity and universal benevolence
shall rule so that the well-being of every individual shall depend
on the prosperity of all, and everyone shall be convinced that he is
working for his own fortune by promoting the wishes of the

others, then no political fanaticism, no false apostle of justice will be able to disturb their blissful peace and disharmony will avoid their peaceful dwellings."

From a number of such and stronger hints we are justified in concluding that some of the early promoters of the settlement movement entertained views of a communistic organization. It will be remembered that no definite organization existed as yet. Everyone was invited to submit his views. From these plans the most feasible was to be selected.

It is not in the least surprising to hear such a communistic note sounded at this time. The air seems to have been full of it. Rapp and other leaders of communities had already brought their societies to the highest point of prosperity. It is safe to assert that almost every German of Philadelphia knew about these societies. From several letters addressed to the temporary officers of the society to be, we glean that the writers feared that a society "à la Rapp" was intended. Soon, however, these allusions and suggestions disappear entirely. The society settled down to work out a sound business proposition. That this task was not an easy one is quite apparent. None of the participants had any experience in such undertakings. First of all it was necessary that a large number of Germans should become interested in the plan. Then the public must be convinced, beyond a shadow of a doubt, of the sincerity of the promoters. The basis of the business must be perfectly sound. All this was understood and appreciated by the committee which was charged to find ways and means to the solution of these problems.

The method of obtaining the necessary money presented much difficulty. It was clear that a large sum of money would be needed. Just how to obtain these funds without giving some capitalists a controlling interest demanded careful reflection. The society was to be for the people and by the people. This much all desired. The plan of forming a stock company appeared to be the most practical and met the most hearty approval. Quite naturally,. however, the details of the plan could mature but slowly. A great number of resolutions were proposed and again recalled. In this manner the affair dragged along until Dr. William Schmoele suggested a sound and practical plan of raising the necessary money to place the whole project on a working basis. This proposition appears in the report the Committee on Ways and Means submitted to the main body.

The report is prefaced thus:

"Brüder nenne ich Euch alle die Ihr hier versammelt seyd, alle, welche sich der deutschen Zunge bedienen, möchte ich zu einem Familienbunde vereinigt sehn."

"I address myself to all of you here assembled as brothers, all who make use of the German language, I would like to see as one family-organization."

After a few paragraphs, rehearsing the purpose of the society, they drew up the resolutions, the essential parts of which follow:

"1.) Dass in einigen der gelesensten Zeitungen Aufforderungen an die Besitzer solcher Ländereien erlassen werden, welche im Staate Pennsylvanien, New York, Illinois, etc. von 150,000 bis 200,000 Acker besitzen, dieselben möchten zum Behufe der Unterhandlung möglichst genaue Beschreibungen und Verkaufsbedingungen einschicken, welche einlaufende Berichte uns in Stand setzen, nicht nur in den Besitz gehöriger Auswahl zu gelangen sondern auch;

2.) Drei Commisaire abzusenden, welche durch möglichst genauen Augenschein alle ortliche Verhältnisse prüfen, und darüber Rechenschaft ertheilen sollen.

3.) Zu Bestreitung dieser, als auch etwaiger weitrer unvermeidlicher Kosten, dürfte von jedem Interessirten eine Beitrags Quota von $3.00 sogleich erhoben werden. Nur auf diese Weise glauben wir den grossen wichtigen Colonisationsplan ausarbeiten zu können, welcher unter brüderlicher Eintracht ausgeführt, das Mittel wird denen sittlichen, wackeren Deutschen, welche die redliche männliche Absicht mitbringen, durch vereinigte Anstrengungen, im Schweiss ihres Angesichtes, sich Unabhängigkeit zu erringen; dann dürfte man sich belebenden Hoffnungen überlassen, dass solche Niederlassungen sich bald, von allen gleichzeitigen anderen, durch ein rasches, fröhliches Gedeihen auszeichnen werden.

Allmählich werden dann alle grossen Landstriche im nordwestlichen Theile von Pennsylvanien, wohl gar unter noch günstigeren Bedingungen, vorzüglich für deutsche Emigranten sich öffnen und in wenigen Jahren vielleicht jener nordwestliche Theil von Pennsylvanien, kürzer und charakteristisch zugleich, mit dem Namen „Deutschheim" bezeichnet werden können und zwar nicht als eine Heimath derer die aus Noth und Bedrängniss eine Heimath suchen, auch für deutsche Volksthümlichkeit und deutsche Nationaltugenden — und eine Zuflucht einst für deutsche Kunst und Litteratur. Das Guthaben des Individuums wird ihm nach seinem Verlangen, entweder in Produkten der Gesellschaft oder wo es thunlich ist, in Geldern oder auch als Capital der Gemeinde gegen Verzinsung, oder zu gemeinschaftlichen Unternehmungen, als Actie gelassen."

"1) That in several of the most widely-read newspapers invitations be addressed to the owners of such land tracts in the states of Pennsylvania, New York, Illinois, etc., as comprise from 150,000 to 200,000 acres; that the same might send us for the purpose of negotiation the most detailed descriptions and terms of sale possible; so that such incoming reports may not only afford us a suitable selection, but also

2) allow us to send three deputies who by most detailed inspection possible shall examine all local circumstances of which they shall give an account.

3) For meeting these, as well as also some probable further additional expenses, a contribution quota of $3.00 is to be immediately levied of everyone who is interested. Only in this

manner do we think we can work out that great important plan of colonization, which, carried out in brotherly harmony, will be the means by which ethical, valiant Germans possessed of honest, manly purpose may win their independence through united efforts and by the sweat of their brow; one could then entertain the invigorating hopes that such settlements would soon, before all contemporary others, distinguish themselves by a rapid cheerful growth.

Gradually then all extensive territories in the northwestern part of Pennsylvania will be opened preferably to German emigrants under even more favorable conditions, and perhaps within a few years that northwestern part of Pennsylvania may be designated shorter and characteristically as "Deutschheim" and indeed not as a home for those who seek a refuge because of poverty and persecution, but also for German national characteristics and German national virtues—and a future refuge for German art and literature. According to his wishes, the outstanding credit of the individual will be paid to him in products of the society, or when feasible, in money or also as a principal on interest of the corporate body, or in shares in common undertakings."

Resolutions 5, 6 and 7 do not interest us here, except for the suggestion relating to communism contained in them. It is therefore unnecessary to quote them here.

"8.) Wenn die Gesellschaft gross genug ist, so werden nach einiger Zeit ein oder mehrere tüchtige, mit soliden Kentnissen ausgerüsteten Schullehrer angestellt, welche zugleich für die Erwachsenen, die Theil am Unterricht nehmen wollen, bestimmt, und auch zweckmässigen Unterricht in der englischen Sprache ertheilen. Musik zur Ausbildung musikalischer Talente, und Gesangübungen für alle jungen Personen möchten mit solchem Unterricht hauptsächlich verbunden werden.

9.) Eine gesellschaftliche Bibliothek ausgewählter, nützlicher Schriften in teutscher und englischer Sprache möge ein wesentlicher Gegenstand der Berathung werden."

"8) When the society is large enough, in due time one or several competent teachers well-informed in sterling knowledge shall be employed, who shall administer to adults wishing to receive instruction, and also impart appropriate instruction in the English language. Above all, music for the development of musical talent and voice lessons for all young people should be combined with the said instruction.

9) A cooperative library of selected, useful publications in German and English languages should become an essential topic of discussion."

Thus the committee outlined the plan of procedure and offered suggestions that should induce others to become interested in the scheme.

In the *Alte und Neue Welt* of August 6th we find the first notice pointing towards the formal organization of the society. It reads thus: "Es wird der Versammlung eine Constitution zur förmlichen Organisirung der Gesellschaft zur Berathung und Abstimmung vorgelegt werden." Signed, "Der Ausschuss." *

At this meeting, which was held on August 9th, fifty persons were found willing to support the scheme as outlined. At that time the following constitution was drafted for the society. The date of its adoption remains undetermined.

Statuten der deutschen Ansiedlungs-Gesellschaft.

Da wir es für sehr vortheilhaft für uns, unsere Freunde, und die Deutschen im Allgemeinen halten, dass in irgend einem passenden Theile der Vereinigten Staaten, wo möglich Pennsylvanien, eine deutsche Ansiedlung angelegt werde, in welcher einer grossen An-

---

*"A constitution for the formal organization of the society will be presented to the meeting for discussion and a vote, Signed "The Committee."

zahl Deutscher Gelegenheit gegeben wird ihren Fleiss und ihre Kentnisse auf einer ihnen vortheilhaften und angenehmen Weise in Thätigkeit und Anwendung zu bringen: so haben wir uns zu einer Gesellschaft vereinigt, deren Zweck ist alle Erkundigungen einzuziehen, Untersuchungen anzustellen und Vorbereitungen zu treffen, welche zur Ansiedlung nothwendig und nützlich sind.

I. *Name.*

Der Name der Gesellschaft soll sein *„Deutsche Ansiedlungs-Gesellschaft."*

II. *Mitglieder.*

Jedermann kann Mitglied dieser Gesellschaft werden, welcher Interesse für die beabsichtigte deutsche Ansiedlung hegt, er mag dahin auswandern wollen oder nicht.

III. *Beiträge.*

Jedes Mitglied zahlt einen Beitrag von $3.00 in die Kasse der Gesellschaft, um die zur Ausführung ihres Planes nothwendigen Ausgaben zu bestreiten. Diese 3 Thaler und alle etwaigen anderen autorisierten Ausgaben der Glieder dieser Gesellschaft sollen denselben bei der späteren wirklichen Anlegung der Ansiedlung als Abschlagszahlung für ihre Landantheile zu gute geschrieben werden.

IV. *Beamte.*

Die Gesellschaft wählt jedesmal in ihrer ersten halbjährigen Versammlung einen Vorsitzer, zwei Stadthalter, zwei Schreiber und einen Schatzmeister. Diese Beamten sollen ihre Aemter unentgeltlich verwalten.

V. *Pflichten und Rechte der Beamten.*

(They are the same as those of any other American organization.)

VI. *Stehender Ausschuss.*

In gleicher Zeit mit den genannten Beamten soll ein stehender Ausschuss von 7 bis 8 Mitgliedern gewählt werden, welcher zwischen den Versammlungen der Gesellschaft die Geschäfte derselben führen

und in wichtigen Angelegenheiten eine ausserordentliche Versammlung der Gesellschaft berufen soll.

Der Vorsitzer, die Schreiber, die Statthalter und der Kassen-
verwalter sollen dem stehenden Ausschuss als Mitglieder beigefügt
werden.

VII. *Versammlungen.*

Die Gesellschaft soll sich alle Monate, je am ersten Samstag-
Abend desselben versammeln um den Gang der Gesellschaft fortzusetzen.

Statutes of the German Settlement Society

Since we consider it very advantageous for us, our friends
and for Germans in general that in some suitable region of the
United States, if possible Pennsylvania, a German settlement be
started, in which large numbers of Germans shall be given
opportunity to employ their industry and skills in activity and
application in a manner advantageous and pleasing to them; so
we have organized ourselves into a society whose purpose is to
collect all information, to carry out investigations and make all
preparations which are necessary and useful for colonization.

I. Name

The name of the society shall be "German Settlement
Society".

II. Membership

Everyone can become a member of this Society who harbors
an interest for the proposed German settlement, whether he
wishes to emigrate there or not.

III. Dues

Every member pays a contribution of $3.00 into the treasury

of the Society in order to cover the necessary expenditures for the execution of its plans. These 3 dollars and all other possible authorized expenditures of the members of this Society shall be accredited to them towards the payment of their land plots at the time of the future actual founding of the settlement.

IV. Officers

The Society shall elect at every first semi-annual meeting a president, two governors, two secretaries and a treasurer. These officials shall perform their duties gratis.

V. Duties and Privileges of the Officers

VI. Standing Committee

At the same time as for the aforesaid officers there shall be elected a standing committee of 7 or 8 members, which between the meetings of the Society shall conduct the business of the same, and in cases of important affairs, shall call special meetings of the Society. The president, the secretaries, the vice-presidents and the treasurer shall be members of the standing committee.

VII. Meetings

The Society shall meet the first Saturday evening of every month in order to promote the progress of the Society.

Pursuant to the call of August the ninth, a meeting was held to discuss the permanent organization. From August 9th to the 27th, seven meetings were held to discuss, alter and amend the proposed constitution. The advice of Samuel Keemle, an attorney at law, was sought, and the most prominent business men of Philadelphia were consulted regarding the practicability of the organization. The chief care was the disposition of the money of the society. The growth as to membership had been steady. No attempt was made to hasten it. The soundness of the basic principles was the chief consideration. Finally on August the 27th, the constitution of the society was formally accepted. Appended to this there appear the names of 225 signers, which we reproduce in their original order.

The following is the constitution of the permanent organization:

Verfassungsurkunde und Nebengesetze der Deutschen Ansiedlungs-Gesellschaft, gegründet zu Philadelphia am 27ten Aug. 1836.

No. 1. *Gesellschaft.*

Wir die Unterzeichneten vereinigen uns zu einer Gesellschaft für die Anlegung einer deutschen Ansiedlung, und wollen den Namen:

„Deutsche Ansiedlungs-Gesellschaft"

führen.

Zur Organisierung der Gesellschaft, zur regelmässigen Geschäftsführung und zur Sicherung der Rechte jedes einzelnen Mitgliedes sowohl als der ganzen Gesellschaft setzen wir folgende Statuten fest:

No. 2. *Actien.*

Die Gesellschaft wird auf Actien gegründet von welchen jede im ersten Tausend fünfundzwanzig und jede im zweiten Tausend dreissig Thaler kosten soll. Die Preise aller übrigen Actien sollen von dem Verwaltungsrath vorgeschlagen und von der Gesellschaft bestimmt werden.

No. 3. *Rechte der Mitglieder.*

Jeder Eigenthümer von einer oder mehreren Actien hat *eine* Stimme. Jedes Mitglied erhält für jede Actie, die es eignet, eine Stadt-lotte in einer von der Gesellschaft anzulegenden Stadt als Eigenthum. Jedoch soll jedes Mitglied, welches eine Bauerei der Gesellschaft unter den nur den Mitgliedern zu bewilligenden Vortheilen ankauft, das Recht haben, eine oder jede seiner Actien zu dem zur Zeit stattfindenden erhöhten Actien Preise, anstatt baaren Geldes, zurückzugeben. Sollte z. B. ein Mitglied vier Actien besitzen und nach zwei Jahren, wenn vielleicht der Preis der Actien auf hundert Thaler gestiegen ist, eine zum Bewohnen fertig gemachte Bauerei für die Summe von vierhundert Thalern von der Gesellschaft ankaufen, so hat er das Recht, seine vier Actien, jede zu hundert Thaler gerechnet, an Zahlungs-Statt zurück zu geben; wodurch seine Bauerei ganz abbezahlt wird.

No. 4. *Beamten.*

Die Beamten der Gesellschaft sollen bestehen in:
    einem Präsidenten,
    einem Vice-Präsidenten,
    einem Secretair,
    einem Vice-Secretair,
    einem Schatzmeister,
und ferner in:
    einem Verwaltungsrathe von neun Gliedern und einem Deputirten-Ausschusse von drei Mitgliedern.

No. 5. *Wahl der Beamten und Amtsdauer.*

Alle Beamten sollen durch Stimmen-Mehrheit in einer constitutionellen, regelmässigen Versammlung der Gesellschaft und zwar derjenigen, welche dem Auslaufe der respectiven Amtsdauer der Beamten zunächst vorher geht, gewählt werden.

Alle Beamten sollen auf ein Jahr gewählt werden.

Das Amt des Deputirten-Ausschusses soll mit der Beendigung seiner Aufträge ablaufen.

Alle diese Bestimmungen über die Amtsdauer der Beamten, mit Ausnahme des Deputirten-Ausschusses, sollen erst in Kraft treten nachdem tausend Actien von der Gesellschaft verkauft sind. Bis dahin sollen alle Beamten, mit Ausnahme der Deputirten, blos provisorisch gewählt werden.

No. 6. *Pflichten der Beamten.*

I. Der Präsident soll
    1.) in den Versammlungen der Gesellschaft den Vorsitz führen und bei Stimmen-Gleichheit die entscheidende Stimme haben.

2.) Er soll dafür sorgen, dass Ordnung und Ruhe erhalten und Beschlüsse der Gesellschaft genau und pünktlich vollzogen werden.

3.) Er soll, gemäss Par. 9, alle Rechnungen und Anweisungen auf die Kasse der Gesellschaft zugleich mit dem Verwaltungsrathe unterzeichnen.

4.) Er soll alle 6 Monate Bericht erstatten über die in dieser Zeit gemachten Fortschritte der Gesellschaft.

II. Der Vicepräsident soll in Abwesenheit des Präsidenten das Amt desselben verwalten.

III. Der Sekretair soll

1.) Das Protokoll der Verhandlungen der Gesellschaft führen.

2.) Er soll die Correspondenz der Gesellschaft besorgen.

3.) Er soll die Constitution und sonstigen Documente der Gesellschaft aufbewahren.

4.) Er soll eine Woche vor dem Ende jedes halben Jahres einen schriftlichen Bericht über die Verwaltung seines Amtes in dem letztverflossenen halben Jahre an den Präsidenten abliefern.

5.) Er soll, nach Par. 9, alle Rechnungen und Anweisungen auf die Kasse der Gesellschaft mit unterschreiben.

IV. Der Vicesecretair soll in Abwesenheit des Secretairs die Stelle desselben vertreten, ihm auch sonst bei überhäuften Geschäften Hülfe leisten.

V. Der Schatzmeister soll

1.) alle Gelder der Gesellschaft in Empfang nehmen und darüber quittiren.

2.) Er soll sobald er eine Summe von 100 Thalern eingenommen hat, dieselbe in einer noch näher zu bestimmenden Bank binnen 24 Stunden niederlegen.

3.) Er soll alle Rechnungen, welche vom Präsidenten, Secretair und Verwaltungsrathe unterschrieben sind, durch Anweisungen auf die Kasse, welche nach Par. 9, von ihm selbst, dem Präsidenten, Secretair und dem Verwaltungsrathe unterschrieben sind, bezahlen.

4.) Er soll über Einnahme und Ausgabe genau Buch führen und jedes Mal auf Verlangen des Verwaltungsrathes, nach zweitägiger Anzeige, diesem die Bücher zur Einsicht vorlegen.

5.) Er soll eine Woche vor dem Ende jedes halben Jahres einen schriftlichen Bericht über den Zustand der Kasse an den Präsidenten ablegen.

Er soll eine verhältnissmässige Bürgschaft leisten.

VI. Der Verwaltungsrath soll:

1.) Die Geschäfte der Gesellschaft zwischen den Versammlungen derselben versehen und alle diejenigen Anordnungen treffen, welche das wohl der Gesellschaft und die Erreichung ihrer Zwecke erfordern. Zu allen seinen Beschlüssen und Anordnungen soll jedoch die Beistimmung des Präsidenten der Gesellschaft notwendig sein.

2.) Er soll nach Par. 9 das Vermögen der Gesellschaft vertreten und alle Rechnungen und Anweisungen auf die Kasse der Gesellschaft unterschreiben.

3.) Er soll in jeder regelmässigen Versammlung der Gesellschaft Bericht erstatten über Alles, was er seit der letzt vorhergegangenen Versammlung angeordnet und geleistet hat.

VII. Der Deputirten-Ausschuss soll die ihm vom Verwaltungsrathe angewiesenen Staaten und Gebiete von Nord-America bereisen und untersuchen ob und wie weit derselbe oder welche Theile derselben zu einer deutschen Ansiedlung geeignet sind.

Der Ausschuss soll zu diesem Zwecke ein Tagebuch führen über Resultate seiner Untersuchungen und während seiner Reise von Zeit zu Zeit einen Auszug daraus an den Verwaltungsrath schicken, bei seiner Zurückkunft aber das Ganze der Versammlung vorlegen.

Der Ausschuss soll ferner, so weit es ihm möglich ist, über diejenigen Landstriche, die ihm zu einer deutschen Ansiedlung am tauglichsten scheinen, provisorische Kauf-Contracte unter den möglichst vortheilhaften Bedingungen abzuschliessen suchen, so dass die Gesellschaft nachher bei der Auswahl eines Landstriches die Kauf-Contracte nach Gutbefinden genehmigen oder verwerfen kann.

No. 7. *Versammlungen.*

Jeden Monat soll eine regelmässige Versammlung der Gesellschaft gehalten werden. So oft bei einer Versammlung der Gesellschaft fünfzig Mitglieder persönlich anwesend sind, soll die Versammlung fähig sein, Geschäfte zu thun.

Nur Mitglieder der Gesellschaft können Stellvertreter für abwesende Mitglieder sein. Kein Mitglied darf mehr als fünf Stimmen repräsentiren, seine eigene eingeschlossen. Sollte daher Jemand von mehr als vier anderen Gliedern zum Stellvertreter ernannt sein, so muss er alle übrigen Stimmen auf anwesende Mitglieder vertheilen. Extra-Versammlungen sollen gehalten und durch den Präsidenten berufen werden, so oft es dieser für nöthig hält oder der

Verwaltungsrath oder fünfundzwanzig Mitglieder der Gesellschaft ihn dazu auffordern.

No. 8. *Verwertung der Gelder.*

Die Gelder der Gesellschaft sollen zum Ankaufe des Landes, zur Urbarmachung und Einrichtung von Bauereien und Dorfschaften, zur Abklärung, und Auslegung von einer oder mehreren Städten, je nachdem die Mittel der Gesellschaft reichen; ferner zu allen solchen Anlagen und Unternehmungen welche das Aufblühen der Gesellschaft befördern: zu Fabriken, Manufacturen, Schulen etc., verwendet werden. Alle Bestimmungen zur Verwendung der Gelder sollen von der Gesellschaft oder vom Verwaltungsrathe gemacht werden. Sobald jedoch im letztern Falle eine Unternehmung über tausend Thaler kostet, soll die Einwilligung einer constitutionsmässigen Versammlung der Gesellschaft unerlässlich sein.

No. 9. *Sicherstellung der Kasse.*

Zur Sicherstellung der Kasse und des Vermögens sollen die neun Verwaltungsräthe als Trusties die Kasse und das Vermögen der Gesellschaft repräsentieren, zu welchem Zwecke ein Trusties-Contract (deed or declaration of trust) durch einen von der Gesellschaft zu erwählenden Ausschuss mit den Verwaltungsräthen abgeschlossen werden soll.

In diesem Contracte soll bestimmt werden, dass alle Einnahmen, sobald sie eine Summe von hundert Thalern betragen, binnen 24 Stunden in einer näher zu bestimmenden Bank sollen niedergelegt werden und dass keine Gelder aus dieser Bank sollen herausgenommen werden können, wenn nicht eine Anweisung zu diesem Zwecke von dem Präsidenten, oder in dessen Abwesenheit vom Vicepräsidenten, von dem Secretaire, von dem Schatzmeister und der Mehrheit des Verwaltungsrathes unterzeichnet worden ist. Ferner sollen in dem genannten Trusties-Contracte, oder (deed or declaration of trust), alle sonstigen Provisionen gemacht werden, welche der zur Abschliessung desselben erwählte Ausschuss zur Sicherung der Gesellschaft für nötig erachtet.

No. 10. *Veränderung dieser Constitution.*

Eine Veränderung dieser Constitution kann nur durch Uebereinstimmung von zwei Dritttheilen sämmtlicher Mitglieder oder ihrer Stellvertreter gemacht werden. Ein Vorschlag zu einer Aenderung kann in jeder constitutionsmässigen Versammlung gemacht werden, ob ein solcher Vorschlag zur Abstimmung kommen soll oder nicht. Im Bejahungsfalle soll darauf der Vorschlag wenigstens einen Monat vor der Abstimmung öffentlich bekannt gemacht werden.

Die Gesellschaft kann durch ein Quorum der bezeichneten Mitglieder Nebengesetze oder Regeln machen, welche jedoch dieser Constitution nicht entgegen sein dürfen, und diese sind stets in das Protokoll der Gesellschaft einzutragen.

No. 11.

Die Gesellschaft soll, sobald als es thunlich incorporirt werden.

Julius Leupold, Präsident.
Wilhelm Schmœle, Vice-Präsident.
J. G. Wesselhoeft, Secretair.
Fr. Lüdeking, Vice-Secretair.
C. G. Ritter
F. L. C. Gebhard
W. H. Leupold
D. W. Wohlein
Adam Schmidt
Ferdinand Heirtz
Johann Conrad Viereck
B. Schmitz
John Bock
F. W. L. Kiderlen
Georg Riefenstahl
Reinhold Koepf
Charles L. Eickhoff
Friedrich Kerschenbach
Jacob Summ
Friedrich Leonhard
Matthäus Krautter
Conrad Ferdinand Kühne
Johann Klumpp
Georg Bader
Adolph Hoehling
Ferdinand Laackmann
Heinrich Christian Schrader
Mathias Birck
Ludwig Sigrist
Gustav Stübgen

Jacob Rommel
Peter Lion
Wilhelm Lemberger
Johann Wittmann
Thadäus Bruder
Ernst Haas
Johann Heinrich Manerke
Georg Schotten
Friederich Hoffmeister
Christ. August Langguth
Christoph Metzger
Joseph Roller
Wilhelm Müller
John Heinr. Schwacke
Adam Siedler
Johannes Hirschmann
Johann Gronhardt
Friedrich Gemf
Johann Oestreicher
Heinrich Köpken
Peter Rau
Friedrich Hoffmeister
Bernhard Schmitz
Joseph Schindler
Wilhelm Tilg
Joseph Nock
Johann Harig
F. W. Wilcke
Sigmund Rutschmann
Friedrich Georg Schaeffer
C. Valetin Presser

Charles Pommer
Jacob Mersinger
Erhard Staffhorst
M. J. Hütz
Jacob Knoll
Michael A. Kerchner
Heinrich Arnsfeld
F. W. C. Seelhorst
Adam Sengenberger
Caspar Knodel
William Henning
Gottfried Krauss
Johann Mayer
Georg Benninghoff
Jacob Ratheusen
Wilhelm Betz
Adam Maag
C. W. Gronau
C. F. Stottmeyer
Ludwig Friedrich Niekerke
Conrad Roos
Wilhelm Kielmann
Bernard Martin Meyer
Johann F. Albrecht
Carl M. Grahn
Joseph Bodenhœfer
Louis Ebstadt
Josef Schmidt
J. Heinrich Bühler
Martin Stephan
Alphonse Libermann
Andreas Dold
Albert Combernass
Herman Schweizer
Louis Gölitz
Gabriel Kowitzky Circovich
Martin Rosienkiewicz
L. A. Wollenweber
Anna Maria Heiner
Wm. Gellert
P. W. Schmidt
Jno. Friedr. Schmidt
Johs. Theiss

Konrad Liebach
Christoph Valet
Lewis Austermell
Hermann Knop
Heinrich Bachmann
Georg Fischer
C. L. Mayer
Philipp Pfister
H. Schmœle
Michael Rohé
Christian Tiemann
Heinrich Gerker
H. Wm. Echternacht
Fr. Leupold
Christ. Hasenpatt
Johann Heinrich Lahring
Georg Ruff
John G. Finn
George Duhring, Dr. M.
Joseph Hiller
Philipp Leidorff
Joseph Engelbert
Hermann Schniedewindt
Franz Arnold
Gottlob Laib
Eduard Koch
Herm. Curtius
Friedrich Viereck
F. G. Schreiber
Franke Franksen
Carl Pommer
Wilhelm F. Pommer
Heinrich Pommer
Martin Petri
Bernhard Schweickert
Christian Klein
Johann Horn
Conrad Wagner
Catherine Viereck
Johann Lemberger
Jacob Schiefer
L. Sommerhalder
F. H. Kühne

Ferd. Riemann
Wilhelm Schubert
Johann Georg Zoller
Johann Georg Zipperer
Karl Becker
F. v. Schrader
Johannes Mayer
Georg Herwig
J. P. Abker
Daniel Heinemann
Friedrich Rebhun
C. F. Heitzmann
Fritz Leibrock
P. Jacob Burkhard
Henry Koch
G. A. Fuss
Friedrich Triebler
Wilhelm Mohl
Friedrich Kühnholz
Georg Schock
Gottfried Ackermann
Christoph Schäfer
Adam Valet
Johannes Knoll
Joseph Baumann
Jacob Hagel
Michael Hagel
Michael Rothrang
Wilhelm Leichmann
Ulrich Stirnemann
Abraham Jenny
Johann Georg Zeller
August Schrader
Daniel Haberstock
Kaspar Müller
H. Diedrichs
Fred. Gentner
G. H. Mecke
Georg Jacob Schneider

David Wittmann
Eduard Seltzer
Joseph Brunner
August Ziegler
Heinrich Gentner
Friedrich Gentner
Georg Supper
Georg Bader
Heinrich Roemer
Friedrich Kaiser
Christian Kraug
Johann Gräbner
Carl Dithmer
F. Gebhard
Leonhard Jung
August Horn
Gottfried Krauss
Carl Metzger
John Hoffmann
Leopold Eckhard
Heinrich Rietze
Joh. Georg Beiszwanger
Marie Elizabeth Viereck
Friedrich Gottlieb
Louis Reiger
Jacob Heinlein
Franz Langendörfer
G. F. Bayer
Friedrich Bok
Adam Martin
John J. Schock
Franz Schellenberg
Fr. Leupold
Heinrich Werklœ
Julius Harnisch
G. H. Mittnacht
F. G. Kaltner
Eleazar Demetrio Artemiews
Charles Libeau

Constitution and By-laws of the German Settlement Society, founded in Philadelphia on August 27th, 1836.

No. 1 The Society

We the undersigned organize ourselves into a Society for the founding of a German settlement and wish to assume the name of "German Settlement Society." For the organization of the Society, for regular conduct of business and the assurance of the rights of every individual member as well as of the organization in its entirety, we establish the following statutes:

No. 2 Shares

The Society shall be founded on shares of which each of the first thousand shall cost $25 and each of the second thousand $30. The value of all other shares shall be recommended by the Board of Managers and determined by the Society.

No. 3 Privileges of the Members

Every owner of one or more share has *one* vote. Every member receives for each share which he owns one city-lot as his property in the city which is to be founded by the Society. Nevertheless every member who buys a building of the Society under the privileges conceded only to the members shall have the right to redeem one or all of his shares at the current increased share value, rather than paying in cash. Should, e.g., a member possess 4 shares, and after 2 years if, say, the value of a share has increased to $100.00 and he wishes to buy a building which has been made habitable for the sum of $400.00 from the Society, then he has the privilege of turning in his 4 shares, each reckoned at $100.00, as payment, whereby his building will be paid in full.

No. 4 Officers

The officers of the Society shall consist of: A president, a vice-president, a secretary, an assistant-secretary, a treasurer, and further of a Board of Managers consisting of 9 members and a committee of Deputies of 3 members.

No. 5 Election of Officers and Term of Office

All officers shall be elected through majority vote in a constitutional regular assembly of the Society, and that the election be held immediately preceding the termination of the respective terms of the officers. All officers shall be elected for one year.

The office of the Committee of Deputies shall terminate with the completion of its assignment.

All these designations concerning the terms of the officers, with the exception of the Committee of Deputies, shall first take effect only after a thousand shares of the Society have been sold. Until then all officers, with the exception of the Committee of Deputies, shall be elected provisionally.

No. 6 Duties of the Officers

I. The President shall

1) serve as chairman in the meetings of the Society and in case of a tie-vote, cast the deciding vote.

2) He shall take measures to ensure order and quiet and have the decisions of the Society enacted carefully and punctually.

3) He shall, in accordance with Par. 9, sign all bills and assignments to the treasury of the Society, as also the Board of Managers.

4) He shall submit a report every 6 months on the progress of the Society made during this time.

II. The Vice-President shall, in the absence of the President, carry out the duties of the latter.

III. The Secretary shall
1) Keep the minutes of the proceedings of the Society.
2) He shall take care of the correspondence of the Society.
3) He shall preserve the Constitution and other documents of the Society.
4) He shall present to the President one week before the termination of each half-year a written report of the management of his office.
5) He shall, in accordance with Par. 9, also affix his signature to all bills and assignments on the treasury of the Society.

IV. The Assistant-Secretary shall, in the absence of the Secretary, perform the duties of the latter, as well as rendering him assistance at other times when duties become unusually heavy.

V. The Treasurer shall
1) take charge of all monies received by the Society and give an account of them.
2) He shall, upon receiving the sum of $100.00, deposit the same within 24 hours in a bank to be designated later.
3) He shall pay all bills which have been authorized by the President, the Secretary, and the Board of Managers by checks upon the treasury, which in accordance with Par. 9 have been approved by the President, the Secretary, and the Board of Managers.
4) He shall keep exact account of income and expense, and upon demand of the Board of Managers, following a two-days' notice, submit his books to the Board for inspection.
5) He shall submit a written report on the financial standing of the treasury to the President one week before the termination of each half-year. He shall furnish an appropriate bond.

VI. The Executive Committee shall

1) Conduct the business of the Society between the meetings of the same, and make all such arrangements which promote the well-being of the Society and the attainment of its purposes. The approval of the President of the Society shall however be necessary for all its decisions and acts.

2) It shall, according to Par. 9, represent the property of the Society and sign all bills and assignments on the treasury.

3) In every regular meeting of the Society it shall submit a report of everything which it has arranged and performed since the last preceding meeting.

VIII. The Committee of Deputies shall visit and examine the states and regions of North America assigned to them by the Board of Managers to ascertain whether and to what extent and which parts of them are suitable for a German settlement.

To this end the Committee shall keep a daily record of the results of its investigations, and during its journeys from time to time send to the Board of Managers a report thereof; but at its return shall present the entire report to the assembly.

Furthermore, the Committee shall, in so far as it is possible strive to procure the most advantageous provisional contracts of purchase under the best conditions of those territories which it deems best suited for a German settlement so that the Society afterwards in its choice of a territory can at its discretion accept or reject the contracts of purchase.

No. 7 Assemblies

A regular meeting of the Society shall be held every month. Whenever fifty members are present in person, the assembly can legally conduct business.

Only members of the Society can be proxies for absent members. No member may represent more than five votes, his own included. If therefore someone is named as a proxy by more than four other members, then he must transfer all other votes to other present members. Special assemblies shall be held and called by the President as often as he deems this necessary, or if the Board of Managers and 25 members of the Society order it.

No. 8 Conversion of the Monies

The monies of the Society shall be used for purchase of land, for clearing and erection of buildings and villages, for making land suitable for cultivation, and for the laying out of one or several cities, depending on the resources of the Society; furthermore, for all such projects and undertakings which promote the growth of the Society: for factories, industries, schools, etc. All decisions for the use of the money shall be made by the Society or by the Board of Managers. In the case of the latter, however, if an undertaking shall cost more than one thousand dollars, then the approval of an assembly of the Society in accordance with the Constitution shall be necessary.

No. 9 Security of the Treasury

For the security of the treasury and the property the nine members of the Board of Managers shall represent the treasury and the property of the Society as trustees, for which purpose a deed or declaration of trust shall be made by a Committee to be elected by the Society with the Executive Committee.

In this contract it shall be stated that all income, as soon as it amounts to a sum of $100.00, shall be deposited within 24 hours in a bank to be designated later, and that no funds can be withdrawn from this bank without an order for this purpose by the President, or in his absence by the Vice-President, by the Secretary, by the

Treasurer, and signed by a majority of the Board of Managers. Furthermore, all other provisions shall be entered into the declaration of trust which the Committee elected for the execution of the same deems necessary for the security of the Society.

No. 10 Amendment of this Constitution

An amendment of this Constitution can only be made by the approval of two-thirds of the entire membership or their proxies. A motion for an amendment can be made in any constitutional assembly, whether or not such a motion comes to a vote. In case the motion is approved, the proposal shall be publicized for at least one month before the vote.

The Society can make by-laws or regulations by a quorum of the registered members, which however may not conflict with this Constitution, and these must always be entered in the minutes of the Society.

No. 11 The Society Shall Be Incorporated As Soon As Is Feasible

On the same evening that the constitution was adopted and signed, the newly created offices were filled. The following were the first officers:

Präsident, Julius Leupold;
Vicepräsident, Dr. Wm. Schmoele;
Secretair, J. G. Wesselhoeft;
Vicesecretair, F. Lüdeking;
Schatzmeister, Dr. Moehring;
Deputirte: C. v. Ferentheil, C. G. Ritter, F. L. C. Gebhard.
Verwaltungsrath: J. C. Viereck, W. Feuring, Adam Schmidt, D. W. Wohlein, B. Schmitz, W. H. Leupold, J. Bock, F. Stark, F. W. L. Kiderlen.

In passing, it should be noted that for some unexplained reason Dr. Moehring did not accept the office of treasurer.

On September 26, Adam Schmidt, then a member of the Board of Managers, was chosen treasurer. The vacancy in the Board of Managers was filled by the election of C. Pommer.

The meeting of August 27th was certainly a memorable one in the history of the society. Enthusiasm for the new cause was running high. One feels something of the feverish nature even in the records of the meeting. Letters of inquiry and commendation seem to have arrived from various parts of the country. Everyone felt certain of the most glorious success. Before retiring from the position of temporary chairman, Dr. Wm. Schmoele delivered a fiery address. He gives a brief résumé of the struggles of the organization. Then he speaks of the future:

"Ja, wahrlich, deutsche Brüder, wenn je etwas Grosses und Glänzendes für die deutsche Nation in diesen Freiheitslanden erstehen soll, so muss diese Gesellschaft es werden. Sie trägt den Charakter des Grossartigen an sich. Sie ist eine reife Geburt des jetzigen ereignissreichen Zeitgeistes, — durch sie ist an's Licht getreten, was in allen deutschen Gemüthern verborgen lebte und dunkel gefühlt ward.

Einigung der Deutschen in Nordamerika, und dadurch die Begründung eines neuen deutschen Vaterlandes — das ist die hohe Aufgabe unserer Ansiedlungs-Gesellschaft! Danach muss, danach soll sie streben aus allen ihren Kräften und mit allen ihren Mitteln. In der Ausführung des ganzen grossen Planes muss Jeder die Begründung seines eigenen Glückes finden. Dann kann, dann muss, dann wird die Sache gedeihen zum Ruhme und zum Wohle der grossen deutschen Nation in Amerika's freiem Schosse."[11]

"Yes, truly, German brethren, if ever something great and splendid shall arise for the German nation in this land of freedom, then this Society must be it. It possesses the characteristic of

---

[11] *Alte und Neue Welt*, Sept. 3, 1836. This paper will hereafter be referred to as A. & N. W.

magnificence. It is the ripe fruit of the present momentous spirit of the age—through it has been brought to the light that which had been lying hidden in all German souls and which had been darkly experienced.

Union of the Germans in North America, and thereby the founding of a new German Fatherland—that is the noble task of our Settlement Society! For this it must, for this it shall strive with all its might and with all its means.

In the fulfillment of the entire great plan each individual must find the establishment of his own fortune. Then the venture can, and must, and shall flourish to the glory and the welfare of the great German nation in America's bosom of freedom."

At an extra session of the newly elected officers, two days after the new constitution took effect, it was decided to take steps to make the movement general in the United States. The minutes record this resolution:

"Der Verwaltungsrath der deutschen Ansiedlungs-Gesellschaft ersucht diejenigen, welche Antheil an dieser Gesellschaft nehmen wollen, und namentlich die deutschen Einwohner Baltimore's, New York's, Pittsburg's etc. Zweig-Vereine zu gründen, die im Geiste unserer Constitution handeln, die Geschäfte dort thun, und die Theilnahme an dieser Gesellschaft dem Publikum erleichtern, die Gelder empfangen, der Central-Gesellschaft überliefern und dafür Actien vom Verwaltungsrathe erhalten."

"The board of Managers of the German Settlement Society requests those who wish to participate in this Society, and particularly the German inhabitants of Baltimore, New York, Pittsburgh, etc. to organize branch societies, which shall function in the spirit of our Constitution, shall carry on business there, and facilitate the participation of the public in this Society, receive monies and transfer these to the Central Society to receive shares from the Board of Managers therefor."

The growth was indeed most encouraging. Less than two weeks after formal organization 350 shares had been sold. Under the date of September 10th the secretary (who was also the editor of the official organ of the society) comments thus:

"Wir freuen uns unsern Lesern mittheilen zu können, dass diese Gesellschaft einen solchen Fortgang nimmt, der unsere Erwartungen weit übertrifft. . . . Wir hoffen und wünschen, dass sie in diesem Geiste fortfahren und ein Bruder den andern auffordern möge, zu diesem grossen Zwecke nach Kräften beizutragen. . . . Mit Recht dürfen wir erwarten, dass unsere auswärtigen Brüder Zweig-Vereine gründen und alles aufbieten werden zu diesem schönen Zwecke nach Kräften mitzuwirken."

"We are pleased to inform our readers that this Society is making such progress as to far exceed our expectations. We hope and desire that it may continue in this spirit and that one brother may exhort the other to contribute to this great cause to the extent of his ability. We may justly expect that our brethren living in other places will organize Branch-Societies and offer their best services to participate in this splendid undertaking to the best of their ability."

GERMAN VILLAGE, 19th CENTURY

Share Book No.

Running No.

18

Issued to

Received the above
Certificate

The

German Settlement Society.

Hermann.

Share Book No. *Running No.*

This is to Certify, that for value received of

is entitled to One Share of the Lands and Tenements of

The German Settlement Society, which entitles him to Lot No. ▓ in the Plan of the City of

HERMANN of said Settlement, transferable on the Books of the Society on surrender of this Certificate

by the said in person or by Attorney, in conformity with the Constitution,

By-Laws, Rules and Regulations of said Society now adopted or which may hereafter be adopted

Witness the Seal of the said Society and the Signature of its President.

this day of **A.D. 18**

President.

Trustees.

Secretary

Attest,

(Actienbuch No.) (Laufende No.)

Uebersetzung.

Die deutsche Ansiedelungs-Gesellschaft.

Es wird hiermit bescheinigt, daß N N für geleistete Zahlung zu einer Actie der „Deutschen Ansiedelungs-Gesellschaft" mit
ihren Ansprüchen auf dieselbe, und namentlich zu Lotte No N. N. im Plane der Stadt **Hermann** in der Ansiedelung, berechtigt
ist. Diese Actie kann in den Büchern der Gesellschaft übertragen werden, entweder bei persönlicher Ueberlieferung dieses Scheins
oder durch gerichtliche Vollmacht, nach den Constitution, den Gesetzen und Regeln der Gesellschaft, welche angenommen sind oder
späterhin noch angenommen werden mögen.
Zur Beglaubigung des Siegel der Gesellschaft und die Unterschrift ihres Präsidenten x. x.

Actienbuch No.
Laufende No.

Ausgestellt an

Empfing die obige Bescheinigung

A SHAREHOLDER'S CERTIFICATE.

2. Various Opinions Regarding the Society.

That the movement caused a great stir among the Germans in all sections of this country, as well as in Europe, is attested by the great number of press notices it received. Not all of these comments were favorable—far from it. Nevertheless they prove that the public was interested.

Immediately after the organization of the society the *Allgemeine Zeitung* of New York comments on the wisdom and far-sightedness of the organization. It approves most heartily the scheme of forming a stock company for this laudable enterprise. It recommends it warmly to all Germans. The editor enumerates its advantages in these enthusiastic terms:

"Betrachten wir die Vereinigten Staaten in ihrem jetzigen Aufblühen, in dem beispiellosen Fortschreiten aller ihrer volksthümlichen Unternehmungen, und erwägen wir dabei, wie viel Antheil daran die Deutschen haben und wie wenig sie im Grunde davon geniessen, wenn wir uns den Deutschen als *Deutschen* denken; ziehen wir ferner in Betracht, wie das Bestreben der Deutschen nach und nach erwacht, um sich ihre Rechte als Bürger zu sichern, um ihre herrliche Sprache zu erhalten und da, wo die Mehrzahl Deutsche sind, vor den Gerichtshöfen geltend zu machen, so müssen wir bei der Masse der hier zu Lande lebenden Deutschen und bei dem steten Drange der Einwanderungen, eine Gesellschaft, wie die obige ist, als eine sehr erfreuliche, als eine höchst zeitgemässe Erscheinung betrachten. Sie giebt den hier Wohnenden eine Gelegenheit, sich näher zu verbinden, die Elemente des deutschen Lebens zu unterstützen und zu verbreiten, wissenschaftliches Bestreben zu fördern, jedes Grosse und Schöne, so weit es hier anwendbar ist, vom Vaterlande hierher zu verpflanzen, dem deutschen Einwanderer gleich bei seinem Eintritt in die Vereinigten Staaten eine Heimath anzuweisen, wo er sich heimischer, als alleinstehend, fühlt, und wo ihm bei Fleiss und Sparsamkeit ein Wirkungskreis angewiesen wird, in welchem er sich bald eine Unabhängigkeit zu erwerben vermag, welches, muss er erst lange darnach suchen, ihm oft schwer fällt. Wir kennen den Stand der deutschen Einwanderer, wir wissen, welche Kämpfe ihrer oft warten und wie Viele im Kampfe erliegen. Anders wird es sein, wenn er weiss, dass er einer Colonie zueilt, wo er befreundete Seelen findet, welche ihn mit Rath und That unterstützen können."[12]

---

[12] *A. und N. W.,* of Sept. 17, 1836.

"When we consider the United States in its present expansion, in its unrivaled progress in all its national undertakings and thereby contemplate the important role which the Germans play in this and how little they in fact profit thereby, if we think of us Germans as *Germans*, if we further take into consideration, how the striving of the Germans gradually awakens in order to safeguard their rights as citizens, in order to maintain their splendid language, and there, where the majority are Germans, to maintain their dignity before the courts, then we are compelled, in viewing the masses of Germans living here in this country and the continual impetus of immigration, to regard a Society as yours is as a most opportune phenomenon. This affords those living here an opportunity to draw closer to each other, to support and disseminate the elements of German life, to promote scientific efforts, to transplant from the Fatherland everything that is lofty and beautiful in so far as it is suitable here, to assign a home to the German immigrant immediately upon his entry into the United States where he shall feel himself more at home than he would standing alone, and where he will be assigned a sphere of action in which, by industriousness and frugality he will soon be able to achieve a measure of independence, which if he first must seek for it a long time, will often be difficult for him. We are acquainted with the state of the German immigrants, we know which struggles often wait upon them and how many fall in battle. It will be different if he knows that he travels to a colony where he will find friendly souls, who are able to assist him with advice and deed."

The *Freiheitsfreund* of Chambersburg, Pa., supports the movement in these words:

"Die Deutsche Ansiedlungs-Gesellschaft hat gewiss die Aufmerksamkeit aller Deutschen und Abkömmlinge von Deutschen auf sich gezogen und durch das Grossartige des Unternehmens und durch die Vortheile die für den Reichen sowohl als für den Armen daraus zu fliessen versprechen, ist wohl jedes biedere deutsche Herz mit Wonne und stolzem Nationalgefühl beseelt worden. Durch ein thätiges und strengvereintes Zusammenwirken der Deutschen muss das wohl durchdachte und weislich geordnete Unternehmen gedeihen und für uns und unsere Kinder die herrlichsten Früchte bringen. Selbst dem Aermsten ist Gelegenheit gegeben, daran Antheil zu nehmen. Kann er sich keine Actie kaufen, so kann er sich eine durch Fleiss und Sparsamkeit verdienen."[13]

"The German Settlement Society has certainly captured the attention of all Germans and descendants of Germans and no doubt every brave German heart has been inspired with rapture and proud patriotism by the nobleness of the undertaking and by the advantages which can be expected therefrom for the wealthy as well as for the poor. By means of an active and strongly-united cooperation of the Germans this well-planned and judiciously organized venture must flourish and bear the most splendid fruit for ourselves and our children. If he cannot purchase a share, then he can earn one by work and frugality."

From Lancaster, Ohio, we find a letter,[14] not so unreservedly enthusiastic. This letter is signed, "Freunde der Ansiedlungs-Gesellschaft." The writers are somewhat informed as to the purpose of the society. They express themselves as ready to support it. But they entertain some doubts, which they desire to have dispersed, and some wishes they would have considered. Their inquiries were not kindly received by the Philadelphians. Nevertheless there was more saneness in their doubts than the society would admit. They spoke as men who had endured the hardships and privations of pioneer life themselves. Experience had taught them many a valuable lesson. They wanted to know how the society proposed to carry out its lofty plans, when brought face to face with facts and reality. They abandoned the visionary views and brought in figures to substantiate their

---

[15] *A. und N. W.*, of Oct. 1, 1836.
[16] *A. und N. W.*, of Oct. 22, 1836.

claims. It appears that the plan of the society was not accurately understood, for these same Ohioans fear "eine Gesellschaft à la Rapp." They also raised the very important question how the members living outside of Philadelphia should be enabled to vote on vital questions. If the society attained to the importance its supporters prophesied for it, it must be self-evident that the greater number of members must live away from the mother society. These and other suggestions and queries, which we believe were made in all sincerity, aroused the displeasure of the Philadelphians, and called forth a cutting, and, as it appears to us, unmerited rebuke. Perhaps the best suggestion they offered was that the greatest care should be given to choose an advantageous location for the settlement. In another part of this work it will be shown how vital this question was. The communication concludes thus:

"Man wähle eine gute Lage, gesundes Klima, gutes Land; man biete den deutschen Ansiedlern reelle Vortheile an, und die Popularität des Planes thut alles Uebrige."[15]

"A good location, a healthy climate, good land should be selected; real advantages should be offered to the German settler, and the popularity of the plan will do the rest."

Many letters appear containing the tone of the communication of Carl Backhaus in Cincinnati, Ohio:

"Welches deutsche Gemüth sollte nicht mit ganzem Eifer der Seele zur Gründung einer Anstalt behülflich sein wollen, in deren wirklichem und baldigem Entstehen allein die sicherste Bürgschaft liegt, deutschen Fleiss, deutsche Geschicklichkeit und vor Allem deutsche Biederkeit, Redlichkeit und Treue, so wie das köstlichste, unsere theure Muttersprache, unverfälscht und rein unsern Nachkommen hinterlassen zu können?"[16]

---

[15] *A. und N. W.*, of Sept. 17, 1836.
[16] *A. und N. W.*, of Oct. 1, 1836.

"Which German mind would not wish with all the zest of his soul to be helpful to an organization in whose actual and imminent genesis alone is found the most certain guarantee that we shall be able to bequeath unalloyed and pure to our descendants German diligence, German skill, and above all German loyalty, uprightness and honesty as well as that which is most precious, our dear mother tongue?"

We could heap up evidence of the interest aroused for the undertaking. We shall, however, content ourselves with citing only a few more instances.

The *Anzeiger des Westens,* of St. Louis, was not a strong supporter of the society. This is shown by an article of October 1, 1836, in which its tone is far from being complimentary. This may have been due to the fact that Illinois was then favorably discussed as the site of the colony. At a later time the *Anzeiger* stepped into line with the enthusiastic defenders and supporters of the society.

In the *New Yorker Staatszeitung* the organization found, from the first, a bitter opponent. In number 52 of the year 1836 this paper issued an article whose basic thought might well be expressed in these terse words:

> "Alles was besteht
> Ist werth dass es zu Grunde geht."

> "Everything which exists
> Deserves to fall into ruin."

This paper seems to have remained the avowed enemy of the society. Its scathing articles elicited the bitterest sort of replies on the part of the supporters of the plan. It does not stand to reason that such a position, by a strong press, should not irreparably injure the undertaking, particularly in New York, a stronghold of German Americans, and that at a time when perfect harmony and united, quick action was most essential to its success.

It will be interesting to note how this movement was looked upon by the European Germans. We fortunately have preserved in the *Alte und Neue Welt* the expressions of at least two prominent individuals. One is a letter by Dr. J. Fr. Hennicke, editor of *Der Allgemeine Anzeiger der Deutschen in Gotha.*[17] The letter was addressed to J. G. Wesselhoeft. It reads as follows:

"Ihre freundliche Zuschrift vom 28. Januar, die am 9. März in meinen Händen war, hat mich sehr erfreut und ich sage Ihnen dafür meinen verbindlichen Dank. Wie sehr ich die edlen Bemühungen der Deutschen Ansiedlungs-Gesellschaft zu würdigen und ihren menschenfreundlichen Zweck zu beurtheilen weiss, ist einigermassen aus meiner Nachschrift ersichtlich. Möchten doch deutsche Regierungen oder wenigstens einzelne edle Deutsche die Wichtigkeit des Unternehmens einsehen und es kräftig zu unterstützen suchen. Ich für meinen Wirkungskreis werde Männer von Einsicht und Einfluss darauf aufmerksam machen und ich habe damit bereits begonnen."

"Your kind message of Jan. 28, which came into my hands March 9, gave me great pleasure and I express my hearty thanks for it. How greatly I value the noble efforts of the German Settlement Society and appreciate its philanthropic purpose will in some measure be evident from my postscript. If only German governments or at least some noble Germans would recognize the importance of the undertaking and attempt to give it strong support. For my sphere of action I shall call the attention of men of insight and influence to it and I have already begun therewith."

---

[17] *A. und N. W.*, of June 9, 1838.

In the columns of his paper Hennicke comments most favorably. After publishing a circular sent out by the Board of Managers at Philadelphia, he continues thus:

"Die von menschenfreundlichen Deutschen in Philadelphia gestiftete Ansiedlungs-Gesellschaft beabsichtigt einen hohen, edlen Zweck, welcher der kräftigen Unterstützung, nicht nur von Seiten gemeinnützig denkender Deutschen, sondern auch einzelner Staatsregierungen, aus deren Gebieten jährlich zahlreiche Schaaren, ohne durchdachten Plan und nur auf gut Glück, nach Nordamerika auswandern, in mehreren, hier nicht näher zu bezeichnenden Rücksichten, würdig ist. Die Bemühungen jener Gesellschaft verdienen aber um so mehr die dankbarste Anerkennung und thätige Unterstützung, da ähnliche, in Deutschland, namentlich in Sachsen und in Hessen-Darmstadt, vorzüglich in Dresden wiederholt versuchte Unternehmungen ohne erwünschten Erfolg geblieben sind. Gleichwohl verdienen die vielen Tausende, die jährlich nach Amerika auswandern, die leitende und unterstützende Hand der Regierungen. Vielleicht entschliesst sich noch eine oder die andere, in die von Dresden aus mitgetheilten und im *Allgemeinen Anzeiger der Deutschen* vollständig bekannt gemachten gemeinnützigen Ansiedlungspläne einzugehen und sie entweder in ihrem ganzen Umfange oder nach ihren wesentlichen Theilen in Ausführung zu bringen. Was der edle William Penn im Jahre 1681 so grossartig, thätig und mit glücklichem Erfolg begann, das sucht nun in unseren Zeiten eine Gesellschaft biederer Männer nach einem durchdachten, menschenfreundlichen Plane fortzusetzen."[18]

"The Settlement Society organized in Philadelphia by philanthropic Germans striving toward a lofty, noble goal deserves for various reasons, which will not be enumerated here, the strong support, not only on the part of unselfish thinking Germans, but also by separate governments of states from whose territories annually large groups emigrate to North America without a coherent plan and only trusting to luck. The efforts of the Society deserve so much more the most thankful recognition and active

---

[18] *A. und N. W.*, of June 9, 1838.

support since similar repeated attempted undertakings in Germany, namely in Saxony and in Hessen-Darmstadt, and particularly in Dresden, have not produced desired results. Notwithstanding, the many thousands who annually emigrate to America deserve the guiding and assisting hand of the goverments. Perhaps one or the other of them will yet decide to participate in the General Promotion of German plans which have been publicized in their entirety in Dresden in the "Allgemeinen Auzeiger der Deutschen" so as to bring them into execution either in their entire scope or at least in their essential parts. What the noble William Penn began so grandiosely and actively and with such fortunate results in the year 1681, this a Society of valiant men now attempts to continue by means of a well-devised, humanitarian plan.

A communication by Advokat F. G. Sprewitz, of Lauenburg on the Elbe, will be inserted later in its proper place.

3. Growth of the Society.

From the consideration of what the public thought of the organization we pass on to a study of its inner and outer development.

The Administrative Board (Verwaltungs-Rath), which was provided by the constitution, was elected, as was pointed out, on August 27, 1836. Their first meeting was held on September 7th. At this meeting they effected their inner organization by electing the following officers:

J. C. Viereck, Vorsitzer; (Chairman)
F. W. L. Kiderlen, Sprecher; (Speaker)
W. H. Leupold, Sekretair. (Secretary)

Just what the duties of the "Sprecher" were cannot be stated. Perhaps he had some of the powers of an attorney. The city register of that time gives Mr. Kiderlen's name as member of the firm of Kiderlen & Stollmeyer, book sellers.

The first duty which this body considered was the safe deposit of the funds of the society. It was unanimously agreed to recommend to the main body that the money be placed in the Girard Trust Company, "wegen ihrer anerkannten Solideté,"* and because it was said "dass einer der Gehülfen in besagter Anstalt 'Deutsch' spräche."* This recommendation, however, was not acted upon favorably until November 3d, when the society voted to remove the funds from the Bank of Pennsylvania to the Girard Trust Company.

Inflated by the many favorable reports that came in, and foreseeing unprecedented prosperity, the members believed that Congress would be only too willing to lend a helping hand. Accordingly, on September 26th, Mr. Kiderlen offered the following motion:

"Dass die Gesellschaft bei dem Congress darum nachsuchen solle, dass dieser ihr soviel Congressland, als die Gesellschaft wünsche und wo sie es wünsche, auf Credit verkaufen möge."

"That the Society petition Congress, that the latter sell it on credit as much land as the Society desires and wherever it desires."

Only the intercession of a Congressman from Pennsylvania, who was a friend of the society, prevented the blunder of such an appeal. This resolution confirmed again what was said concerning the opinion of the possibilities of this undertaking.

It will be remembered that the question of branch societies was early and frequently discussed. As early as November 3,

---

*"Because of its recognized solidarity"

*"that one of the help in said institutions speaks German."

1836, we meet with the confirmation that an auxiliary was established at Albany, New York. And later in the same month Baltimore reports a like organization. Concerning the inner workings of the Albany branch we are, unfortunately, left almost totally uninformed. Some of the minutes of the Baltimore society have come down to us. We know the Baltimore officers to have been Christoph A. Medinger, President; G. H. Mittnacht, Secretary; Johannes Berger, Treasurer. Most of these men became quite prominent in the society later on. At a later period Pittsburg also had a branch society.

The auxiliaries were, of course, under the restrictions of the general constitution. Regarding the disposition of the money collected by the auxiliaries for shares, etc., the Board of Managers passed the following order on November 17th:

"Sobald eine Summe von wenigstens Einhundert Dollars eingegangen ist, soll ein Bank Check of New York, payable to the President of the German Settlement Society Julius Leupold or order — eingesandt werden: worüber nach specifirter Angabe der respectiven Namen, in der deutschen Zeitung *Neue und Alte Welt* quittirt werden soll."

"As soon as a sum of at least $100.00 has been collected, a Bank Check of New York, payable to the President of the German Settlement Society, Julius Leupold or order shall be sent in; concerning which after specific listing of respective names a receipt of account shall be published in the German newspaper 'Neue und Alte Welt'."

Great activity was also manifested in New Orleans, Montreal, Cleveland, Cincinnati and other cities of the Union, but we have no proof that other auxiliaries than the three above-named existed.

Early in December of 1836 the Board of Managers recommended most heartily the advertising of the plan of colonization through the medium of newspapers in Germany. The thirteen publications which they regarded as best adapted to these advertisements were the following:

Die Bremer Zeitung,
Der Hamburger Correspondent,
Die Dorfzeitung,
Anzeiger der Deutschen in Gotha,
Das Frankfurter Journal,
Der Schwäbische Merkur,
Die Augsburger Allg. Zeitung,
Der Schweizerbote,
Die Speyrer Zeitung,
Die Preussische Staatszeitung,
Elberfelder Zeitung,
Breslauer Zeitung,
Karlsruher Zeitung.

The main body sanctioned this plan, but decided to delay its execution until the purchase of property had been effected.

Previous to this, Nos. 43-45 of the *Alte und Neue Welt* of 1836 contain a most interesting article enumerating the possible and probable advantages accruing from sharing in this undertaking. It was signed by the president and secretary and the nine members of the Board of Managers. At its close this request was subjoined:

"Alle deutschen Zeitungen werden ersucht obige Anzeige für 2 Thaler 3 Mal in ihre resp. Blätter einzurücken."

"All German newspapers are requested to publish the above announcement 3 times in their respective papers for 2 dollars."

After pointing out that the society had been making slow but sure and successful advancement, the article said:

"Daher laden wir alle deutschen Brüder aller Orten freundlichst ein Mitglieder dieser grossartigen National-Unternehmung zu werden."[19]

"Therefore, we most heartily invite all German brethren in all places to become members of this grandiose national undertaking."

The chief advantages of this society over others, this article proceeds to delineate under four principal heads:

1. Absolute equality of the rights and privileges of all members.

Detailed under this head stands this:

"Jedes Mitglied der Gesellschaft bekommt ausser einer eigenthümlichen Stadtlotte für jede Actie noch das Miteigenthum am ganzen Vermögen der Gesellschaft, durch welches nicht nur eine Menge Vortheile durch gemeinschaftliche Anlagen von Dorfschaften, Fabriken, Manufacturen, Schulen u. s. w., sondern höchst wahrscheinlich auch eine immerwährende Freiheit von Taxen und Schulgeld für alle Mitglieder bewirkt werden kann."

"Each member of the Society receives for each share not only a city lot, which is his exclusive property, but also a share in the common property of the Society by means of which a large number of advantages can accrue from common establishments of city buildings, factories, industries, schools, etc., but also in all probability perpetual freedom from taxes and general obligations for all members."

2. The number of participants which this movement is sure to have:

---

[19] *A. und N. W.*, of Oct. 22, 1836.

"Je schneller und stärker die Bevölkerung einer Gegend wächst, und besonders eine fleissige und ausdauernde Bevölkerung wie die deutsche, desto raschere Fortschritte macht sie an Reichthum und Blüthe."

"The faster and stronger the population of a region grows, and especially an industrious and persistent population like the German people, the swifter progress it will make in wealth and vigor."

3. The capital of the society is always secure, being invested in real estate:

"Die Mitglieder der Gesellschaft haben daher nie Grund zu befürchten, dass je ihre Einlage könnte verloren gehen — dagegen haben sie vollen Grund zu hoffen, dass ihr Kapital mehr als tausend Procent Zinsen tragen wird!"

"The members of the Society therefore will never have cause to fear that their investment might be lost—on the contrary they have all reason to expect that their capital will pay more than a thousand percent interest."

4. The poor man can pay for his shares by working for the society.

Early in 1837 steps were taken to become incorporated under the laws of the State of Pennsylvania.

The question of prime importance appeared now to be the acquisition of land. This is but natural, for upon this choice depended, in a great measure, the success or failure of the enterprise. It was evident that many persons declined to join because the site for the colony had not been determined upon. It became difficult to solicit new shareholders, and also difficult to hold those members who were growing lukewarm. Illinois, Indiana, Pennsylvania and Missouri had long been considered as having suitable locations. On January 5, 1837, the Province Tamulipas in Old Merico was recommended to the society. A committee of nine investigated the claims of this locality, and reported favorably on the strength of the information at their command, but recommended more minute inquiry. This action did not find favor with President Leupold, however. Quite autocratically he ruled that further inquiry be dispensed with, holding it as the opinion, "es sei nie der Plan der Gesellschaft gewesen eine Ansiedlung ausserhalb der Vereinigten Staaten zu gründen."* For this dictatorial, flat-footed decision he was compelled to offer apologies later. Nevertheless he succeeded in checking, most effectually, all attempts to extend the landed interests of the society beyond the borders of the United States. After this abrupt and rather disagreeable decision, which almost had the result of bringing about a serious rupture between the rulers and the ruled of the society, the Verwaltungs-Rath issued the following recommendation:

"Nach näherer Prüfung und Ueberlegung, nach Erwägung der Vor- und Nachtheile des Bodens, Climas, Communication etc. kam der Verwaltungs-Rath zu dem Resultate, dass alle anderen Kosten zu sparen und folgende Staaten nur zu bereisen ihm als zweckmässig erscheine: Pennsylvania, Ohio, Arkansas, Missouri, Illinois, Wisconsin, Indiana, der östliche Theil Michigan's und der westliche Theil New York's."

"After closer examination and deliberation, after consideration of the advantages and disadvantages of the soil, climate, communications, etc., that to avoid all other expenses it seemed suitable to the purpose of the executive committee to visit only the following states: Pennsylvania, Ohio, Arkansas, Missouri, Illinois, Wisconsin, Indiana, the eastern part of Michigan and the western part of New York."

---

*"that it had never been the intention of the Society to found a settlement outside the United States."

Early in March, C. G. Ritter was commissioned to go to Washington to confer with certain land agents, but more particularly to make inquiry at the government land office and even to apply to Congress for information and to actually appeal for its assistance. It will be recalled that Mr. Ritter was one of the deputies elected on August 27, 1836. Hence the action of this body was stayed until his return. He returned on the 11th of March and reported to the Board of Managers. He had gained much valuable information, but, as a matter of course, had not interviewed the Congress of the United States. Now the society decided, encouraged by recent information, to authorize the deputies to visit these States and Territories, viz.: Illinois, Indiana, Missouri, Michigan, Wisconsin. It was also urged that the representatives set out on their long and difficult journey in the early part of April, "da Aufschub nur Erkaltung zu Folge haben würde."* Dr. Wm. Schmoele, G. F. Bayer and Fr. Klett were appointed to draft a set of instructions for the government of the deputies.

On April 14, 1837, they set out on their wearisome journey. They departed with this last word of instruction from the Board of Managers:

"Beschlossen: Dass die Deputirten zuerst in die Gegend des Wabash gehen, um die Ländereien daselbst in Augenschein zu nehmen, und von dort aus direkt nach dem Staate Missouri, wo sie entweder von Jefferson City, oder von St. Louis aus an den Verwaltungs-Rath Bericht erstatten sollen, wie das Resultat ihrer Untersuchungen in den Staaten Indiana, Illinois und Missouri ausgefallen ist."

---

*"since delay would only create disinterest."

"RESOLVED: That the deputies should first go to the region of the Wabash in order to see at first hand the landed properties there, and from there go directly to the state of Missouri where they shall, either from Jefferson City or from St. Louis send to the Board of Managers a report giving the results of their investigations in the states of Indiana, Illinois and Missouri."

The following are the instructions of the deputies, subscribed to by the parties concerned:

Instruction für die reisenden Deputirten der Deutschen Ansiedlungs-Gesellschaft.

Da Sie seit der Gründung der Gesellschaft Mitglieder derselben waren und daher Gelegenheit hatten, mit dem Geiste, dem Streben, so wie den gegenwärtigen und künftigen Mitteln der Gesellschaft sich genau bekannt zu machen; so wird von Ihnen vorausgesetzt, dass Sie den Endzweck Ihrer Sendung vollkommen richtig verstehen.

Ihr Auftrag ist kurz follgender:

Sie sollen in den durch einen Beschluss der Gesellschaft vom 16. März bestimmten und namhaft gemachten Staaten und Territorien nämlich: Indiana, Illinois, Missouri, Wisconsin und Michigan, einen für die Ansiedlung der Gesellschaft passenden Landstrich aufsuchen und den möglichst vortheilhaften Ankauf desselben nach eingeholter Instruction vom Verwaltungs-Rathe, einleiten.

Den Plan für Ihre Reise, die Wahl und Lage des Landes und alle andern dahin sich beziehenden Punkte müssen Ihnen, als den auserwählten Sachverständigen zur Bestimmung überlassen bleiben.

In formeller Hinsicht hat der Verwaltungs-Rath die Bestimmung gemacht, Ihnen die genaue Führung eines Tagebuches über alle Ihre Arbeiten, Reisen, Ansichten und Urtheile in Beziehung auf ihre Sendung zur Pflicht zu machen.

Ferner sind Sie beauftragt, so oft Sie es für nothwendig erachten, mindestens aber alle 8 Tage ein Mal, Bericht zu erstatten.

Hinsichtlich Ihrer Ausgaben und Reisekosten haben Sie sich an die von der Gesellschaft gemachten Bestimmungen zu halten, nämlich folgende:

1.) Laut Beschluss der Gesellschaft vom 25. März erhalten Sie alle drei bei Ihrer Abreise baar $450.00 (vierhundert und fünfzig dollars), also jeder $150.00 und können Sie ausserdem durch eine Bank in St. Louis oder Cincinnati $450.00 beziehen.

2.) Laut Beschluss der Gesellschaft vom 6. April erhält ein jeder von Ihnen $5.00 per Tag während Ihrer Reise von der Gesellschaft.

3.) Alle Extra-Auslagen oder Opfer, welche Sie bei provisorischer Abschliessung von Contracten für die Gesellschaft zu bringen für nöthig erachten werden, sollen Ihnen von der Gesellschaft wieder vergütet werden, jedoch dürfen diese Auslagen nicht die Summe von $500.00 (fünf hundert dollars) übersteigen.

4.) Sie werden angewiesen, bei Auswahl des Landes nur Grundeigenthum im Bereich eines schifbaren Flusses zu berücksichtigen, und von diesem Lande muss wenigstens so viel am Flusse selbst gelegen sein, um darauf eine Handelsstadt gründen zu können.

5.) Sie haben nur auf eine Strecke Landes zu reflectiren, welche nicht weniger als 25,000 (fünf und zwanzig tausend) Acker in sich fasst.

6.) Zur Bestreitung der Ihnen während Ihrer Reise vorstehenden Auslagen wird Ihnen vom Verwaltungs-Rathe ein Credit von $950.00 (dollars neun hundred und fünfzig) in St. Louis oder Cincinnati eröffnet.

7.) Sie werden angewiesen in jedem Ihrer Briefe dem Verwaltungs-Rathe zu bemerken an welchem Orte Sie dessen Antworten entgegensehen wollen.

8.) Sie werden angewiesen bei der Auswahl des Landes besonders zu berücksichtigen, dass Getreide- Wein- und Obstbau, wie Vieh- und Schafzucht mit Vortheil betrieben werden können.
Zu Ihrer Organisation soll nach Ihrer eigenen Wahl ein Mitglied als Vorsitzer Ihre Berathungen und Untersuchungen leiten, ein anderes als buchführender und das dritte als correspondirender Secretair agiren.

Diese Instructionen sind in duplo ausgefertigt und von beiden Theilen wohl verstanden und genehmigt worden.

So geschehen. Philadelphia am 10ten April 1837.

> *J. Leupold,* Präsident.
> *J. G. Wesselhoeft,* Secretair.
> *Adam Schmidt,* Schatzmeister.
>
> *G. F. Bayer,*
> *J. C. Viereck,*
> *E. W. Wohlein,* ⎬ Verwaltungs-Rath.
> *Wm. Feuring,*
> *C. Staffhorst,*
>
> *C. Ferentheil,*
> *C. G. Ritter,* ⎬ Deputirte.
> *F. L. C. Gebhard,*

Instructions for the traveling deputies of the German Settlement Society Center.

As you were members of the Society since the founding of the same and have therefore had opportunity to become well acquainted with the spirit, the striving and the present and future means of the organization, the assumption will be made that you thoroughly and correctly understand the purpose of your task.

Your task in short is the following:
You shall locate according to a resolution of the Society of March 16 in the designated and named States and territories, namely: Indiana, Illinois, Missouri, Wisconsin and Michigan, a domain of land suitable for the settlement of the Society and initiate proceedings for the most advantageous purchase of the same after receiving instructions from the Board of Managers. The plan for your journey, the selection and situation of the land and all other involved details will be left to your decision as being the most competent judges. As a formal consideration the Board of Managers has resolved to make it your duty to keep an exact daily record of all your tasks, journeys, views and judgments in connection with your mission. Furthermore, you are charged to send a report as often as you deem it necessary, but at least once every 8 days.

As regards your expenses and traveling costs, you are to observe the decisions made by the Society, namely the following:

1) According to a resolution of the Society of March 25, the three of you will receive $450.00 cash; i.e., each one $150.00 and in addition you can draw from a bank in St. Louis or Cincinnati another $450.00.

2) According to a resolution of the Society on April 6, each one of you receives $5.00 per day on your trip for the Society.

3) All additional expenditures or down-payments which you deem necessary for the settlement of temporary contracts for the Society shall be reimbursed to you by the Society; these expenditures, however, may not exceed the sum of $500.00.

4) You are charged in the selection of the land to consider only landed real property in the domain of a navigable river and of this land at least so much must lie along the river itself as to afford space for the establishment of a commercial city.

5) You are to consider only a piece of land which is not less than 25,000 acres in area.

6) For payment of expenditures during the journey ahead of you, the Board of Managers will place $950.00 to your credit either in St. Louis or in Cincinnati.

7) You are charged to notify the Board of Managers in everyone of your letters as to which place you will receive their answer.

8) You are charged in the selection of the land to note especially whether it is advantageous to the growing of grain, wine and fruit and to the raising of cattle and sheep. For your organization there shall be chosen in accordance with your own

election one member as chairman of deliberations and investigations, another as recorder, and the third shall function as corresponding secretary.

These instructions have been made in duplicate and have been well understood and approved by both parties.
Subscribed to in Philadelphia, April 10, 1837:
G. Leupold, President
I. G. Wesselhoeft, Secretary
Adam Schmidt, Treasurer

G. F. Bayer	)	
G. C. Viereck	)	Board of Managers
E. W. Wohlein	)	or
Wm. Feuring	)	Administration Board
C. Staffhorst	)	
C. Ferentheil	)	
C. G. Ritter	)	Deputies
F. L. C. Gebhard	)	

With the departure of the deputies enthusiasm was more aglow than ever. An actual step had been taken towards the accomplishment of the great undertaking. The optimists were now certain of success. The pessimists were at least silenced.

It was also deemed prudent to supplement the constitution with two amendments. Paragraph II was now made to read thus:

"Die Gesellschaft wird auf Actien gegründet von welchen jede im ersten Tausend fünfundzwanzig und jede im zweiten dreissig Thaler kosten soll; *jedoch soll* NACH *Ankauf des Landes der Preis von den noch nicht verkauften Actien* von dem Verwaltungs-Rathe vorgeschlagen und von der Gesellschaft bestimmt werden."

"The Society shall be founded upon shares of which each of the first thousand shall cost $25.00 and each of the second $30.00;

however, after purchase of the land the price of the shares not yet sold shall be proposed by the Board of Managers and determined by the Society."

This was done on May the 4th, 1837. On July 6, 1837, a much more radical amendment was passed upon:

"Wo es erwiesen werden kann dass ein Mitglied zum Nachtheil der Gesellschaft spricht, schreibt oder druckt, mit einem Wort, der Gesellschaft *oder ihrem guten Fortgang zu schaden sucht,* soll es der Gesellschaft frei stehen, ein solches Mitglied — wenn es die Mehrheit wünscht — aus der Gesellschaft auszuschliessen. Doch behält sich die Gesellschaft vor, über die Art und Weise wie dies geschehen und namentlich wie viel einem solchen Mitglied von den eingezahlten Geldern abgezogen werden soll, näher zu bestimmen."

"Where it can be proved that a member seeks to disparage the Society by speech or writing or printing, in short, tries to harm the Society or its good progress, then the Society shall have the right—if the majority wishes it—to expel such a member from the Society. But the Society reserves the right to determine the ways and means for doing this and in particular, to determine the amount of the refund of the fees paid up."

This amendment was destined to cause a great deal of unpleasantness and demanded many explanations. For instance, the editor of the *Alte und Neue Welt* was compelled to write many articles in its defence. One, the most memorable, he prefaces: "Wer reines Herzens ist, hat das Gesetz nicht zu fürchten, und wer seine Stimme in die Wagschale der Mehrheit bei der Gesetzgebung legte, hat nicht Ursache über Tyrannei zu klagen."[20]* The point of contention was, of course, that the mem-

---

[20] *A. und N. W.,* of August 12, 1837.

*"Whoever has a clear conscience need not fear the law, and whoever placed his vote on the scale of the majority for the promulgation of the law, has no reason to complain about tyranny."

bers interpreted it as an encroachment on their freedom of speech. Though much was said for and against it, the law remained unchanged. But the records show no account of its enforcement or any expulsions.

The instructions required the deputies to report at least once every week to the society. Naturally these reports were looked forward to with great interest. Their first letter arrived from Cincinnati on May the 4th, and their second one from St. Louis May the 31st. From this last date to July the 3d not a word was heard from the men. It was manifestly impossible to live up to the letter of their instruction. Their investigation carried them far from all established mail routes. Perhaps, too, they did not have much to report. Their friends were, of course, much concerned as to their welfare and whereabouts. The Board of Managers had already prepared to issue a call of inquiry, giving minute descriptions of the men and stating their mission, appealing to their western friends for co-operation in clearing up this mysterious disappearance. The letter of July 3d explained the silence completely. It was evident that letters Nos. 3 and 4 had been lost or delayed. The content of these letters, which arrived later, was kept a profound secret. Only the Board of Managers was initiated into its secrets. Even yet we do not know the full amount of information or description they contained. This is very much to be regretted. Doubtless they contained many interesting items. But unfortunately they are lost, and what the deputies held as their opinion regarding Illinois, Indiana, or any other region they may have visited, must remain a secret. In their final report not a syllable occurs to satisfy our curiosity concerning their experiences.

On July 12th, Ritter and Gebhard returned. Ferentheil, who remained on business in Pittsburg, was delayed four days by a break of the canal, arriving on July 16th.

The members were, of course, extremely anxious to hear

the detailed account of their representatives. Much dissatisfaction prevailed because the content of the previous reports had been withheld from them. The reason for withholding the specific information from the general public was well founded. It was simply to prevent conniving land agents and unprincipled speculators from foiling their plans. This was, however, not well understood by the members. Many of them were only too ready to suspect foul play. On July 17th the deputies submitted their complete report, which reads as follows:

Allgemeiner Bericht über das von den Deputirten der Deutschen Ansiedlungs-Gesellschaft zur Ansiedlung als geeignet vorgeschlagene Land.

Das Land liegt im Missouri Staate, an zwey schiffbaren Flüssen. Das zur Anlage einer Stadt am besten geeignete Land fängt auf dem rechten Ufer des einen Flusses, etwa 5 Meilen von dessen Mündung in den anderen Fluss, an. Der erstere Fluss wird bis jetzt nur bis auf etwa 5 Meilen von dessen Mündung mit Dampfschiffen befahren. Im Frühjahr dürften Dampfböte auch höher hinauf gehen können, doch nur eine kurze Zeit. Versuche sind bis daher noch nicht gemacht worden. Das rechte Ufer dieses Flusses ist bis auf 5 Meilen von dessen Mündung fast durchgängig so hoch, dass es gegen Ueberschwemmungen gesichert sein soll, wie von einem 20 Jahre an diesem Flusse bereits wohnenden Manne versichert wurde, wenn nicht Wasserschwellungen, wie bei Cincinnati vor einigen Jahren der Fall war, eintreten. Oberhalb stösst an das eben beschriebene Land ein etwa 5 Meilen langer von ½ bis 1 Meile breiter Bottom. An der Mündung des Flusses fangen steile, steinigte Ufer an, die sich auch an dem andern Flusse hinziehen. Das linke Ufer ist fast durchgängig niedriger als das rechte und darum auch wenig geeignet zur Anlage einer Stadt. Um indess fremden Anlagen niergends Raum zu geben, ist nothwendig, dass sich die Gesellschaft nicht nur den Besitz beider Ufer des Flusses, von dessen Mündung bis auf etwa 9 Meilen hinauf, sichert, sondern sich auch den Besitz des Ufers an dem andern Flusse, an beiden Seiten der Mündung so weit sichert, dass an der Mündung nie eine fremde Anlage Platz nehmen kann.

Zunächst dem Flusse ist das Land bis auf eine halbe Meile etwa durchschnittlich, auf dem rechten Ufer meist eben und sehr gut. Auf dem linken Ufer sind einige kleine, steile Stellen. Die ganze Gegend ist ausserdem gebrochen und zum Theil stark hügelich. An den Bächen findet sich überall einiges Bottom Land. Das Hügelland ist theilweise sehr gut und so auch einige grosse Bergflächen, wie der Baumwuchs, die Baumarten und das hin und wieder gefundene Getreide beweisen. Ist das Land nicht überall durchaus günstig für den Ackerbau, so ist es um so besser für Grasswuchs und also für die Viehzucht. Meist in der ganzen Gegend findet sich Kalkstein. Eisenerz soll viel da seyn. Die Bleimienen sind nicht entfernt und also möglich, dass sich auch in der besagten Gegend dieses Metall findet. Die wenigen in der Gegend vorgefundenen Obstbäume haben einen sehr guten Wuchs. Weinbau wird wahrscheinlich gedeihen, wenn das Land mehr angebaut ist. Quellen sind in dieser Gegend mehr als in anderen Gegenden. An dem rechten Ufer, da, wo die Stadt anzulegen ist, sind nur 2 Plätze, die zusammen 220 Acker messen und die die Eigner für den Preis von 15 Doll. per Acker zum Verkauf anbieten, aber gewiss mit einem geringeren Preis zufrieden seyn werden.

Ab vom Ufer auf 4 und mehreren Meilen liegen nur einige kleine Farmereien, welche die Gesellschaft nicht nothwendig kaufen müsste; alles andere Land ist bis auf kleine Strecken Congress-Land. Im südlichen Theile des Counties sind mehr Ansiedlungen, aber auch da ist noch viel Congressland vorhanden. Auf dem linken Ufer, das Bottom-Land am Flusse ausgenommen, ist das Land weniger gut als auf dem rechten Ufer, doch ist auch da noch einiges gute Congress-Land zu finden. Am linken Ufer des Flusses ist eine kleine Farm, deren Besitz für die Gesellschaft wichtig ist."

"General Report by the Deputies of the German Settlement Society concerning the proposed land suitable for settlement.

The land lies in the state of Missouri along two navigable rivers. The land most suited for the site of a city begins on the right bank of the one river about 5 miles from its confluence with the other river. The first-named river is at present navigable with steamboats only for about 5 miles above its mouth. In spring steamboats can probably proceed further up, but only for a short time. Up to now such attempts have not been made. The right bank of this river is almost everywhere so high for 5 miles from its mouth as to make it secure from flooding, as has been assured us by a man who has already lived here at this river for 20 years, unless a water swell occurs, as was the case at Cincinnati several years ago. The above described land is bounded on the upper side by a ½ to 1 mile wide bottom about 5 miles long. At the mouth of the river rise steep, stony banks which also extend along the other river. The left bank is for almost its entire length lower than the right and therefore little suited for the site of a city. In order not to yield space for foreign establishments it is necessary that the Society receives possession not only of both banks of the river from its mouth to about 9 miles upstream, but also obtains possession of the bank of the other river on both sides of the confluence so far as to preclude the occupation of the mouth by any foreign establishment.

Alongside the river on the right bank the land is on the average for about ½ mile mostly level and very good. On the left bank are several small, steep places. Otherwise the entire region is rugged and in part hilly. Everywhere along the creeks is found some bottom land. The hill land is in part very good and so also some extensive hilly plateaus as the growth and species of trees and the grain found here and there testify. If the land is not everywhere favorable for cultivation it is so much the better for pasture and cattle raising. Limestone is found in the greater part of the region. It is reported that iron ore occurs. Lead mines are located at no great distance and it is, therefore, possible that this metal is also found in the above described region. The few fruit trees found in this region have a good growth. Vineyards will probably flourish when more of the land has been cleared. There are more springs in this region than in other places. On the right bank, there, where the city is to be situated, are only 2 sites which together comprise 220 acres and which the owners offer for sale at a price of $15.00 per acre, but they will certainly be satisfied with a smaller offer.

Away from the shore for 4 or more miles are located only several small tracts of small farms which the Society is compelled to purchase; all other land with the exception of several small tracts is Congress-land. More settlements are located in the southern part of the county, but much Congress-land is available there also. On the left hand, except for the bottom land along the river, the soil is not as good as on the right bank, but there also some good Congress-land can still be found. On the left bank of the river is located a small farm, the possession of which is essential to the Society."

Whether the deputies did or did not follow their instruction to visit Michigan and Wisconsin cannot be stated. Neither do we know what was the result of their investigation along the Wabash.

It is indeed an interesting problem why Missouri should have been selected. It must be remembered that Missouri was a slave state and that the German mind had a natural antipathy for the institution of slavery. Other States, in free territory, had land at just as liberal terms as Missouri. It must not be overlooked, however, that one prime factor in the instructions issued to the agents of the society was that they should consider only such sections as were adjacent to a navigable river. For this reason, no doubt, the Wabash and the Missouri were specifically mentioned. We would further venture the assertion that Missouri was more in the public mind than the other sections suggested for the colony. It was yet on the very frontier. The struggle which ended in the Missouri Compromise was not forgotten. The Mormon settlement of 1832 in western Missouri gave notoriety. Undoubtedly Gottfried Duden's idealized account of his paradisiacal trans-Mississippi home, published under the ponderous title: *"Bericht über eine Reise nach den westlichen Staaten Nordamerikas und einem mehrjährigen Aufenthalt*

am Missouri (in den Jahren 1824, 25, 26 *und* 27) *in Bezug auf
Auswanderung und Urbevölkerung, oder: Das Leben im Inneren
der Vereinigten Staaten und dessen Bedeutung für die häusliche
und politische Lage der Europäer, dargestellt,* a.) *in einer
Sammlung von Briefen,* b.) *in einer besonderen Abhandlung
über den politischen Zuständen der nordamerikanischen Freistaaten, und* c.) *in einem rathgebenden Nachtrag für auswan-
dernde deutsche Ackerwirthe und Diejenigen, welche auf Hand-
unternehmungen denken, von Gottfried Duden,** pointed like a
giant index to Missouri, for the first edition was scattered far
and wide among the eager readers of Germany. Furthermore,
just one year previous to the organization of the Deutsche Ansiedlungs-Gesellschaft, Tr. Bromme published, at Baltimore, with
E. Scheld & Co., his book: *Missouri eine geographische — statistische — topographische Skizze für Einwanderer und Freunde
der Länder- und Völkerkunde,* 1835. This author, too, is quite
liberal with his praises. He discusses various portions of the
State as especially fitted for German settlements. He depicts in
bright colors Missouri's natural resources. We can easily con-
ceive how his description of a wild grape vine 36 inches in cir-
cumference would provoke comment among his German readers.
Nor does it require a very vivid fantasy to imagine that a de-

---

*"*Report of a journey to the western states of North America and a several
year's sojourn on the Missouri (in the years 1824, 25, 26 and 27) in relation to
emigration and original settlers, or life in the interior of the United States and
its signification for the domestic and political situation of the Europeans
portrayed: (a) in a collection of letters (b) in a special treatise on the political
conditions of the North American states, and (c) in an advisory appendix for
emigrating German farmers and those who intend to pursue manual trades,
by Gottfried Duden.*"

scription of a veritable Eden would be perused with interest. On page 37 Bromme says, speaking of Missouri's population:

"Auch hier findet man die Bewohner aller Länder Europas und der Union vereinigt, keiner sehnt sich zurück in die früheren Verhältnisse und das Gross der Bevölkerung lebt glücklich und zufrieden. Was sollte auch ein Missourier vermissen! Er bewohnt ein reiches, fruchtbares Land, welches er um den geringen Preis von 1¼ Dollar von der Regierung, oder, je nachdem Verbesserungen darauf angebracht waren, um 4—25 Dollars den Acre, von Privaten kaufte; — er führt bei mässiger Arbeit ein angenehmes, sorgenfreies, patriarchalisches Leben, und wenn er gleich seinen Dienstleuten einen hohen Lohn von 100—150 Dollars, ja oft noch darüber geben muss, vermehrt sich doch sein Kapital mit jedem Jahr! — Kam er arm in's Land, so setzte ihn zweijährige Arbeit in den Stand eines unabhängigen Farmers, und hat er Intelligenz, in Kurzem ein Beamter seines neuen Vaterlandes zu werden. Ein weites Feld der Thätigkeit steht hier Jedem offen, und wer nicht darnach trachtet, Reichthümer aufhäufen zu wollen, kann hier in wahrhaft philosophischer Ruhe ein herrliches beneidenswerthes Leben führen. Mit 4—500 Dollars kann man 80—100 Acres erwerben, von denen ein Theil schon in Kultur gesetzt ist, und einem Familienvater, welchem nach Abzug der Reisekosten ein solches Kapital bei seiner Ankunft übrig bleibt, braucht, und wenn er noch so viel Familie hätte, nicht vor der Zukunft zu bangen."

"Here also one finds united the inhabitants of all European countries and of the Union; no one wishes himself transferred back into his former circumstances and the mass of the population lives happily and contently. For what should be lacking to a Missourian! He inhabits a rich, fruitful land which he has bought for the insignificant price of $1¼ per acre from the government, or depending on the improvements made upon it, for 4-25 dollars per acre from private individuals;—with moderate work he leads a pleasant, carefree patriarchal life, and even though he has to pay his helpers a high wage of 100-150 dollars per year, or in many cases even more, his capital still increases every year!—If he came into the country poor, two years' work placed him in the position of an independent farmer, and if he possesses intelligence, of becoming an official of his new Fatherland. A wide field of action stands open to everyone here, and whoever does not strive to pile up riches for himself can here lead a splendid enviable existence in veritable philosophic peace. With 4-500 dollars one can obtain 80-100 acres, of which a part has already been placed in cultivation; and the head of a family who, after the deduction of his traveling expenses, still possesses that amount of capital on his arrival, need not fear for the future regardless of how many persons are in his family."

One spot which Bromme finds worthy of particular description lies in Montgomery County, directly opposite the present site of Hermann. Duden's settlement,[21] too, it must be remembered, was only a few miles east of the section the deputies found favorable for the colony. Furthermore, Münch[22] and Follenius,[23] the leaders of the unfortunate Giessner-Gesellschaft, lived near there. And the Berliner-Gesellschaft was only 30 miles to the east.[24]

It stands to reason that the Philadelphia society was familiar with all these facts. In the light of these facts we believe that Missouri would suggest itself naturally to them. Indeed, we find Cullmann recommending Missouri to the Executive Committee as early as the 14th of June, 1836. We have, however, no further insight into the discussions regarding the proposed sites, nor do we know who championed the cause of Missouri.

The report of the deputies was received amid the most enthusiastic plaudits. The very evening when the report became known the Board of Managers resolved as follows:

---

[21] Gert. Goebel, *Länger als ein Menschenleben in Missouri*, p. 6.
[22] Gert. Goebel, *ibid*, Chapter 2.
[23] Friedrich Münch's *Gesammelte Schriften*, p. 101.
[24] Gert. Goebel, *Länger als ein Menschenleben in Missouri*, p. 7.

"Auf diese Gründe gestützt, hält der Verwaltungs-Rath es für äusserst nothwendig, dass sobald als möglich ein Deputirter nach besagtem Lande abgeschickt werde, um der Gesellschaft den Besitz des Landes zu sichern und scheint es ihm daher erwünscht, dass die Absendung schleunigst geschehe."

"Relying on these arguments, the Board of Managers deems it most necessary that a deputy be sent to the described region as soon as possible in order to secure the possession of the land for the Society and it holds it as desirable that the dispatch take place as soon as possible."

After a committee of nine had examined the report in detail, the Board of Managers was authorized to deputize some responsible and capable person as agent plenipotentiary to lay claim to the aforesaid land. The choice of this Board fell upon G. F. Bayer, a schoolmaster by profession—at that time engaged by the Zions-Gemeinde of Philadelphia. This recommendation on the part of the Board was heartily confirmed by the society. A committee, composed of Adam Schmidt and Dr. Schmoele, drew up the instructions for this representative. The document was signed by Bayer and the members of the Board of Managers. On the 27th of July, Bayer started out on this difficult and extremely responsible mission. He generously enough asked for no compensation, contenting himself with the defraying of his actual expenses.

The instructions by which he was governed are the following:

Instruction für Herrn G. F. Bayer, Agent des Verwaltungs-Rathes der Deutschen Ansiedlungs-Gesellschaft um Land zu kaufen.

Zu Folge eines Beschlusses der Deutschen Ansiedlungs-Gesellschaft vom 18. July d. J. (1837) hat der Verwaltungs-Rath Sie zum Agenten gewählt, um den von den kürzlich zurückgekommenen Deputirten der Gesellschaft aufgefundenen und näher beschriebenen Landstrich, soweit als möglich, durch Ankauf für die Gesellschaft zu sichern.

Sie wollen daher direkt nach St. Louis reisen und von dort über folgende Punkte so schnell als thunlich an den Verwaltungs-Rath berichten:

1.) Ist der von den Deputirten bezeichnete Landstrich ganz oder zum Theil und wie weit Congress-Land?

2.) Auf welche Weise kann die Bezahlung dieses oder eines Theiles desselben am zweckmässigsten gemacht werden?

3.) Sollten Sie ausserdem noch passende Nachrichten mitzutheilen haben, so werden Sie solche zu thun gebeten.

Im Falle, dass Ihre Erkundigungen in St. Louis so ausfallen, dass Sie glauben, dass der ganze von den Deputirten bezeichnete Landstrich oder ein hinreichend grosser Theil desselben vom Congresse zu haben ist, so wollen Sie direkt hinreisen und sich mit der Localität des Landes so genau als möglich bekannt machen. Alsdann wählen Sie die für die Gesellschaft tauglichsten Striche zum Ankauf aus, und zwar in der Art dass Sie sowohl innerhalb der Ihnen bekannten Kräfte der Gesellschaft bleiben, als auch das nicht gleich gekaufte Land für den künftigen Ankauf so viel als möglich sichern.

Sollten Grundstücke, die Privatpersonen gehören, innerhalb des von Ihnen für die Gesellschaft ausersehenen Landstriches liegen, so wollen Sie mit den Eigenthümern möglichst vortheilhaft provisorische Kauf-Contracte abschliessen und die Resultate so schnell als möglich an den Verwaltungs-Rath berichten.

Zugleich wollen Sie angeben wie viel Geld unbedingt nöthig ist, um den von Ihnen auf dem Platze selbst gemachten Kaufplan am vortheilhaftesten auszuführen, und wohin, zu welcher Zeit, und auf welche Weise dieses Geld an Sie geschickt werden möge.

Sollten Sie schon in St. Louis oder späterhin erfahren, dass der obige Plan zum Ankaufe des von den Deputirten bezeichneten Landes unausführbar ist, so sind Sie beauftragt dieses dem Verwaltungs-Rathe unverzüglich zu berichten und direkt zu dem zweiten von den Deputirten bezeichneten Landstriche am Cuivre Flusse zu reisen. Hier werden Sie dasselbe oben beschriebene Verfahren in Beziehung auf provisorische Kauf-Contracte einschlagen und die Mittel bestimmen, den von Ihnen vorzuschlagenden Kaufplan durchzuführen.

In dem Falle dass beide erwähnten Landstriche entweder für unbrauchbar oder unerlangbar für die Gesellschaft befunden werden sollten, so sind Sie beauftragt, nach den besten von Ihnen eingezogenen Erkundigungen einen andern passenden und erlangbaren Landstrich für die Gesellschaft aufzusuchen und nach den oben niedergelegten Grundsätzen entweder provisorisch anzukaufen, oder auf andere Weise den Ankauf derselben zweckgemäss vorzubereiten. Hierbei haben Sie nach den Grundsätzen zu verfahren, welche in der, den früheren Deputirten gegebenen Instruction niedergelegt sind. Jedoch sollen Sie überhaupt die Vollmacht haben, in einzelnen Fällen nach Ihrer eigenen besten Einsicht und in dem Ihnen bekannten Geiste unserer Gesellschaft zu verfahren, ohne jedoch unautorisirte Verbindlichkeiten einzugehen.

Sollten Sie in der Ausführung Ihrer Aufträge die Hülfe anderer Personen, z. B. eines Begleiters, Feldmessers etc. bedürfen, so haben Sie alle Gewalt, sich dieselben auf Kosten der Gesellschaft zu verschaffen.

Es steht ferner die Summe von zweihundert und fünfzig Thalern zu Ihrer Disposition welche Sie zu ausserordentlichen Ausgaben, die Sie zur Erreichung Ihrer Zwecke für nöthig erachten, ganz oder theilweise zu verwenden Erlaubniss haben.

Alle in dieser Instruction Ihnen zur Abschliessung aufgetragenen Contracte haben Sie auf Ihren Namen abzuschliessen zum Besten der „Deutschen Ansiedlungs-Gesellschaft."

In einem besonders dazu bestimmten Tagebuch wollen Sie die Fortschritte Ihrer Bestrebungen täglich niederschreiben und, so oft Sie es für rathsam halten, wenigstens aber jede Woche einmal, von Ihrer Ankunft in St. Louis an, einen Auszug aus demselben an den Verwaltungs-Rath schicken, wobei Sie zugleich anzugeben haben, wohin allenfalsige fernere Instructionen für Sie gesandt werden mögen.

Instructions for Mr. G. F. Bayer, Agent of the Board of Managers of the German Settlement Society for the purchase of land.

In accordance with a resolution of the German Settlement Society of July 8, 1837, the Board of Managers has elected you as agent to secure for the Society, in so far as possible, through purchase that tract of land selected and more closely described by the recently returned deputies of the Society.

You are, therefore, to travel directly to St. Louis and from there inform the Board of Managers as soon as feasible on the following points:

1) Is the tract of land designated by the deputies entirely or only in part, and to what extent, Congress-land?

2) In which manner can the payment of this or a part of the same be made so as to best suit the purpose?

3) If in addition you have other pertinent information to communicate, you are requested to do this.

In the case that your investigations in St. Louis lead to the result, that you believe, that the entire tract or a sufficiently large part of the same, which has been designated by the deputies, can be obtained from Congress, then you are to proceed directly there and make yourself acquainted with that locality of the land as closely as possible. Then select for purchase those tracts most suitable for the Society and indeed in such a manner that you not only remain within the limits of the resources of the Society which are known to you, but also secure as much as possible that land not immediately bought, for future purchase.

If tracts of land belonging to private individuals lie within the territories selected by you for the Society, then you are to make the most advantageous provisional contracts of purchase with the owners and dispatch the results as soon as possible to the Board of Managers.

Simultaneously you are to state how much money is absolutely necessary in order to carry out to the best advantage that plan of purchase which you yourself have formulated on the spot, and whither at what time and in which manner this money is to be sent to you.

If you already discover in St. Louis, or later, that the aforesaid plan for the purchase of the land designated by the deputies is impractical, then you are charged to immediately inform the Board of Managers and to travel directly to the second tract of land selected by the deputies, along the Cuivre River. Here you will observe the same procedure described above in relation to provisional contracts of purchase and determine the measures to put into effect the plan of purchase proposed by you.

In the case that both of the above mentioned tracts are either unsuitable or unobtainable for the Society, then you are charged to find some tract suitable and available to the Society in accordance with the best of observations you have made, and in conformity with the above established principles either pro-visionally purchase the same or otherwise make preparations in the most suitable manner for the purchase. To this end you are to proceed in accordance with the principles laid down in the instructions to the former deputies. However, you are in general empowered in special cases to act according to your own best discernment and in the spirit of our Society as understood by you without, however, entering unauthorized involvements.

If in the performance of your duties you require the assis-tance of other persons, e.g., a guide, surveyor, etc., you shall be empowered to obtain these at the expense of the Society.

"Furthermore, the sum of $250.00 is placed at your disposal, for which you have permission to use for extraordinary expenses which you deem necessary for the attainment of your purposes.

All the contracts which are to be entered into, as charged in these instructions, are to be signed in your name for the benefit of the "German Settlement Society."

You are to record progress of your efforts daily in a journal designated especially for this purpose, and as often as you think it advisable, but at least once a week, beginning with your arrival in St. Louis, to send an extract from the same to the Board of Managers, in which you are to note whether possible further instructions are to be sent you.

The first weeks after Bayer's departure were weeks of anxiety and suspense. It was generaly felt that the society was approaching a crisis. Upon Bayer's success or failure as agent hinged the future of the whole undertaking. The weekly reports, requested of the agent, did not flow in any more freely than those of the three deputies had on their prospecting tour. This, of course, heightened the desire for information. On August 21st Bayer's first letter arrived. It was dated at St. Louis, the 12th of August. In this letter he states that in his opinion the purchase of the land should be made without delay. The society, of course, complied promptly with the agent's wishes. The necessary steps were taken to forward the money. The treasurer's report submitted in connection with this action shows the society to have been prosperous. Up to September 7th, 1837, 823 shares had been sold. There had been deposited with the treasurer $12,-396.11. It goes without saying that this was not the full amount due. It will be remembered that the lowest share was worth $25. Therefore, the entire amount due was almost double the amount collected. This difference is explained by the fact that partial payments were permitted. Each installment was at the rate of $5.

After Bayer became acquainted in St. Louis, his letters seem to have been punctually written, but were often seriously delayed on the way. We have record of letters dated August 19th and

THE UNITED STATES OF AMERICA.

To all to whom these Presents shall come, Greeting:

WHEREAS George H. Bayer of Philadelphia County Pennsylvania

ha_ deposited in the GENERAL LAND OFFICE of the United States, a Certificate of the REGISTER OF THE LAND OFFICE at St Louis

whereby it appears that full payment has been made by the said George H Bayer

according to the provisions of the Act of Congress of the 24th of April, 1820, entitled "An act making further provision for the sale of the Public Lands," for Section five in

Township forty five of Range five West, in the District of lands subject

to sale at St Louis Missouri, containing Six hundred and sixty five acres

and sixteen hundreths of an acre

according to the official plat of the survey of the said Lands, returned to the General Land Office by the **SURVEYOR GENERAL**, which said tract has been purchased by the said

George H Bayer

NOW KNOW YE, That the

UNITED STATES OF AMERICA, in consideration of the Premises, and in conformity with the several acts of Congress, in such case made and provided, HAVE GIVEN AND GRANTED,

and by these presents DO GIVE AND GRANT, unto the said George H Bayer

and to his heirs, the said tract above described: TO HAVE AND TO HOLD the same, together with all the rights, privileges, immunities, and appurtenances of whatsoever nature, thereunto

belonging, unto the said George H Bayer

and to his heirs and assigns forever.

IN TESTIMONY WHEREOF, I, Martin Van Buren

PRESIDENT OF THE UNITED STATES OF AMERICA, have caused these letters to be made PATENT, and the SEAL of the GENERAL

LAND OFFICE to be hereunto affixed.

GIVEN under my hand, at the CITY OF WASHINGTON, the first day of October, in the year of our

Lord one thousand eight hundred and forty, and of the **INDEPENDENCE OF THE UNITED STATES**

the Sixty fifth

Martin Van Buren

BY THE PRESIDENT:

Recorded, Vol. 19 Page 395.

CERTIFICATE OF PURCHASE OF GOVERNMENT LAND.

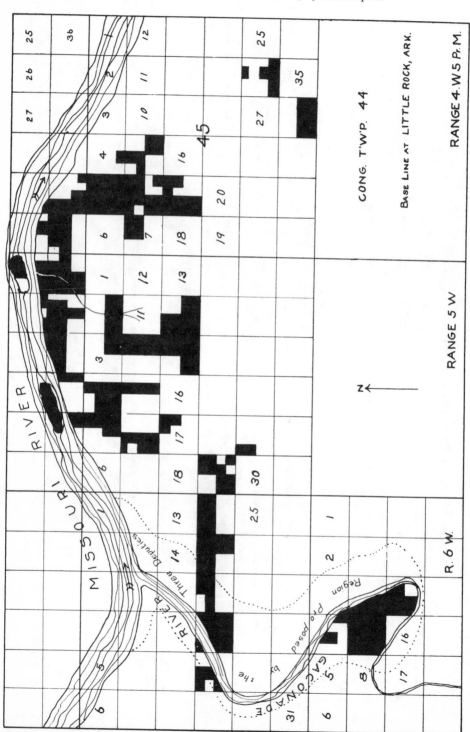

CHART SHOWING LAND PROPOSED AS SITE OF THE COLONY AND LAND ACTUALLY PURCHASED BY THE SOCIETY.

26th, and September 4th, 8th, 17th, 18th. But, like the letters of the deputies, they seem to have been misplaced when the papers were carried to Hermann, or they were destroyed. Of all the many letters that the agent then wrote, and those which he later sent to the superior in office, only three are known now to exist. They are a few of the many he wrote from Hermann. They will be inserted in their proper place in this article. We cannot refrain from expressing our regret that these old historic relics are not to be found. The most diligent search has failed to reveal the slightest clue to their whereabouts. Vandalism has even dared to encroach upon the archives at Hermann at a late date, and has delayed honest investigation most unpardonably.

As it stands, we can but infer, and often only conjecture, as to what these letters contained, by the action of the Board of Managers and the society. Thus, for instance, we cannot do better than merely surmise the reasons why Bayer did not follow the recommendations of the deputies more closely.

The land designated by the deputies lies along the Gasconade River, and along the point of confluence of this river and the Missouri. (This region is indicated on the accompanying chart by a dotted line.) From this same chart it will be seen also that only a comparatively small part of the Bayer purchase actually lies in this scope of territory. Why this was done is an unanswered and perhaps unanswerable question. It will be remembered that in their report the deputies mention the fact that 220 acres of this region were already in the hands of private owners. These owners offered this land at $15.00 an acre. However, it is not at all improbable that they declined to dispose of their possession under any consideration, whatever, seeing a prospect of profiting by the society later; or that they refused to sell at the price previously quoted by them, asking, indeed, a much higher price. Even $15.00 an acre must have appeared exorbitantly high then, when millions of acres could be entered at just one-twelfth of that price. At any rate, Bayer met with some serious hinderance. This he must have reported to the society, for the Board of Managers hastened to forward additional instructions to him.

„Dass Herr Bayer benachrichtigt werde, die auf dem von ihm erlesenen Landstriche aufgenommenen Plätze anzukaufen, im Falle sie durch keine andern ersetzt werden können."

"That Mr. Bayer be instructed to purchase occupied sites on the tract of land selected by him, in case no others can be substituted for them."

This was done on September 18th. It is plain from the connection of these minutes and what followed, that this has reference to some of the land he actually purchased from private owners, and not to the 220 acres above mentioned. This view is confirmed by another resolution, passed later that same evening:

„Dass Herr Bayer angewiesen werde, dass am Missouri und Gasconade gelegene Land, wenn es unter gleich vortheilhafter Bedingung zu haben, zu kaufen; doch seiner Einsicht die Entscheidung zu überlassen."

"That Mr. Bayer be instructed to purchase the land situated along the Missouri and the Gasconade, if it is obtainable under equally advantageous terms; nevertheless, the decision shall be left to his judgment."

This reference is clearly to the land visited by the three deputies, and also shows that pecuniary matters formed the barrier against a speedy purchase.

The accompanying chart shows and locates every acre of ground Bayer bought for the society. It is based on data found in the original patents, yet preserved at Hermann, and in an old deed of the society. A glance at the chart will show how the land was scattered. The reason for this is not well known. Bayer certainly did try to buy the land indicated by the deputies, and he had succeeded in acquiring several sections in this region. But most of the purchase lies near the present site of Hermann. Hermann is located on parts of Sections 25 and 26, 35 and 36, of Township 46, Range 5, West. In choosing the land thus scattered, the agent doubtless had in mind the fundamental principle of the body that sent him, namely, that agriculture and manufacture should go hand in hand. The regions along the Gasconade and the interior of the county were much better adapted to agriculture than the extremely broken land along the Missouri. On the banks of the Missouri he hoped the manufacturing establishments would spring up. The great river was to be the public highway on which the finished products should reach the market.

From a record at Hermann we learn the exact dates when the land was entered. On September 21st, 1837, the following certificates were issued at the St. Louis Land Office: Nos. 9636 to 9642, conveying seven separate tracts of land, containing 1594.81 acres; on September 22d, Nos. 9643 and 9644, conveying 480 acres; on October 4th, Nos. 9689 to 9694 and 9699 to 9710, conveying 5537.47 acres; on October 9th, Nos. 9728 to 9738, conveying 2640.26 acres; on October 10th, Nos. 9752 and 9753, conveying 560 acres. There is a further record, stating that on May 10th, 1838, he entered three more tracts, embracing 200 acres, on certificates Nos. 10,385 to 10,387. Though this entry was made many months after the first, the land must have been bought for the society, as Bayer was still its agent. This gives us a total of 11,012.54 acres, which were obtained from the government for the sum of $14,077.73. But this was not all the land acquired by the agent. From a deed whereby the trustees of the society took formal possession of the land, we learn that five further tracts, containing in all 288.09 acres, were bought from private owners. Therefore, the grand total of acres of which the society became possessor was 11,300.63. The persons who conveyed their land to the society were Stephen Atkins, William Guyler, Charles Roark, Willis Hensley and Polly Phillips.

Bayer's ledger account informs us that he expended $1535.00

in purchasing land from private individuals. A man named Jarvis refused to sell his farm. He foresaw a rapid increase in the value of land, and hoped to profit by the prosperity of the colony. He retained his claim, and later became the cause of much vexation and annoyance to the settlers.

Whether Bayer ever visited the Cuiver River country, indicated in his instruction, or not, is unknown.

We have, in several places, referred to the favorable report of the deputies, regarding the Gasconade River country. We desire to say that, from personal examination, we can confirm the opinion that it would be admirable for a settlement of the kind proposed. The land along the Gasconade is, in part, very fertile. This, then, would have satisfied the requirements which stipulated the purchase of farming land. The other demand—that of a site for manufacturing possibilites—could easily be met along either of the rivers. The statements of the deputies were entirely true and accurate. Only one fact did they fail to report, which, owing to the season in which they made their visit, they were unable to observe, namely that the lowlands of this region are quite miasmatic. As in other river bottoms, fevers play havoc among the inhabitants during the autumn. For this reason, it was doubtless a blessing that Bayer could not make agreeable terms of purchase. As it was, hundreds suffered intensely from ague during the first years of residence.

Bayer selected the site for the new town in the comparatively narrow valley of a small stream called Frain Creek. It is located seven miles to the east of the point of confluence of the Gasconade and the Missouri, on the south or right bank of the latter. The topography of the surrounding country is very irregular. Fr. Münch's rather poetical description of the physical environments of Missouri's "Deutschheim" when he says: "Hermann ist auf der Südseite amphitheatralisch von Hügelreihen umgeben," * is scarcely strong enough. Some of the land is extremely broken.

But very little of the land around the site of the proposed town is adapted to extensive agriculture. Other sections of the purchase have very good farm land. But they are far away, making communication and transportation difficult and laborious. To the unprejudiced observer it seems quite doubtful that Bayer was a good judge of land. He was by profession a schoolmaster. Most probably he knew more of "the three R's" than of the business of buying land for a corporation. Various conjectural explanations have been offered to account for his decision and the choice of this land. Some surmise that he selected it because it reminded him of his old Bavarian home.* Others say he selected it because it promised well for horticultural pursuits. Still others that he intentionally avoided the vast tracts of level land of West and North Missouri in order that there might be no temptation or possibilty for the settlers to own slaves. Still others believe and quite justly, that the nearness of St. Louis, "the Gateway of the West," led him to the choice. In addition to these views, we should like to refer again to some of the reasons we have previously enumerated, when we spoke of the choice of Missouri. We believe that the settlement of the Berliner Gesselschaft at Washington, Missouri, and that of Münich, Follenius and Bock, in Warren County, had more to do in fixing his choice than any other reason that has been suggested. The cheapness of the land

---

"Hermann is surrounded amphitheatrically on the south side by chains of hills."
* Fr. Münich, *"Der Staat Missouri,"* p. 204.

Note: The reference to Bayer's home being in Bavaria is probably erroneous. Goodspeed states: George F. Bayer, born in Weingarten, Baden, September 27, 1800 and died at Hermann, Missouri, March 18, 1839. His widow, in 1841, was married to Joseph Doyon. She died in 1880.

*Quote referred to: *Some surmise that he selected it because it reminded him of his old Bavarian home."*

of that locality cannot have been an inducement to him, for all the government land of Missouri sold then at the price of $1.25 to $2.50 per acre. The restriction that the settlement should be on a river, of course, hampered the agent more than one might think at the first glance.

We must now return again to the society itself, in Philadelphia.

The meeting of October 5th, 1837, was another memorable one in the annals of the Deutsche Ansiedlungs-Gesellschaft. After the president's order, that the society enter into secret session, had been obeyed, he announced:

„Dass er die frohe Nachricht mitzutheilen habe, dass ein grosses Stück Land für die Gesellschaft gekauft sei."

"That he could communicate the glad tidings, that an extensive tract of land had been purchased for the Society."

The enthusiasm of the members knew no bounds. "Land! land!" they cried, like anxious mariners after a dreary journey. New hope, new expectations, filled them all. A giant stride had been made towards the coveted goal. Here was, at last, a tangible proof of the sincerity of the undertaking. The dormant ones became aroused, the faithful stimulated and encouraged. The organization had gained a new lease on life. The world beheld that the Germans were, indeed, in earnest, and that their perseverance was about to be crowned with glorious success. So favorable was the prospect and so bright the outlook that the Board of Managers felt justified soon after in resolving:

„Dass, da das Land für die Gesellschaft an einem sehr günstigen Platze am Missouri Flusse angekauft ist, jede Actie vom 1. October d. J. an, bis auf weitere Anzeige, 35 Dollar kostet."

"That, since the land purchased for the Society was situated at a very favorable site on the Missouri, every share beginning with Oct. 1 of the current year, would cost $35.00, until further notice."

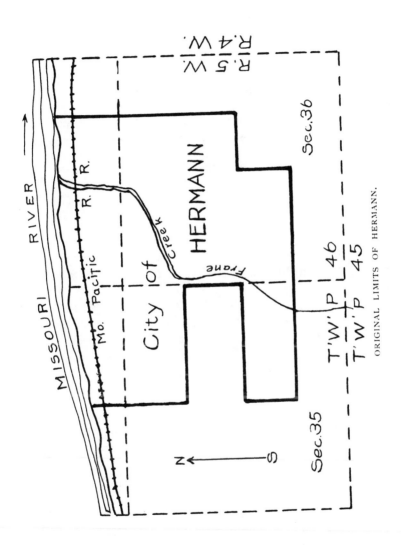

ORIGINAL LIMITS OF HERMANN.

The society accepted this recommendation, and even went a step farther, and on November 2d decreed:

„Der Preis der Actien soll vom 1. December d. J. an, auf $50, bis auf weitere Anzeige, festgestellt werden."

"Beginning on Dec. 1 of the current year, the price of a share shall be set at $50.00 until further notice."

On the same day that the announcement of the purchase was made, the name of the town was to be discussed. Only a name typically German would do. After a brief deliberation, this decision was reached:

„Dass die auf dem von der Deutschen Ansiedlungs-Gesellschaft gekauften Lande zu erbauende Stadt den Namen HERMANN erhalten soll."

"That the city to be built on the land purchased by the German Settlement Society shall receive the name HERMANN."

Under these prosperous conditions, it became apparent that to promote the undertaking still further, a responsible supervisor was a positive necessity. This officer was to be styled "General Agent." He should conduct their business at the prospective colony. In casting about for a suitable person for this very important business, it became clear to the members, "dass man keinen schicklicheren General Agenten als Herrn Bayer finden würde."* The election was, however, postponed until Bayer's return.

On the evening of October 30th, Bayer reported to the Board of Managers, having made the trip from St. Louis in seventeen days. He presented a sketch of the proposed town, described the land he had bought, and also the environments in which it was

---

*"That one would find no General Agent more competent than Mr. Bayer."

found.   On November 2d he made a written report to the "General Versammlung"*concerning the trip.   (Unfortunately, this report is not to be found.)   A committee took his report into closer scrutiny.   Every one was well pleased with the services of the agent, and it was at once moved to make G. F. Bayer the "General-Agent" of the society.   At first it was suggested that he should hold his office for an indefinite period, during good behavior.   Later the time was limited to one year.   As a matter of fact, he held it less than a year.   On October 2d, 1838, he laid down his extremely difficult task.

GEO. F. BAYER, THE AGENT OF THE SOCIETY.

General Assembly.

Todes-Anzeige.

Starb, nach langem Leiden, am Freitag Abend um 10 Uhr

Christopher Siems

im Alter von 77 Jahren.

Die Beerdigung findet am Sonntag Nach=mittag um 3 Uhr auf der Farm statt, und sind Freunde und Bekannte freundlichst eingeladen derselben beizuwohnen.

Die trauernden Kinder

Peter Siems nebst Geschwister.

Hermann, Mo., den 9. Sept. 1905.

ODD METHOD OF ANNOUNCING FUNERALS STILL
PREVALENT IN HERMANN.

In a town with a weekly newspaper, the news of some events must be put before the public without waiting on the next newspaper. The death notices are still printed as they were in 1907, the only change being that the notices are now on printed cards distributed to all of the business houses. In Bek's day the above notice was tacked onto the telephone poles.

Another form of notification is the tolling of the death bell when a death occurs in the congregations of St. Paul's and St. George's parishes.

Another delightful custom of both churches is the ringing in of the Sabbath at sundown on Saturday.

HARMONIE MEMBERSHIP CARD
HENRY BOCK 1886

SCHOOL RULES AND REGULATIONS

He was instructed to depart for the colony at the earliest possible date. The remuneration he was to receive for his services is itemized under four heads:

1. Herr Bayer erhält einen jährlichen Gehalt von $600 so lange er seine Pflicht erfüllt.

2. Es werden ihm 80 Acker Land von der Gesellschaft zu dem Ankaufspreise gelassen.

3. Er erhält $300 für sich und seine Familie als Reisegeld.

4. Er erhält ein im Bezirk der Stadt unvollendetes Blockhaus als Geschenk.

1) Mr. Bayer receives a yearly salary of $600.00 as long as he performs his duties.

2) He shall be allowed 80 acres of land at cost price by the Society.

3) He receives $300.00 as traveling expenses for himself and his family.

4) He receives as a gift an unfinished log house within the limits of the City.

All the land which Bayer had procured for the society still appeared in his name. November 3, 1837, the Board of Managers created a Board of Trustees, to whom the property of the society should be deeded. As security of the trust of these men their own personal property should be held. The society gladly and quickly ratified this appointment. The new board consisted of four enthusiastic supporters of the movement. Adam Maag, Adam Schmidt, Jakob Hummel, and Frederich Klett. It was deemed advisable that these four men should be added to the Board of Managers of the society. As it happened, most of them already belonged, so that the Board of Managers did not become too unwieldy a body. The deed, remarkable for its length, containing the itemized record of the transfer of forty-five separate tracts of land, is written, with exemplary neatness, on two pieces of parchment, each measuring 27x34 inches.

For the reason that it contains some historical facts, and because of its quaintness, we subjoin a short part of the deed here:

This Indenture made the fourteenth (14) day of November in the year of our Lord one thousand eight hundred and thirty-seven, Between George F. Bayer of the city of Philadelphia and the State of Pennsylvania, Merchant, and Catharine, his Wife, of the One Part, and Adam Maag, of the District of Spring Garden in the County of Philadelphia, Bottler; Adam Smith, of the Northern Liberties of the City of Philadelphia, Morocco Dresser; Jacob Hummell, of the Northern Liberties aforesaid, Morocco Dresser, and Frederick Klett, of the Northern Liberties aforesaid, Druggist, of the other part, witnesseth, That the said George F. Bayer and Catharine, his Wife, as well for and in consideration of the sum of One Dollar lawful money of the United States of America unto them at or before the Sealing and Delivery hereof by the said Adam Maag, Adam Smith, Jacob Hummel, and Frederick Klett, well and truly paid, the Receipt whereof is hereby acknowledged, as for divers other causes and considerations them thereunto moving have granted, bargained, and sold, aliened, enfeoffed, released and confirmed, and by these Presents do grant, bargain and sell, alien, enfeoff, release and confirm unto the said Adam Maag, Adam Smith, Jacob Hummel, and Frederick Klett and the Survivor and Survivors of them, and the Heirs and Assigns of the Survivor of them, All those Forty-Five Certain Tracts or Pieces of Land situated, lying and being in the County of Gasconade in the State of Missouri, to wit:"

It will be noticed that Bayer is spoken of as a merchant. This was doubtless an error. The City Directory of Philadelphia of 1837 gives his occupation as "teacher," his residence, 432 N. Second. In all other connections, when his name is mentioned with a profession, it is that of teacher. While he was away on his tour of inspection, and purchased the land, he wrote to the Board of Managers to send word to the "Zions-Gemeinde" that he would not be able to return in time to open the school. In a letter of August 10, 1838, to the Board of Managers, he says:

„Handel werde ich nie treiben auch wenn ich nicht mehr Agent bin, indem es mit meinen Principien nicht übereinstimmt."

"I shall never conduct a business even when I am no longer agent, as it does not harmonize with my principles."

It certainly sounded more businesslike to say "merchant" instead of "teacher" in connection with a big land deal.

It will also be noted that some of the proper names are Anglicized. The parties concerned were, however, all German.

The closing months of the year 1837 were marked by the intensest interest in the society. It was, indeed, a feverish interest. There was an eagerness that seems almost unnatural, a rush almost ridiculous. And all this, too, in a year when a fierce storm swept the financial world. But the panic of 1837 did not pass without marring even this institution. Of this we shall speak later. The transactions of the society impress us now as rather too eager. It seemed as if they wished to reach the ultimate goal by one single bound. They fired the imagination and exaggerated the possibilities and built up hopes which they were not certain they could fulfill. They realized, of course, that the time to strike is when the iron is hot. But we know how fatal the collapse is when hopes are shattered, promises unfulfilled, and expectation meets disappointment.

Many resolutions were passed regarding the government of the proposed town, and regarding the land, which all attest the keen interest taken in the affair, but which are uncalled for and premature. Thus without knowing anything of the land which they found themselves possessors of, save what the necessarily meager and perfunctory report of Bayer had told them, they arbitrarily ruled that the land should be divided into classes one and two, class one to cost $3.00 per acre and class two $2.00. It goes without saying that only the most loyal supporters would agree to take such land at such prices, when, in almost any quarter of the vast Louisiana Purchase any one could gain the ownership of two acres of land instead of one from the society, and that, too, of land that was of superior quality. Another drawback was the ruling which decreed that every owner should build a house valued at $300 on his lot or lots during the first year of ownership. The lots bordering on the wharf and costing $150.00 each were required to have a house valued at $500 by the expiration of the first year. Failure to comply with this decree forfeited the property to the society.

It would be expected that the board of managers would be very deliberative and conservative in their proposals, but it appears that they were most speculative. And the society sanctioned and accepted blindly most of their propositions. In their minds' eye Hermann was the rival of St. Louis—in reality its proposed site was a howling wilderness. Before they had any definite knowledge of the topography of the land around Hermann, they planned public squares, laid out streets (all on paper) and dignified these squares and streets by naming them after great German and American celebrities. Upon motion of Mr. Maag it was decided:

„Dass die grosse Strasse, welche von Norden nach Süden laufe, den Namen „Marktstrasse" bekomme, dass aus dieser Strasse das Viereck (Square) wegfalle, in der Mitte die Markthäuser gebaut und diese Strasse 10 Fuss breiter als die Marktstrasse von Philadelphia gemacht werde."

"That the main street, which runs from north to south, receive the name "Market Street"; that the Square be omitted from this street, that market houses be erected in the center, and that this street be made 10 feet wider than the Market Street in Philadelphia."

Mr. Klett moved to set aside four squares, one in each quarter of the plot chosen for the town, to be used as public places of recreation. It was further resolved that promenades 150 ft. wide should be arranged east and west along the town. As a matter of fact such promenades are absolutely impossible owing to the extremely broken condition of the ground in question. The streets running parallel to Market Street should bear these names: Washington, Franklin, Tell, Blücher, Philadelphia, Friedrich, Gutenberg, and Mozart. (The streets we do actually find in Hermann now are Market, Schiller, Gutenberg, Franklin, Gilbert, Mozart, Washington, Goethe, Jefferson and Wein, other streets being numbered.) The proposed squares (which, however, were never laid out) were to bear these names: Schiller, Goethe, Wieland and Herder. This was all very commendable to demonstrate their enthusiasm and zeal but it certainly was impractical and extremely visionary. Before a year had elapsed the board of managers had received intelligence that their plans were inapplicable to the new town. The actual conditions had foiled their ideals. On April 12th, 1838, they ask for an accurate insight into the physical conditions at Hermann, in these words:

„Dass Herr Bayer die Veranstaltung treffe: eine topographische Karte (nebst Plan der Stadt Hermann) von den sämmtlichen Ländereyen für die Gesellschaft anzufertigen oder anfertigen zu lassen und diese Zeichnungen dem Verwaltungs-Rathe hier einzuschicken."

"That Mr. Bayer make arrangements for: the completion of a topographic map (in addition to the plan for the City of Hermann) either by himself or by someone else of the entire territories for the Society and to send these drawings here to the Board of Managers."

At this time, too, the board of managers resolved to make another effort at popularizing the organization in the Fatherland. They decided to have 500 notices printed setting forth the prosperous condition of the society and encouraging participation in the same. These notices were to be distributed among the Philadelphia members who should enclose them in their letters to European friends and kinsmen. This idea found favor. At a subsequent meeting it was agreed to have another lot of 500 such notices struck. They were designed to be sent to European ports, like Bremen, Hamburg, and Havre, where "Schiffsmackler" should distribute 10 to 15 of them on each ship sailing for North America.

There was no doubt whatsoever in the minds of the officers, that Hermann would soon become a booming city. For the comfort and safety of the prospective residents they ordained the following:

"Dass keine Schlächterei, keine Leim-, Licht-, Seifen-, Oel-, Terpentin-, Pulver- oder Stärkefabrik, oder irgend eine Anstalt, welche das Leben der Nachbarn fährdet oder unangenehm macht, innerhalb der Stadt angelegt werden dürfen."

"That no slaughterhouses, no factories for the production of glue, candles, soap, oil, turpentine, gunpowder or starch, or any other institution whereby the lives of the neighbors are endangered or inconvenienced, shall be permitted to be established within the city."

The promoters of the undertaking were "Grossstädter"[*] and took account of a host of things which would not occur to residents of a small town until the specific case presented itself, when they would know how to meet the emergency.

The river was their great highway by which their wilderness was connected with civilization. This the colonists realized and thus early provided to reserve its use wholly to the society, and not allow the monopoly of any man or a collection of men to mar their progress or inconvenience them.

4. The Founding of the Colony and its Early Growth.

The year 1837 was nearing its close. It was necessary that

[*]"Ship Agents."

[*]"Inhabitants of large cities."

Bayer should return to the site of the colony with the earliest dispatch. New instructions were now needed for the new "General Agent" to be governed by. On November 30th the following committee was appointed to draw up these instructions: Fegenbusch, Gentner, Kiderlen, Wollsiefer, Maag, Klett, Schmidt and Hummel. The adoption of these instructions marks the beginning of a new chapter in the history of the society.

The instructions were these:

INSTRUCTION

des General-Agenten der Deutschen Ansiedlungs-Gesellschaft zu Hermann, Missouri.

Par. 1.

Der General-Agent verpflichtet sich, so bald es die Gesellschaft wünscht, an den Ort zu reisen, wo dieselbe Land gekauft, um die Geschäfte der Gesellschaft zu besorgen, so, wie nachstehend bestimmt ist.

a) Der General-Agent verpflichtet sich alle Einkäufe und Verkäufe für die Bevollmächtigten der Gesellschaft zu machen, nach ausführlicher Instruction derselben.

b) Alle Vierteljahre soll er ausführliche Rechnung über den Stand seiner Kasse ablegen und der Gesellschaft übersenden.

c) Der General-Agent verpflichtet sich über alles Eigenthum der Gesellschaft ein ausführliches Lagerbuch zu führen.

Par. 2.

Sobald 10 Mitglieder der Gesellschaft auf dem Ansiedlungs-Platze ankommen soll der General-Agent eine Versammlung derselben berufen und aus ihnen ein Committee von 3 Personen wählen lassen, die das Recht und die Verpflichtung haben, die Geschäfts-Führung des General-Agenten zu revidiren und, falls dieselben nicht nach dem Sinn dieser Instruction sein sollten, darüber an die Gesellschaft zu berichten.

a) Genannte Committee soll jede vierteljährige Rechnung des General-Agenten durchsehen und deren Richtigkeit bescheinigen.

Im Falle die Committee die Rechnung des General-Agenten nicht richtig findet, soll sie einen speciellen Bericht gelangen lassen.

b) Im Falle der General-Agent durch Krankheit oder auf andere Weise geschäftsuntüchtig gemacht werden solle, oder seinen Verpflichtungen gegen die Gesellschaft nicht nachkäme, so kann die Committee bei vollkommener Uebereinstimmung aller ihrer Glieder und mit Zustimmung der Mehrheit der dortigen Mitglieder der Gesellschaft, den General-Agenten suspendiren und überhaupt solche Schritte gehen wie dieses der Vortheil der Gesellschaft erheischt.

c) Diese Committee in Vereinigung mit dem General-Agenten hat zu bestimmen, zu welcher Klasse ein Stück Land gehören soll.

Par. 3.

Der General-Agent soll kein Geschäft betreiben, ausser das für die Gesellschaft, weder in seinem noch in eines Andern Namen, mit Ausnahme des Ackerbaues.

Par. 4.

Sollte ein Fall vorkommen, wo der General-Agent nothwendig handeln müsste, ohne für den besonderen Fall Instruction von der Gesellschaft zu haben, so soll er mit Zuziehung und Berathung der dortigen Committee so handeln, wie es für die Gesellschaft am vortheilhaftesten ist.

Par. 5.

Der General-Agent soll alle Land-Vermessungen auf dem Gebiete der Gesellschaft besorgen.

Par. 6.

Der General-Agent soll sowohl der englischen als der deutschen Sprache mächtig sein.

Instructions for the General Agent of the German Settlement Society of Hermann, Missouri.

Par. 1

The General Agent obligates himself as soon as the Society desires it, to travel to the place where this land has been purchased in order to manage the business of the Society as set forth below:

a) The General Agent obligates himself to perform all necessary purchases and sales for the representatives of the Society according to detailed instructions concerning the same.

b) Every quarter he shall compile a detailed account of the standing of his treasury and submit it to the Society.

c) The General Agent obligates himself to keep a detailed merchants' stock book of all property of the Society.

Par. 2

As soon as 10 members of the Society have come to the site of the settlement the General Agent shall call a meeting of the same and have a committee of 3 persons elected by them who shall possess the privilege and the duty of reviewing the business management of the General Agent, and, in the case that this should not be in accordance with the intent of these instructions, to notify the Society thereof.

a) Said committee shall examine every quarterly report of the General Agent and verify its accuracy. In case the committee finds the report of the General Agent incorrect, they shall arrive at a special report.

b) In case the General Agent should become incompetent for his duties through sickness or some other cause, or should not fulfill his obligations towards the Society, then the Committee can by unanimous vote of its members and with the approval of a majority of the members of the Society there, suspend the General Agent and in general take such measures as the welfare of the Society demands.

c) This committee, acting with the General Agent, must determine the classification of a tract of land.

Par. 3

The General Agent shall conduct no business, except that for the Society, either in his or in some other name, except that of farming.

Par. 4

Should an incident arise for which the General Agent must necessarily take action without having any instructions from the Society for the special case, then he should with the cooperation and advice of the Committee there, take such action as is most advantageous to the Society.

Par. 5

The General Agent shall conduct all land surveys on the domains of the Society.

Par. 6

The General Agent shall be versed in the English as well as in the German language.

With these instructions Bayer, accompanied by his family, started out for his new field of labor, early in December, 1837. At Pittsburg personal illness delayed him many weeks. This delay worked great inconvenience and hardship to a number of pioneers who had already journeyed to the site of the new settlement. Bayer alone had authority to lay out lots and assign them to colonists. But now he was a thousand miles away. Winter was setting in, and build they must, to protect their wives and children. But where should they build? Everywhere was wilderness. They were not certain that the houses, they erected, with great toil, stood on parts of two lots, instead of one. No wonder they wrote pleadingly to the mother society for an Agent.

With the approach of the new year Bayer was able to depart for the colony. In midwinter he undertook the gigantic task that was assigned him. Poor man! Alone he found himself placed in almost unexplored wilds. The responsibility that rested on his shoulders was enormous. The success of the whole undertaking rested largely on his decisions and his judgment. What made the task still greater is (as we are led to conclude from report) that he was hardly qualified for such an important position. The demands were too appallingly great for one man. It is quite improbable that any other man in the society would have been many sided enough to engineer an undertaking so great as this one was. What was it the society asked of him? He was required to oversee everything that pertained to the property of the society, to superintend the surveying, not only of the town site, but of all the 11,000 acres of ground, to assign the property to colonists and record their claims, to hear and adjust a thousand complaints of the settlers, to answer innumerable communications of prospective colonists and shareholders, to furnish food-supplies for all, to arrange for the building of saw and grist mills, and a thousand other things. No wonder that his reports to the home society came in meagerly and irregularly. When it is remembered that the colonists were subject to human erring, and that some of them had none of those noble, lofty sentiments, which actuated the founders, but that selfishness often impelled them to unreasonable and unjust demands, we wonder that any man had the persistence to stay at his post as long as Bayer did.

The pioneers who had the hardihood to venture into the Missouri wilds in 1837, even before the General-Agent had gone out, were:

Conrad Baer, Georg Conrad Riefenstahl, with wife and five children, John George Prager, with wife and two children, Gottleib Heinrich Gentner, with wife, Daniel Oelschlaeger with wife and one child.

These seventeen persons left immediately after the purchase became assured, confident that Bayer would speedily follow and regulate and supervise their settlement. This program was broken into by Bayer's sickness which confined him at Pittsburg,

Pa., for many months. Communication was slow in those days, and in the cold season it almost ceased entirely. Just how these first colonists eked out an existence during this first winter is unchronicled. Their discomfort must certainly have been great, great enough to embolden them to ask retribution from the society later. In an early record mention is made of a half-finished log house on the site of the proposed town. This some of them are said to have occupied. It is perfectly safe to assume that the English speaking settlers gave them all the aid and comfort in their power to give. The Missourian is remarkably hospitable today, and he was even more so in the pioneer days. The latch string always hung on the outside for the needy and distressed. At any rate Bayer found them later, sound in body, though not quite contented in mind.

A number of other enthusiastic colonists left the east later. But they had the good judgment not to enter the wilderness at such an inhospitable season. They remained comfortably in St. Louis awaiting Bayer's arrival there and finding what temporary employment they could in the city. They had come this far west to be on the grounds in the earliest spring in order to secure the best choice of farm land or town lots. Selfishness is a human characteristic. This corporation was no more exempt from it than any other land-seeking body. All desired a place on the "ground-floor."

Quite naturally, the failure on the part of the General-Agent to arrive at the colony on scheduled time did even more than work hardship to the pioneer settlers, it shook the confidence, not only of the enrolled members but also of those about persuaded to join the organization. As was stated above, the colonists did not know the reason for Bayer's delay because of lack of communication.

On the 22nd of February, 1838, Bayer had not arrived at St. Louis. This we learn from a letter of D. Widersprecher written there and then to Secretary Wesselhoeft.

„Wir warten schon seit einigen Monaten vergeblich auf die Ankunft des Herrn Bayer und befinden uns so ziemlich in einer ungewissen Lage. Auf jeden Fall hat diese Angelegenheit bereits sehr dadurch gelitten, dass niemand vorhanden ist, die Geschäfte zu superintendiren.

Sie werden sehr wohl wissen, dass die Meinung für die Ansiedlung im Allgemeinen nicht günstig ist und wenn das Werk nicht mit Eifer und Patriotismus angegriffen wird kann man sich keine grossen Aussichten versprechen."

"You will very likely know that in general the opinions concerning the settlement are not favorable and if the work is not pursued with zeal and patriotism, no great expectations can be realized from it.

We have already been waiting in vain for several months upon the arrival of Mr. Bayer and are placed in a rather uncertain situation. In any case this affair has suffered greatly in that no one is present to supervise the business."

Just when Bayer arrived in Missouri, is not known. The first record of a letter from him, which the minutes contain, speaks of a communication dated at Hermann, March 28. Allowing him a few days to arrange the most necessary things and to look over the situation, we should say he arrived about the middle of March. From the action taken by the society and the reply the officers sent to Bayer, we infer that the agent experienced a very unpleasant reception at Hermann, and that some extraordinarily presumptuous and unjust demands were made upon him. It is to be sincerely regretted that the lofty aims of the founders of the society did not actuate every one of its members; that the appeal of the unselfish ones: "Seid einig, einig, einig!"*fell upon stony hearts; that the principle of give little and gain much permeated so many of the early colonists; that the spirit of sacrifice was not in the land; that it was not felt and appreciated that such an organization could prosper only by the strictest adherence to the

---

"Be united, united, united!"

principles of equal rights to all and special privileges to none. It appears that those who had spent that comfortless winter of 1837-8 on the banks of the Missouri, not only desired, but demanded special favors of the agent. They even appealed for commiseration to the society, claiming that through the unfortunate and unforeseen delay of Bayer they had endured more hardships and were thus entitled to special recognition, and favors. Such advantages could not be granted, if for no other reason than that of the precedent it established. President Schmoele, in a letter written at Philadelphia, April 12th, 1838, clearly instructs the agent as to his action:

„Geehrter Herr!

Ihr Schreiben, datirt: Hermann, den 28ten März 1838, an die Deutsche Ansiedlungs-Gesellschaft, nebst den Beschlüssen einer auf der Ansiedlung gehaltenen Versammlung ist richtig empfangen worden, und ich werde beide Dokumente dem Verwaltungs-Rath, und der nächsten monatlichen Versammlung der Ansiedlungs-Gesellschaft vorlegen.

Als vorläufige Antwort auf Ihren Brief dient folgendes:

Obgleich es mir, wie der Gesellschaft Wunsch ist, dass Sie durch Freundlichkeit, Gefälligkeit und vernünftige Nachsicht die Lage derjenigen Mitglieder, welche schon lange auf der Ansiedlung sich befanden, Ihrer, durch Unglück verhinderte Ankunft entgegenharrend, zu erleichtern streben möchten, so muss doch auf strenge Beobachtung Ihrer Instruction gedrungen werden. Namentlich kann und wird sich die Gesellschaft in keiner Hinsicht auf Bevorrechtigung einzelner Mitglieder einlassen, diese mögen mit den Gesetzen der Gesellschaft bekannt sein oder nicht. Alle auf die Rechte der Mitglieder bezüglichen Beschlüsse der Gesellschaft sind in unserem gewöhnlichen Organ, der *Alten und Neuen Welt,* regelmässig bekannt gemacht worden. Es ist daher Pflicht der Mitglieder, dieselben zu kennen; wenigstens kann Unkenntniss derselben kein Vergehen gegen sie entschuldigen; und am wenigsten Vorrechte oder Anmassungen begründen. Suchen Sie vorkommende Fälle dieser Art auf die günstigste und gelindeste Art zu beseitigen."

"Dear Sir!

Your letter dated March 28, 1838 to the German Settlement Society in addition to the resolutions of a meeting held in the Settlement has been safely received and I shall present both documents to the Board of Managers and to the next monthly meeting of the Settlement Society.

The following may serve as a temporary answer to your letter. Although it is my desire, as well as that of the Society, that you would by friendliness, amiability and sensible forbearance strive to ameliorate the situation of those members who have been in the settlement for a long time anxiously awaiting your arrival which was delayed by ill fortune, it is nevertheless necessary to insist upon strict obervance of your instructions. In particular the Society cannot and will not in any respect tolerate privileges for individual members, whether they are acquainted with the laws of the Society or not. All the decisions of the Society regarding the rights of the members have been regularly published in the "Alte und Neue Welt", as our official organ. It is, therefore, the duty of the members to be acquainted with them; at least ignorance of them cannot excuse the transgression of them; and least of all be grounds for special privileges or usurpations. Attempt to settle cases of this kind that may arise in the most favorable and mildest way.

In the spring of 1838 a large number of colonists journeyed to Hermann. Statistics of the town show that during this year 230 persons—men, women and children—arrived. Of this number 29 were unmarried men. Two were widows with 3 and 5 children, respectively. This was the banner year of the colony so far as numerical growth was concerned. The record for the years 1839 and '40 is not so complete in detailed accounts. The books show that 21 shareholders arrived. We can not say how many persons came with them. Nor do we know just how many more shareholders purchased colony land. A letter from Hermann, May 15, 1839, asserts that the population then was 450.

This is encouraging enough, considering that travel was slow and laborious.

It will be remembered that Par. 2 of the instructions to Bayer provided for the organization of an executive committee of three to be chosen as soon as 10 persons of the society had arrived. Bayer was slow in carrying out this injunction. Dr. Schmoele's letter, which we continue to quote here, reminds him of this duty as well as others expressed in the instructions.

„Da nunmehr schon so viele Ansiedler eingetroffen sind so werden Sie Ihrer Instruction gemäss so bald als möglich die Organisation einer kontrolirenden Committee veranlassen. Es scheint am zweckmässigsten, dass Sie zu diesem Ende eine Versammlung sämmtlicher dort anwesenden Mitglieder berufen, dieser dann Ihre Instructionen sowohl wie alle die Organisirung der Ansiedlungs-Gesellschaft betreffenden Verordnungen und Beschlüsse der Gesellschaft vorlegen und sie zu einer nächsten Versammlung nach einer gebührlichen Frist einladen, um die Wahl der Committee zu vollziehen.

Die Resultate wollen Sie, sowohl als die Committee selbst, unverzüglich, an mich berichten.

Ueberhaupt wird es sehr gewünscht, und würde das Vertrauen der Gesellschaft dadurch verstärkt werden, dass Sie uns durch häufige und ausführliche Berichte erfreuen. Vor Allem wurde ein unverzüglicher Bericht Ihrer geschehenen Abreise von Pittsburg, sowie Ihre Ankunft in Hermann dringend erwartet. Ebensosehr wünscht die Gesellschaft zu wissen, welche Massregeln Sie getroffen haben, um das untere, an unserem Lande liegende, zum Stadtplatze nothwendige Landstück für die Gesellschaft zu sichern.

Bei dem jetzigen blühenden Zustande unserer Gesellschaft, möchte der Gedanke gewagt werden dürfen, das grosse Jarvische Claim für die Gesellschaft anzukaufen. Alle Extra-Bemühungen, welche Sie zu diesem Zwecke machen würden, möchten Ihnen im glücklichen Falle von der Gesellschaft mit der grössten Liberalität belohnt werden.

Ich brauche wohl den möglichst schnellen Betrieb der Vermessungen nicht zu erwähnen, da dieses unter Ihrer ersten und wahrscheinlich schon zum grossen Theile erledigten Pflicht gehört.

In der Hoffnung, dass Sie in der Erfüllung Ihres wichtigen und beschwerlichen Amtes nicht müde werden, und mit dem Wunsche, dass etwa vorkommende Zwistigkeiten auf die gelindeste

und menschenfreundlichste Weise beseitigt werden mögen, bin und
bleibe ich Ihr ergebener und treuer Freund

Wilh. Schmoele,

(Beglaubigt Fr. Schreiber.)   Präs.

Sekretair.

Since so many settlers have already arrived you will in accordance with your instructions arrange for the organization of a
controlling Committee. It seems best suited to the purpose that to
attain this end you call an assembly of all members present there,
and then submit to them your instructions as well as the organization of the regulations and the decisions of the Settlement
Society, and then to invite them to the next meeting after a
suitable time to hold the election of the Committee.

You, as well as the Committee itself, are to inform me of the
results without delay.

It is generally greatly desired, and the confidence of the
Society would be greatly strengthened, if you would cheer us by
numerous and detailed reports. Above all, an immediate report of
the journey you made from Pittsburg, as well as of your arrival in
Hermann, was anxiously awaited. Likewise, the Society desires to
know which measures you have taken to secure for the Society the
lower tract of land adjoining our domain which is necessary for
the site of the city.

In view of the present flourishing condition of the Society the
thought might now be ventured of purchasing the large Jarvis
claim for the Society. All extra exertions which you make toward
this end would, in the case of a fortunate result, be rewarded with
the greatest liberality by the Society.

I probably need not remind you to carry out the work of the

survey, as this was one of your first tasks and has probably been partly completed by now.

In the hope that you will not become weary of the fulfillment of your important and difficult office, and with the wish that possible differences may be settled in the mildest and friendliest manner possible, I am and remain your devoted and faithful friend.

Wilh. Schmoele
President

Attested by: Fr. Schreiber
Secretary

Parts of this letter show again how much was expected of Bayer and how very varied were the capacities in which he was supposed to be proficient. What a presumption is expressed in this letter. The Agent—a schoolman by profession—doubtless little acquainted with the duties of a surveyor, is expected to have surveyed the enormous tract of more than 11,000 acres of ground in the short period of less than one month, and besides performing a multitude of other complex duties. And this is the attitude of the society for the greater part of Bayer's activity as agent. It only goes to prove how inexperienced the founders of the society were in problems of this nature. We do not champion the cause of Bayer. It is our opinion that he was not competent to cope with the many-sided problems. But we also wish to point out that no one man could meet efficiently the requirements of this organization.

The colonists were not in harmony with the agent and did not co-operate in the difficult tasks that presented themselves. They lacked the ability to adjust themselves to primitive conditions, were often and in many things extremely impractical, and worst of all were selfish, fault finding, without the good of the cause at heart. Under such conditions and among people of such dispositions, protests naturally followed protests. The disappointed, the discontented and the "wise" ones soon registered their objections with the home society. Some of these objections were trivial, foolish, puerile and malicious. This will be made clearer by giving, in toto, the complaints of one Binz. Binz had been at Hermann. Returning to Philadelphia he regarded it his solemn duty to report his grievances. As he was too ignorant to make an intelligent statement, the society appointed a committee of three to confer with him, to bring his accusations to writing, and "mit dessen eigenhändiger Unterschrift versehen zu lassen und der nächsten Versammlung vorzutragen."* We have decided, after considerable hesitation, to insert it here. We do it because it shows how malicious and asinine some of the colonists were. Also because it is typical of the nature of many complaints presented. Some of the complainants had not yet been purged of the "Kleinelei"* of another Fatherland. The accusations read as follows in the report:

Herr August Binz sagt aus wie folgt:

1. Dass Herr Bayer (General-Agent in Hermann) durchaus in der Erfüllung seiner Pflichten keine Genugthuung gebe, und meist nur seinen eigenen Geschäften nachgehe.

2. Dass Herr Bayer in "company" mit Herrn Widersprecher einen "Stohr" halte, die Tageszeit auf seinem Lande zubringe und die Abendzeit auf seinen "Stohr" verwende.

3. Dass die vier Gesellschafts-Ochsen, Herrn Bayer's Pferd, Kuh, und zwei Schweine mit ihren Jungen täglich zu Gaste haben.

4. Dass drei Herren in Hermann waren um Actien zu kaufen, dass aber die Bekanntschaft mit Herrn Bayer ihr Vorhaben verleidet.

"To have him affix his signature in his own handwriting and to present it to the next assembly."

"Triviality, provincial outlook"

5. Dass Herr Bayer dem Herrn Schindahler aus Gefälligkeit 160 Ackers, nah an der Stadt für den Ankaufspreis in der Office habe zuschreiben lassen.

6. Dass Herr Bayer seinen Pflichten gegen ihn selbst nicht nachgekommen sey.

7. Dass Herr Bayer in einer Zeitung in St. Louis alle Sonntag eine regelmässige Versammlung angekündigt habe, in den letzten fünf Wochen aber nie erschien.

8. Dass alle Ansiedler es wünschen, da sie wussten dass Herr A. Binz nach Philadelphia gehen wollte; besonders eine Gesellschaft zu halten, um Nachrichten an die Muttergesellschaft mit zu nehmen; Herr Bayer aber nicht erschien; Herr Binz verweilte bis den Freitag, es konnte aber keine Versammlung zusammengebracht werden, weil Herr Bayer mit seinen eigenen Geschäften zu viel zu thun hatte.

9. Dass nicht fünf Mann auf der Ansiedlung seyen die mit der Handlung und dem Betragen des Herrn Bayer zufrieden wären.

10. Dass Herr Bayer das Ausmessen gar nicht verstehe, eine solche Verwirrung hervorbrachte, dass durch einen Sachkundigen die schon gethanen Vermessungen noch einmal vorgenommen werden mussten; und so sich zeigte, dass ein neugebautes Blockhaus auf zwei Lotten stand.

11. Dass Herr Binz die Muttergesellschaft in Philadelphia versichere, dass im Allgemeinen eine grosse Unzufriedenheit wegen Herrn Bayer's Nichtsthun dort in Hermann herrsche, und er als Mitglied der „Deutschen Ansiedlungs-Gesellschaft" sich verpflichtet fühle, dies offen und frei zum Wohle der ganzen Gesellschaft auszusprechen, und mit seiner Namens-Unterschrift zu unterzeichnen.

August Binz.

Committee:

    G. Zimmermann, Präs.
    J. C. Viereck, Sekretair.
    J. Andreas Kehr.

Mr. August Binz states as follows:

1) That Mr. Bayer (General Agent in Hermann) absolutely gives no satisfaction in the performance of his duties, and spends most of his time with his own business affairs.

2) That Mr. Bayer conducts a store in company with Mr. Widersprecher, spends the daytime on his farm and the evening in his store.

3) That the four oxen belonging to the Society have as daily guests Mr. Bayer's horse, cow and two hogs along with their progeny.

4) That three gentlemen were in Hermann to buy shares, but that their acquaintance with Mr. Bayer had changed their intentions.

5) That Mr. Bayer had made a deed in the office for 16 acres near the city at cost price to Mr. Schindabler as a favor.

6) That Mr. Bayer was unable to take care of his own business affairs.

7) That Mr. Bayer had announced in a St. Louis paper a regular meeting every Sunday, but had himself not appeared in the last five weeks.

8) That all settlers desired, as they knew that Mr. Binz wanted to go to Philadelphia, to hold a special assembly, to send news to the Mother Society along with him. Mr. Bayer, however, did not appear.

Mr. Binz delayed till Friday, but no meeting could be held because Mr. Bayer was too preoccupied with his own affairs.

9) That there were no five men in the settlement who were satisfied with the management and the conduct of Mr. Bayer.

10) That Mr. Bayer did not understand surveying at all; that he caused such confusion that the surveys which had already been made had to be repeated by a professional surveyor, so that it was discovered that a newly-built log house stood on two lots.

11) That Mr. Binz assures the Mother-Society in Philadelphia that, generally speaking, a great dissatisfaction prevails in Hermann over Mr. Bayer's inactivity; and that as a member of the German Settlement Society he feels himself obligated to express this openly and freely for the sake of the welfare of the Society, and to affix his signature in his own handwriting.

August Binz

Committee:
C. Zimmermann, President
J. C. Viereck, Secretary
J. Andreas Kehr

Some of the accusations are perhaps justifiable, but others are too trivial, gossipy and evidently concocted to make up a respectable list of complaints, to merit recognition.

Upon hearing the report, which was presented early in June, the society passed this resolution of June 8th:

„Dass der General-Agent aufs dringendste ersucht werde *sogleich* einen speziellen Bericht über die ganze Ansiedlung zu geben, indem die Gesellschaft sehr unzufrieden über das Benehmen des Herrn General-Agenten sei und diese Berichte von 14 zu 14 Tagen fortzusetzen habe."

"That the General Agent be most urgently requested to furnish *immediately* a special report about the entire settlement, as the Society was very dissatisfied with the conduct of the General Agent, and these reports were to be repeated every 14 days."

The society had no longer any confidence in Bayer. At this same meeting we learn that the agent's instructions are to be copied, and the copy sent to the "Controlierende Committee,"*(which Bayer had evidently organized now, in comformity to his instructions) "mit der Bemerkung" (to execute them) "da Herr Bayer es doch vernachlässigen würde."*

The Board of Managers, too, took a thrust at the agent, when they, as early as the middle of May, resolved:

„Dass der General-Agent Herr Bayer ersucht werde, seinen Verpflichtungen in dem Masse nachzukommen, in Zukunft pünktlicher Bericht über den Fortgang der Colonie Hermann abzustatten. . . . . dass wenigstens alle 4 Wochen ein, auf Wahrheit gegründeter Bericht von der kontrolierenden Committee unterzeichnet, dem Verwaltungs-Rathe eingeschickt werden müsse.“

"That the General Agent, Mr. Bayer, be requested to fulfill his duties to the extent of furnishing in the future, detailed reports concerning the progress of the Colony in Hermann . . . that at least every four weeks a creditable report signed by the Controlling Committee would have to be sent to the Board of Managers."

From the very beginning, some of those who could reasonably be regarded as the best the society numbered among its own and who on the whole were enthusiastic enough, give expression to views, that are wholly unwholesome in a body of this nature. So for instance D. Widersprecher, in the letter from which was quoted above, having heard a false rumor that some one had received favors, at once wrote to Secretary Wesselhoeft:

"Since Mr. Bayer would neglect it anyway."

"Controlling Committee"

"With the notation"

„Wenn ich für mich keinen guten Bauplatz bekommen kann, gehe ich nicht nach Hermann, und (he adds a thread) es werden dann meine Freunde auch nicht hingehen.

Ueberdies wollen wir nichts mit der Sache zu thun haben, wenn wir finden, dass Begünstigungen stattfinden und wenn wir dort unsere Grundsätze von Recht und Billigkeit verfolgt sehen."

"If I cannot get a good building site for myself, I shall not go to Hermann and (he adds a threat) then my friends shall also not go there.

Moreover we want nothing to do with the affair, if we find that favors are granted and that our principles of right and justice are perverted."

The author of the letter demands favors which he would not grant. Such language was ill becoming a man who on the site of the colony became a rich man. This shows again the disposition of many of the participants who were to be the pillars of strength of the social structure.

From day to day the discontent with Bayer's régime grew stronger. The derogatory reports came faster. The censure became more and more vehement. Even President Schmoele, who in his semi-annual report, delivered on April 14, expressed the utmost confidence in Bayer, and called attention to his "allegemein anerkannte Ehrlichkeit, Umsicht und Menschenfreundlichkeit,"* began to suspect the agent as neglectful of his duties.

It appears that Bayer did not know who his accusers were— at least not for a long time. He endeavored to carry the fearful burden that was placed upon his shoulders without a murmur. The changed attitude of the home society soon became known to him through the tone of their communications. His friend Adam Schmidt visited the colony in June and to him he poured out his heart's sorrow, with him he discussed the best steps to be taken for the good of the whole.

---

*"*Universally recognized honesty, insight and philanthropy.*"

When Schmidt returned to Philadelphia many of the unexplained acts, and the apparently unpardonable neglect of the agent
were explained. After Schmidt's report the Board of Managers
resolved:

„Dass, da die Obliegenheiten des General-Agenten in Hermann von einer solchen Ausdehnung und zeitraubend sind und da
der General-Agent unmöglich alles dieses übersehen kann, Nachtheile für die Gesellschaft entstehen könnten, so hält der Verwaltungs-Rath es für nothwendig die Gesetzgebung und Verwaltung
den Mitgliedern in Hermann soweit zu übertragen, als es die Localität und die Bedürfnisse der Mitglieder erheischen.

Dass folgende Mitglieder in Hermann, die Herren: E. C. Staf-
horst, Julius Leupold, M. Krauter, W. L. Henrich, W. Senn und
―― Gentner, mit Hinzuziehung des General-Agenten, bevollmäch-
tigt sind, die sämmtlichen Mitglieder zu einer Versammlung zu
berufen und förmlich zu organisiren, um regelmässige Beamten zu
wählen."

"That, since the obligations of the General Agent in Hermann are of such an extent and are time-consuming, and since it is
impossible for the General Agent to fulfill all of them, disadvantages could result for the Society; therefore, the Board of
Managers deems it necessary to transfer the legislative powers
and management to the members in Hermann insofar as the
locality and the necessities of the members require it.

That following members in Hermann, the gentlemen: E. C.
Staffhorst, Julius Leupold, M. Krauter, W. L. Henrich, W. Senn
and Gentner, with addition of the General Agent, be empowered
to call all members to a special meeting to formally organize
themselves in order to elect officers."

This was done June 2nd, 1838. It marks a big concession
on the part of the home society—a concession which the colony
eagerly took hold of, and which encouraged them to ask for still
more powers, before the year had gone by.

We are fortunate in having handed down to us three letters from the former agent—Bayer. We insert them here because they will speak for a most sorely abused man, and will in a measure vindicate him, if he needs vindication, but best of all they present a glimpse into the actual workings of this body.

Hermann, June 25th, 1838.

Herrn Doctor Schmoele, Präsident der deutschen Ansiedlungs-Gesellschaft zu Philadelphia.

Geehrter Herr!

Die Beschlüsse der Colonie dahier, im Verlauf dieses Monats gehalten, werden Ihnen zugekommen seyn. Dringende Geschäfte veranlassten eine Verzögerung der ersten Beschlüsse dieses Monats, und da die Erledigung mehrerer Punkte derselben Eile forderte, so schien es mir passender die nächste Sitzung abzuwarten. Herr Schmidt, welcher seinem Versprechen gemäss persönliche Berichte bei seiner Zurückkunft an die Gesellschaft erstatten wird, indem wir Manches mit einander besprochen, dass, meines Erachtens, nicht an die grosse Glocke gehört, wenn nicht unserem nunmehr schönen Gelingen unserer Sache entgegen gearbeitet werden soll. Ich muss mir dabey freylich einen Vorwurf machen, nemlich: dass ich Ihnen und der Muttergesellschaft Wünsche (öfter zu schreiben) nicht nachkommen konnte. Indessen wird Herr Schmidt und Herr Arnold der Wahrheit gemäss gewiss bezeugen, dass der Arbeiten viele auf mir liegen, und dass ich in der Hauptsache gewiss meine Schuldigkeit thue. Wenn man dann noch annimmt, wie viele ungesetzliche Anforderungen von zwei unverständigen Glücksrittern und Abentheurern, die hie und da auch bey uns ihr Heil versuchen wollen, gemacht werden, und die gewöhnlich mit Grobheiten enden, so möchte man am Durchsetzen der Sache verzweifeln. Doch Muth und Besonnenheit hat mich schon durch manches Labirinth geführt, und wenn die Muttergesellschaft so wie früher fortfährt meine scheinbaren Schwächen zu tragen und keinem ungegründeten Misstrauen Platz giebt, so ist gar kein Zweifel, dass die Vorhersagungen aller Vorurtheils freyen Männer, sowohl Deutschen als Amerikanern, in dieser Gegend in Erfüllung gehen, und die Stadt Hermann schon in den ersten Jahren mit irgend einer im Westen, St. Louis ausgenommen, weteifern kann. — Obgleich schon viele edle Männer hier sind, so wäre es nach meiner Ansicht doch noch nicht zu wünschen, dass die Muttergesellschaft aufhören würde, das Oberhaupt der Colonie zu seyn. Die statistischen Verhältnisse der Colonie sind freylich glänzend genug um auf den ersten Ueberblick einen solchen Wunsch zu hegen, aber sowohl in moralischer als finanzieller Hinsicht scheint es mir noch zu früh daran zu denken. Nach und nach werden sich die verschiedenen Ideen, die fast Jeder mit nach Hermann bringt, verschmelzen und ein nach den Grundgesetzen der Muttergesellschaft geformtes Ganze herauskommen, das die Basis zu allen erspriesslichen Folgerungen abgeben wird. Mögen auch der Sache Missgünstige, oder Zweifler oder boshafte Verläumder über mich herfallen, es stört mich nicht, wenigstens nicht auf die Dauer, denn ich kann mit Recht stolz darauf seyn, dass ich, durch kräftige Mitwirkung edler deutscher Männer, eine Colonie gegründet habe, die der Nachwelt zeigen wird, dass der Deutsche, auch ohne fanatisch angefeuert zu seyn, ein Muster der Einigkeit und des Fleisses ist, sobald nur die Art und Weise denselben moralisch zu leiten nicht verfehlt wird.

Nur schade, dass die meisten unserer jetzt hier angesiedelten Glieder so viel mit sich selbst zu thun haben, und gerade oft Diejenigen, welche ihrer Talente und Moralität nach am meisten leisten könnten, durch Geschäfte ausserhalb verhindert werden, Theil an dem politischen Thun und Treiben der Gesellschaft zu nehmen, in Folge dessen es denselben dann unmöglich wäre, auch Aufsätze zur Veröffentlichung zu geben.

Alles dieses wird später besser, und es wäre nach meiner Ansicht auch nicht gut, wenn die Einwanderung in unsere Colonie vor dem Herbste stärker gienge, als sie jetzt geht. Die Lebensmittel werden rar, und wir haben jetzt vor der Erndte oft viele Mühe solche zu bekommen, besonders das Mehl macht uns viel zu schaffen. Mehrere Bestellungen, die ich in St. Charles machte, wurden nicht befördert. Soeben komme ich von einer Reise, auf welcher ich alle Mühlen im westlichen Theile von Warren County aufsuchte, ohne glücklichen Erfolg, am Ende doch, nahe an der grossen Prairie in Montgomery County hatte ich das Glück mit einem virginier Mühlenbesitzer einen Contrakt für Mehllieferung zu machen. Alles dieses muss auf der linken Seite des Missouri geschehen, was besonders mir, der für all dieses zu sorgen hat, sehr viele Mühe macht. Vorige Woche reiste ich nach Washington (Mo.), und hatte das Glück ein neues ferryboat zu kaufen, das nächster Tage herauf kommen wird und uns gewiss Manches erleichtert. So wie ich bey dem nun beynahe vollendeten Brückenbau abkommen kann, reise ich in die Countystadt um eine Lizens für eine Ferry einzuholen, vorher aber will ich mit den gegenüber liegenden Besitzern, so viel wie möglich vortheilhafte Contrakte abschliessen, was ich schon eingeleitet habe. Statistische Ueber-sicht der Stadt und des Landes soll nächstens verfertigt werden und vielleicht schon im nächsten Briefe kommen.

Uebrigens empfehle ich mich Ihnen so wie der ganzen Ge-sellschaft.

Hochachtungsvoll,

G. F. Bayer,

G. A.

Hermann, June 25, 1838

Doctor Schmoele, President of the German Settlement Society in Philadelphia

Dear Sir!

The decisions of the Colony here, made during this past month, have no doubt reached you. Pressing business caused a delay of the first decisions of this month and since the dispatch of several matters demanded the same speedy attention, it seemed advisable to me to await the next session. Mr. Schmidt, in accordance with his promise, will on his arrival submit reports to the Society in person concerning much that we have discussed with each other which, in my opinion, should not be proclaimed to the entire world if the present outstanding success of our endeavors is not to suffer damage. Indeed, I must thereby make an accusation against myself, namely that I was unable to fulfill your wish and that of the Mother-Society (to write often). Meanwhile, Mr. Schmidt and Mr. Arnold will in conformity with the truth certainly testify that many tasks lie upon me and that I perform my duties in the essentials. If one then also considers how many illegal demands are made by two irresponsible adventurers and upstarts, who occasionally wish to seek their fortunes here with us also, and which generally end in squabbles, then one almost despairs of succeeding in the business. But courage and resolution have already shown me the way through many a labyrinth and if the Mother-Society continues as formerly to bear with my apparent weaknesses and gives no room to unfounded suspicions, then there is no doubt at all that the prophecies of all unprejudiced persons, Germans as well as Americans in the region, will be fulfilled and the City of Hermann, even in its first years, will compare with any City in the West, St. Louis only excepted.

Although many fine men are already here, it is my opinion that it is not yet desirable that the Mother-Society would cease to be the master of the colony. The statistical circumstances of the colony are to be sure attractive enough in order to generate at first sight such a wish, but from a moral, as well as the financial viewpoint, it seems to me still too early to think of that. Gradually the various ideas which almost everyone brings along to Hermann will coalesce and a totality formed in harmony with the principles of the Mother-Society will ensue from it, which will be the basis of all salutary consequences.

Even if persons antagonistic to the undertaking, or doubters, or malicious caluminators oppose me, it does not disturb me, at least not for long, for I can justly be proud of this, that I, with powerful cooperation of noble German men, have founded a Colony which shall demonstrate to posterity that the German, even without being fanatically aroused, is an example of harmony and industry if only the ways and means of moral guidance of the same are not missing.

It is a pity that most of our members now settled here are so engrossed in their own affairs and often just those who because of their talents and character could render the best service, are prevented by extraneous business from participating in the political working and striving of the Society, in consequence of which it would then be impossible for them to give articles for publication.

All of this will improve later, and in my opinion it would not be good if the influx into our Colony before autumn would become greater than it now is. The means of livelihood are becoming scarce, and now before the harvest we are often in difficulty to obtain the same, it is especially difficult to obtain flour. Several orders, which I placed in St. Charles, were not delivered. I have just returned from a trip during which I visited all mills in the western part of Warren County, without satisfactory results, until finally near the large prairie in Montgomery County I had the good fortune to be able to make a contract for delivery of flour with a Virginian owner of a mill. All of this must be arranged on the left side of the Missouri, which causes me especially, who must take care of all this, very much trouble. Last week I travelled to Washington, (Mo.) and had the good fortune to buy a new ferryboat which will come up here within a few days and certainly make many things easier for us. As soon as I can get away from the now almost completed building of the bridge, I will travel to the County Seat in order to get a license for a Ferry, previously however I wish to make as many advantageous contracts as possible with the property owners on the other side, the beginning of which has already been made.

A statistical abstract of the city and of the country will be completed in the near future and will perhaps be sent in the next letter.

As for the rest I pay my respects to you as well as to the entire Society.

Most respectfully
G. F. Bayer, G. A.

Hermann, July 3rd, 1838.

Herrn Doctor Schmoele, Präsident der deutschen Ansiedlungs-Gesellschaft zu Philadelphia.

Geehrter Herr!

Ich benutze den Vorabend des für uns Deutsche so gehaltvollen Festes, das auch morgen hier nun von der ganzen Colonie mit Einschluss der uns umgebenden Amerikanern gefeiert werden soll, um Ihnen die Fortsetzung des unterm 25ten v. M. datirten Briefes zu liefern. Der Gedanke an den grossen, edlen Befreyer unserer jetzigen Heimath, hat viel für mich, sollte es für jeden Deutschen haben. Er handelte frey und recht mit seinen Landsleuten und wurde doch verkannt, sogar vom damaligen Congress. Warum soll *ich* mich beklagen, dem so Vieles abgeht, was ihm eigen war, wenn ich verkannt werde. Warum soll ich mich beleidigt fühlen, wenn Einer dem ich nicht nach seiner Pfeife tanzen konnte, ohne meine Instruction zu verletzen, in der St. Louiser Zeitung von Gewalt herunter schwatzt, die ich nicht kenne noch kennen mag? Oder ist das Gewalt, wenn ich ihm 200 Acker Land die er verlangt nicht auf Credit gebe, weil er nur zu 80 berechtigt ist? Ist das Gewalt, wenn ich dem Begehren eines Herrn von Philadelphia, der für zwei Actien drei gewöhnliche und eine Wharflotte und noch 120 Acker Land wollte, kein Gehör gab? Oder wird das Gewalt genannt, wenn ich nicht Jedem der es verlangt Mehl und Fleisch u. s. w. fort und fort auf Credit gebe und noch Geld dazu leihe wenn es ihm beliebt?

Sehen Sie mit solchen Leuten habe ich hie und da zu kämpfen und gerade solche spielen manchmal auf kurze Zeit die Hauptrolle bis sie die Mehrzahl kennt. Als Mann von Erfahrung wissen Sie das eben so gut wie ich und Sie werden mir gewiss auch diese missmuthige Abschweifung zu Gute halten.

Wie ich Ihnen im letzten Briefe andeutete, ist nun alle Vorkehrung zu einer Ferry getroffen. Auf welche Weise solche betrieben werden soll muss die Erfahrung lehren und die Verwaltungskommittee wird mir dabey an die Hand gehen. Das Landausmessen, welches mit vielen Schwierigkeiten verknüpft ist, da die meisten Eckbäume durch das Waldfeuer zerstört sind, wird nächste Woche wieder seinen Anfang nehmen und ich werde keine Mühe scheuen Alle die rechtlich Land anzusprechen haben, zufrieden zu stellen, nach den Vorschriften die mir dieserwegen in meiner Instruction gegeben sind. Mancher der bisher die Deutsche Ansiedlungsgesellschaft als eine melkende Kuh betrachtet hat, wird sich freylich getäuscht fühlen und, wie gewöhnlich, räsonieren. Doch das scheert mich nicht.

In der Stadt sind nun 142 gewöhnliche Lotten und 19 Wharflotten in Beschlag genommen, die doch nach der Vorschrift innerhalb eines Jahres bebaut werden müssen. Das Land an der Frain Creek ist alles, an der Little Berger Branch sehr bedeutend, und an der Coal Creek beynahe alles aufgenommen.

Die grössten Bedürfnisse könnten durch eine Sägemühle und Mahlmühle beseitigt werden. Zu diesem fehlt uns aber die Wasserkraft an der Frain Creek. Solche an die Big Berger oder First Creek zu setzen, wo wir auch Mühlsitze haben, ist von keinem wesentlichen Nutzen, da solche bey den noch unfahrbaren Wegen von der Colonie nicht benutzt werden könnten. Herr Setzer von Washington (Mo.), der früher eine Dampfsäge- und Mahlmühle beabsichtigte, ist zu ängstlich in der Sache, da er gar keine Kenntniss von solchem Betrieb hat. Herr Schiefer zeigte bey seinem Hierseyn grosse Lust etwas derartiges ins Werk zu setzen und ich versprach ihm, dass die Muttergesellschaft gewiss alles mögliche thun wird, ihn zu unterstützen. Den Fuss Bretter müssen wir zu 2½ bis 3 Cents bezahlen, wo wir es hier zu 1 bis 1½ Cents gesägt bekommen könnten, und das Holz kostet uns nichts. Der Buschel Weizen würde uns zu $1.00, das Buschel Korn oder Rocken zu 50 Cents, und Mais oder Welschkorn zu 40 Cents geliefert bey grossen Quantitäten, und so müssen wir für Weizenmehl $4.00 per 100 lbs., Rockenmehl $3.00 per 100 lbs., und Maismehl ¾—1 Thlr. per Buschel bezahlen und noch dazu 10 bis 20 Meilen weit dafür gehen, da die Mühlen in der Nähe herum meistens in einem unbrauchbaren Zustande sind. Wenn nur irgend Jemand von den vielen Capitalisten im Osten etwas in der Lage thun würde oder die Gesellschaft im Stande wäre einige tausend Thaler darauf zu verwenden, dass wir eine gute Dampfsäge- und Mahlmühle bekämen. Herr Hoch oder High in Reading, welcher auch in der Gesellschaft betheiligt ist, soll eine ganz neue Dampfmaschine besitzen, welche man sehr billig und unter vortheilhaften Bedingungen auf Credit bekommen könnte. In einem Jahr hätte sich die Sache bezahlt und der Colonie bliebe vieles Geld in der Tasche.

Eine Bittschrift für eine Postoffice ist bereits eingeschickt und da zu gleicher Zeit eine solche in der Gegend von Lyle westlich des Gasconade abgesandt wurde, so ist es ohne Zweifel, dass wir bald unsern Wunsch in dieser Hinsicht erfüllt sehen. Ja der Posthalter in Washington (Mo.) versicherte mich, dass die Poststation für unsern Platz schon besprochen und bestimmt worden sey ehe nur unsere Suplick an Ort und Stelle gelangt sey.

Wir haben manches durchzukämpfen, doch wird Alles gut gehen. So haben im Anfang die Capitaine der Dampfboote unsere Landung verschrieen und es wurden mir manche Vorwürfe desshalb gemacht. Jetzt landen sie alle nach Herzenslust wenn sie Fracht oder Pasagire für uns haben und werden später wenn wir ihnen Lebensmittel zum Verkauf anbieten können, auch bey uns übernachten.

Mit vieler Achtung grüsst Sie mit dem Wunsche mich der Muttergesellschaft zu empfehlen

Ihr G. F. Bayer, G. Ag.

Dr. Schmoele, President of the German Settlement Society in Philadelphia.

Dear Sir!

I am making use of the evening before the holiday which is so generally observed by us Germans, which is also to be celebrated here by the entire colony in conjunction with surrounding Americans, in order to furnish you the continuation of the letter dated on the 25th of the preceding month. The remembrance of the great noble liberator of our present homeland means much to me, as it should for every German. He acted openly and justly with his countrymen and yet was maligned, even by the Congress of his time. Why should *I* accuse myself, who lacks so many of his qualifications, when I am maligned? Why should I feel offended if someone to whose piping I could not dance without violating my instructions, babbles in the St. Louis newspaper about tyranny, which I do not know, nor wish to know? Or is that tyranny if I do not give him 200 acres of land which he demands on credit, because he is only entitled to 80? Or is that tyranny if I lend no ear to the request of a gentleman from Philadelphia who for two shares wanted three ordinary lots and one wharf lot and in addition 120 acres of land? Or will that be called tyranny if I do not give to everyone who demands it flour and meat, etc. on and on for credit, and in addition, lend him money whenever he desires it?

You see it is with just such people that I occasionally must struggle and it is just those who obtain the upper hand for a short time until the majority learns to know them; as a man of experience you know that as well as I, and you will certainly pardon this gloomy digression.

As I indicated to you in the last letter all preparations for a ferry have been made. In which manner this shall be operated will have to be learned from experience and the Administrative Board will assist me in this. The land survey, which is accompanied by many difficulties as most of the corner-trees have been destroyed by the forest fire, will again be resumed next week and I shall spare no pains to satisfy all those who have rightful claims to land according to the regulations pertaining thereto as given in my instructions. Many a person, who has hitherto regarded the German Settlement Society as a cow to be milked, will to be sure feel himself cheated and as usual make a great noise. But that will not disturb me.

In the City 142 ordinary lots and 19 wharf lots have been taken in possession, which in conformity with the regulations must have improvements within one year. All of the land along Frene Creek, much of that along the Little Berger Branch, and most of that along Coles Creek has been taken.

The greatest needs could be met by a saw-mill and a grain mill. But we lack the necessary water power on the Frene Creek. To place these along the Big Berger or First Creek, where we have such mill sites, is of no essential benefit since, due to the yet impassable roads they could not be used by the Colony. Mr. Setzer of Washington (Mo.) who at first had some plans for a steam-powered sawmill and grain mill is too doubtful of the matter, as he has no knowledge at all of this occupation. Mr. Schiefer during his presence here showed great interest in beginning something of the kind and I promised him that the Mother Society would certainly do everything possible to support him.

We must pay from 2½ to 3 cents a foot for boards, whereas we could get them sawed here for 1 or 1½ cents, and the wood costs us nothing. A bushel of wheat delivered to us in large quantities would cost $1.00, a bushel of grain or rye would cost 50¢ and maize or corn 40 cents; as it now stands we must pay $4.00 per 100 lbs. for wheat flour, $3.00 per 100 lbs. for rye flour, and ¾ to one dollar per bushel for cornmeal and in addition have to travel 10 to 20 miles for it, since most of the mills in this neighborhood are in an unusable condition. If only someone of the many capitalists in the east would do something toward this situation, or the Society had the means to spend several thousand dollars thereon, so that we could obtain a good saw mill and grain mill. Mr. Hoch or High in Reading, who is also active in the Society, is said to possess a brand new steam engine which could be obtained very cheaply and on credit under advantageous conditions. Within one year this business would have paid for itself and much money would remain in the pocket of the Colony.

An application for a post office has already been sent in and since simultaneously a similar one was sent away from the region of Lyle west of the Gasconade, there is no doubt that we shall soon see our wish fulfilled in this matter. Indeed, the Postmaster in Washington (Mo.), assured me that the station for our place had already been discussed and determined even before our petition had arrived at its destination. We have much to contend with, but everything will work out alright. At first the captains of the steamboats gave a bad name to our landing and many reproaches were made against me on account of it. Now they all land as they please when they have freight or passengers for us and later when we can offer them merchandise for sale they will also spend the night with us. With great respect and greetings to you and the wish that you convey my kindest regards to the Mother Society, I remain

Yours truly,

G. F. Bayer,

Hermann, August 19ten, 1838.

An den Verwaltungsrath der deutschen Ansiedlungsgesellschaft.

Geehrte Herrn!

Durch die neuen Ankömmlinge sind mir Briefe zugekommen, die mir endlich doch einmal die Quellen zeigen, woraus die Heimlichkeiten entsprangen, die der Verwaltungs-Rath besonders in der letzten Zeit gegen mich beobachtete.

Warum, meine Herrn, verdammt man mich ohne mich über die mir aufgebürdeten Verläumdungen zu hören. Ich muss freylich hier oft energisch handeln, wenn nicht das gesellschaftliche

Vermögen allen nach Belieben preissgegeben werden soll. Z. B. im Aufang verlangte man, dass ich für Arbeit per Tag $1.25 zahlen solle. Ich that es nicht, weil Amerikaner sich für bedeutend weniger anboten. Es giebt wirklich noch solche die unverschämt genug sind, den Tagelohn zu verlangen, wenn ihnen Land angewiesen wird. Herr Krauters Monopol $1.75 per Tag ist nun gebrochen, da die Leute welche bauen nicht gerne mehr bezahlen als hier üblich ist. Was die Association mit Widersprecher betrifft, so erkläre ich jeden als einen infamen Lügner der solches sagt. Der Bretterhandel mit demselben ist ebenfalls eine erdichtete Lüge; ja ich kann sogar beweisen, dass derselbe mir die Bretter höher ansetzte als er sie Andern verkaufte, was mich veranlasste, keine von ihm zu kaufen, wodurch ich nun ausserordentlich gehindert bin im Baue meines Hauses. Wenn Widersprecher sein merkantilisches Interesse so hoch stellt als Andere ihr persönliches und während meiner Abwesenheit Bretter kauft, die Krauter mit sammt seinem Anhang nicht kaufen konnte und sich dann für seine Mühe bezahlen lässt, so kann ich das nicht hindern, besonders wenn derselbe solche um einen Preiss erlässt, den wir alle jetzt gern bezahlen würden wenn sie nur zu bekommen wären.

Handel werde ich nie treiben, auch wenn ich nicht mehr Agent bin, indem es mit meinen Prinzipien nicht übereinstimmt. Ueberhaupt Jeder der sagt dass ich meine Instruction überschritten habe ist ein Lügner, und zwar so lange bis er mir es beweisst. Glauben Sie ja nicht, dass es mir einerlei ist was man von mir spricht und in einem Körper spricht mit dem ich Hand in Hand zu gehen mir vorgenommen habe, und denen nützlich zu seyn, die jetzt, zum Theile, so undankbar an mir handeln.

Was das Land betrifft, so bin (ich) eben so wenig im Stande, andern Leuten zu verwehren Land zu enteriren wenn sie Lust und Geld dazu haben, so hat z. B. Schönthaler, Setzer und noch mehrere andere Amerikaner und Deutsche seit der Zeit, ja vor kurzer Zeit drey Herrn von Charleston über 600 Acker in der Nähe unserer Besitzung aufgekauft. Leimer der nun durch Umgehung unserer Gesetze 300 Acker hat und auf den Namen seines Vaters und Bruders noch zweymal 80 Acker nehmen will, sobald die von mir verlangte Vollmacht da ist, soll letzte Woche bedeutend Congressland gekauft haben und namentlich ein 40 Ackerstück das ich, nächstens wenn ich nach St. Louis kommen würde mir vorgenommen hatte zu enteriren, und vorläufig an Herrn Staffhorst abgegeben hatte. Bekommen wir noch einige auf den Hals wie Herr Leimer, so hat die Ansiedlung einige Landspekulanten in ihrer nächsten Nähe, und die Armen können ihre 40 Acker Stückchen 8—10 Meilen weit suchen.

Wenn nicht die Certificate und die Duplicate hierher geschickt werden so weiss ich nicht wie Ordnung in die Geschäfte kommen soll. Alles was ich bisher gethan, habe ich memorirt, so gut es sich thun liess, in das Rekordbuch kann aber doch nur solches Land eingetragen werden für welches mit Actien-Certificaten bezahlt worden ist. Nun haben viele Glieder nicht einmal eine bestimmte Quittung oder sind blos in der *Alten und Neuen Welt* quittirt, was soll man da machen, besonders wenn man sich auf die Liste nicht verlassen kann. Alle die Leute hier bestehen darauf, dass man ihnen, da sie nun auf dem Platze der Ansiedlung eingetroffen sind, ihre Actien-Certificate ohnentgeldlich zuschicken müsse.

Ferner fehlen uns die Notifikationen der Muttergesellschaft über die im Laufe der Monate Mai, Juni und Juli eingeschickten Beschlüsse unserer Colonie.

Hinsichtlich der Stadt selbst muss ich bemerken, dass ich solche nach den Lokalitätsveränderungen ausgelegt habe, und mit Herrn Wesselhoeft den neuen Plan an die Muttergesellschaft gelangen zu lassen gedenke, der nun ausgeführt werden kann.

Auf das Reserveland haben wir den Begräbnissplatz gelegt, und was uns nun südlich der Stadt an solchem fehlt, indem wir nur über unser Eigenthum und nicht über fremdes zu disponiren haben, so wurden dafür westlich über 400 Acker reservirt, und Land dem Flusse entlang ist der Stadt von grösserem Nutzen als Land einwärts.

Herr Wagenschwanz ist angelangt und es scheint, dass er mir viele Mühe machen wird. Derselbe hat eine Vollmacht oder vielmehr Ueberschreibung von Rosenberg für 4 nicht ganz bezahlte Actien und 4 spricht er selbst an. Den Rest meint er solle man ihm schenken für seine grosse Mühe die er mit der Gesellschaft gehabt habe. Ich sagte ihm dass wenn er noch $20 bezahle so seye er berechtigt zu 6 Actien was ihm aber nicht zusagt.

Wir müssen uns nun sehr beeilen wenn wir uns dieses Jahr incorporiren lassen wollen, ob als Stadt oder als Gesellschaft ist eine Frage über die man sich verständigen sollte, ebenfalls, wenn ersteres der Fall, was denen auf dem Lande für Gerechtsame zugestanden werden könnten. Herr Leupold ist derowegen nach St. Louis gereist um Rath bey einem Advokaten einzuholen, der unser Interesse so wenig kennt, als ich die Wälder von Polen. Ich empfehle mich bestens als

Ihr ergebener

G. F. Bayer, G. A.

Hermann, August 19, 1838

To The Board of Managers of the German Settlement Society
Dear Sirs!

Through the new arrivals letters have reached me which finally indicate to me the sources of the secrecy which the Board of Managers, especially of late, harbored against me.

Why, my gentlemen, am I condemned without even hearing of the calumnies heaped upon me. I must, to be sure, often act energetically if the property of the Society is not to be alienated for the benefit of anyone who wants it, E.G., at first it was demanded that I should pay $1.25 for a day's wages. I did not do it because Americans offered themselves for considerably less. There are actually such who are impudent enough to demand the day's wage when they are offered land. Mr. Krauter's monopoly of $1.75 per day has been broken, as the people who are building do not wish to pay more than is customary here. Insofar as concerns the association with Widersprecher, I proclaim everyone who says this as a vile liar. The lumber deal with the same is likewise a fabricated lie; indeed I can even prove that the same offered me the boards at a higher price than he charged others, which was the reason that I bought none from him, because of which I am now very greatly hindered in the building of my house. If Widersprecher places his mercantile interest as high as others do their personal interest, and during my absence buys boards which Krauter with his accomplices could not buy and then takes payment for his services, then I cannot prevent that, especially if he sells them at such a price as we would now all be happy to pay, if they were only obtainable.

I shall never conduct a business, even when I am no longer Agent, as it does not harmonize with my principles. Moreover, everyone who says that I have violated my instructions is a liar and indeed so long until he can prove that to me. Do not think that it is a matter of indifference to me what is said of me and what is said in a body with which I have intended to work hand in hand, and to be helpful to those, who now in part act so ungratefully towards me.

As concerns land, I am just as powerless to prevent other people from entering land if they have the desire and the money to do it, as for example Schönthaler, Setzer and several other Americans and Germans have done since that time; indeed, not long ago three gentlemen from Charleston purchased more than 600 acres near our properties. Leimer, who by evasion of our laws has now 300 acres and wishes to take two more 80 acres in the names of his father and brother as soon as he receives the demanded power of attorney from me, is said to have bought considerable Congress-land last week and in particular a 40-acre tract which I had intended to enter the next time I would come to St. Louis and which he has for the time being turned over to Mr. Staffhorst. If we are plagued with several more like Mr. Leimer the Settlement will have several land speculators in its immediate neighborhood and the poor people can look for their little 40-acre tracts 8 to 10 miles away.

If the Certificates and the duplicates are not sent here then I do not know how the business affairs can be conducted in an orderly way. Everything that I have done up to now I have memorized as much as possible; in the book of records, however, only such land can be entered which has been paid for with Certificates of shares. Now many members do not even have a definite receipt or have only been acknowledged in the "Alte und Neue Welt". ("Old and New World") What is there to do, especially if one cannot rely upon the list? All the people here insist that, since they have now come to the place of the settlement, their Share-Certificates must be sent to them gratis.

Moreover, the notifications of the Mother-Society concerning the resolutions of our Colony during the month of May, June and July have not been received by us.

As concerns the city itself, I wish to note that I have laid out the same according to the variations of the locality and intend to send the new plan, which can be realized, to the Mother-Society in care of Mr. Wesselhoeft.

We have placed the cemetery on the reserved land, and to make up what was lacking of this south of the town, as we can only dispose of our own property and not that of others, more than 400 acres of land towards the west were reserved and land alongside the river is of greater benefit to the City than land towards the interior.

Mr. Wagenschwanz has arrived and it seems that he will cause me much trouble. The same has power of attorney or more properly a quit-claim from Rosenberg for 4 not fully paid shares and 4 he himself claims. He thinks that the remainder should be given him gratis for the great difficulties which he has had with the Society. I told him that if he would pay an additional $20.00 he would be entitled to 6 shares, but this does not satisfy him.

We shall have to make great haste if we are to incorporate ourselves this year; whether as a City or as a Society is a question which should be resolved; likewise, if the former should be the case what rights can be granted to those living in the Country? Mr. Leupold has on that account traveled to St. Louis to obtain advice from a lawyer who is as little acquainted with our interests as I am with the forests in Poland.

       With kindest compliments, I remain
               Yours truly,
               G. F. Bayer, G. A.

We are indeed fortunate in having these few letters. They are like brands rescued from the fire. They corroborate our statement regarding the disposition and characteristics of the colonists.

They defend the agent, if he need a defense, against the virulent attacks of his adversaries. It is our private opinion that some of the settlers were narrow enough to heap their vituperation upon this man, because, of the six hundred dollars, the 80 acres of land at cost price, and the unfinished log-house which were offered him for his hundred-fold services to the corporation.

Despite all the objections made to the controlling officer, the colony seems to have grown and flourished. The proof for this we will take largely out of the mouths of the colonists themselves. The *"Alte und Neue Welt"* contains the substance of a letter of those very pioneers of 1837-38:

> „Wir haben einen Brief, unterzeichnet von mehreren Mitgliedern der „Deutschen Ansiedlungs-Gesellschaft" aus Hermann, Staat Missouri, erhalten. Diese Herren schreiben, dass ihnen der Platz der Ansiedlung sehr gefällt, dass das Wasser gut, die Gegend gesund und eine der schönsten zum Bau einer Stadt am Missouri ist, soweit sie die Ufer dieses Flusses besucht hätten. Sie bemerken in ihrem Briefe, nachtheiligen Gerüchten über die Gegend keinen Glauben beizumessen und ziehen den Ort der Ansiedlung den Ufern des Gasconade vor, wo es lange nicht so gesund sei."*

"We have received a letter signed by several members of the German Settlement Society of Hermann, State of Missouri. These gentlemen write that they are pleased with the site of the Settlement, that the water is good, the region healthful and one of the finest along the Missouri for the building of a city, insofar as they have explored the shores of this river. They note in their letter to lend no credence to disparaging reports about the region, and they prefer the site of the Settlement to the banks of the Gasconade, where it is not nearly as healthful."

In all these reports we are made to feel, that the chief desire is to push the undertaking to its wished-for culmination. This tone likewise prevails in the report of the president as well as in the appeals of the secretary.

---

* *A. und N. W.* of January 27, 1838.

Just one instance may be given here. On April 25, '38, a committee, composed of Julius Leupold, F. Schreiber and C. Staffhorst, appointed to examine the books of the treasurer, reported:

„Dass diese Bücher auf eine Weise geführt worden sind, welche keine verständliche Uebersicht derselben zulässt."

"That these books have been kept in a manner which permits of no intelligent supervision."

(This condition was later adjusted according to sound business principles.) But in the semi-annual report of the president, submitted April 14, '38, when he could not have had reliable information concerning the treasury, he nevertheless indulges in a glowing account, which as he proceeds becomes quite speculative and even visionary. We quote from it here:

„Unsere Kasse hat schon jetzt nach Tilgung aller Schulden einen reinen Ueberschuss von mehr als Tausend Thaler. Dazu kommen noch die Rückstände einzelner Mitglieder, deren Betrag ich im Bericht nicht angegeben finde, die aber ebenfalls eine nicht unbedeutende Summe ausmachen. Ausser diesem hat die Gesellschaft noch über tausend Aktien" (blank slips of paper merely) „die nach dem jetzigen Preise mindestens 50,000 Thaler Werth sind, so wie über 80 Wasserstrassen-Lotten in Hermann" (building lots along the Missouri River) „wie über 12,000 Acker Landes, dass zum mindesten Preise 24,000 Thaler einbringt, zu verkaufen.
Im Ganzen stellt sich also nach Befriedigung aller persönlichen Ansprüche sämmtlicher Aktionäre, ein reines Vermögen von circa 90,000 Thalern Werth heraus, welches Gemeingut der Aktionäre ist."

"Our treasury already has, after payment of all debts, a clear surplus of over one thousand dollars. To this are to be added the arrears of several members, the amount of which I do not find recorded in the report, which however amount to no insignificant sum. In addition to this the Society still has over one thousand shares (blank slips of paper merely) which at the present price are worth at least $50,000.00 dollars, as well as more than 80 water-street lots in Hermann (building lots along the Missouri River), as well as over 12,000 acres of land to sell, which at the lowest price will bring at least $24,000.00.

Therefore, there is shown on the whole, after satisfaction of all personal claims by all shareholders, an unencumbered property of about $90,000.00 in value, which is the common property of the shareholders."

To the cool-headed business man such a summary could not appeal. Some of the shareholders understood and appreciated the conditions, but, with but few exceptions, all desired the accomplishment of the undertaken task, either for the sake of preserving and fostering things German in America, or (and in this rubric falls the greater number) to gain a more comfortable and independent livelihood than had been theirs in Europe. A letter from Hermann, printed anonymously in the *"Anzeiger des Westens"* and copied in the *"Alte und Neue Welt,"* bears evidence to both phases of the question discussed.

Hermann, d. 1. Juni 1838.*

Werther Herr Weber!

. . . . . Ich will Ihnen eine getreue Ansicht von dem Zustand und den Hoffnungen Hermann's geben.

Es ist nicht alles so wie der Präsidial-Bericht vom 14. April d. J. meldet. Es war ein Fehler, Einem Manne, ohne gehörige Kontrole, so viel Macht einzuräumen. Diesem ist jetzt abgeholfen, weil wir dem General-Agenten eine Verwaltungs-Kommittee zur Seite gesetzt. Gewiss ist's, dass ein besserer Platz für die Zwecke der Gesellschaft nicht leicht hätte gefunden werden können. Die Lage der Stadt Hermann verspricht viel als eine Stadt im Innern, der Platz ist gesund, geschützt vor Ueberschwemmungen, reich an Wasserquellen, und von einem fruchtbaren und romantischen Land-

---

* *A. und N. A.* of July 7, 1838.

striche umgeben. Die finanziellen Verhältnisse der Gesellschaft sind bei weitem nicht so gut als man erwartet, aber dessen ungeachtet wird für mehrere Jahre ein hinreichender Fond vorhanden sein, um die Stadt verschönern und vielen Arbeitern Verdienst geben zu können; zumal wenn alle Rückstände einkommen. . . .

Es wohnen hier bereits neben Ober- und Niederländern, Schweizer, Franzosen, Schotten und Amerikaner, welche aber sicherlich nicht mit den „Natives" zu verwechseln sind. Es ist ein treuer unverdorbener Menschenschlag, wie man östlich nicht mehr findet. Die innwohnenden Amerikaner interessiren sich sehr für Hermann, welches indess schon in ihrem eigenen Interesse liegt. Aus Obigem werden Sie schon ersehen, dass die Aussichten für Hermann nicht anders als sehr gut sein können.

Von den Fremden, welche hierher kamen, ist fast keiner wieder fortgegangen, ohne vorher einen Bauplatz oder Land genommen zu haben, in der Absicht, sobald als möglich zurückzukommen und sich anzusiedeln. Viele sind schon häuslich eingerichtet und betreiben bürgerliche Geschäfte. Man kann hier alle möglichen Sachen billig bekommen, es giebt bereits gute Boardinghäuser, und unser Cigarrenfabrikant liefert sehr gute Ware zu 4 Doll. pr. 1000 Stück. Die innwohnenden Amerikaner liefern uns Lebensmittel, die nicht theuer sind. Butter 12½ cent, Eier 12½ c., Schweinefleisch 8 c., Hirschfleisch 2 c., Mehl 4 c., Welschkorn 50 c. pr. Bushel.

Es wäre zu wünschen, dass wir die ganze Verwaltung jetzt bald hierher bekämen und dass recht bald über den Zustand der Kasse der Deutschen Ansiedlungs-Gesellschaft hinreichende Auskunft gegeben und förmliche Rechnung abgelegt würde. Wir würden dann im Stande sein unsere Mittel besser zu übersehen um unsere Unternehmungen darnach einrichten zu können.

Wir wollen jetzt um Einrichtung einer Postoffice nachsuchen. Bis jetzt werden unsere Briefe nach Bridgeport, Warren County, Mo., adressirt."

Hermann, June 1, 1838

"Dear Mr. Weber!

I wish to give you an accurate view of the condition and the expectations of Hermann.

It is not all so as the President's report of April 14th of this year announces. It was a mistake to grant so much power to a man with insufficient means of control. This has now been remedied because we have placed an Administrative Committee by the side of the General Agent. It is certain that a better site for the purposes of the Society could not easily have been found. The site of the City of Hermann is very promising for an interior city; the place is healthful, protected against floods, rich in springs and is surrounded by a fruitful and picturesque landscape. The financial circumstances of the Society are not nearly as good as expected, but nevertheless there shall be sufficient funds available for several years to beautify the City and to give work to many laborers, especially if all arrears are paid.

There now live here in addition to High and Low Germans— Swiss, French, Scotch and Americans, who however are certainly not to be confused with the "natives". It is a real, unspoiled haven for people, as is no longer to be found in the East. The Americans living here are greatly interested in Hermann, as this promotes their own interests. From the aforesaid you will readily perceive that the expectations for Hermann cannot be other than very good.

Of the strangers who have come here, almost none have departed without first having acquired a building site or land in the expectation of returning as soon as possible and settling here. Many have already established homes and conduct civic businesses. One can here obtain all imaginable things cheaply; there are already good boarding houses and our cigar factory delivers good products at $4.00 per 1000 cigars. The Americans living here furnish us with food which is not expensive. Butter 12½ cents, eggs 12½¢, pork 8¢, deermeat 2¢, flour 4¢, maize 50¢ per bushel.

It would be desirable if the entire administration would be transferred here and that sufficient information concerning the treasury of the German Settlement Society be furnished very soon and formal accounting thereof be made. We would then be in a position to better estimate the means at our disposal in order to be able to arrange our undertakings accordingly.

We now wish to attempt the arrangement of a Post Office.
Up to now our letters are addressed to Bridgeport, Warren
County."

In the next to the last paragraph of the above letter, we
have an early outcropping of a sentiment which soon grew into a
demand. Of this demand we shall have yet to speak at length.
However, before we deal with this graver side of our theme we
desire to give place to some more information regarding the
growth of the colony. This information coming as it does from
presumably authentic and veracious individuals must prove valuable as well as interesting. We must regret that for reasons
known to himself the editor has not published the names of the
authors of some of these letters.

Hermann, Mo., den 13. März 1839.*

Unsere Ansiedlung geht prächtig von Statten; täglich treffen
neue Ankömmlinge hier ein; über 50 neue Häuser sind dem Aufrich-
ten nahe und unsere unheilverkündenden Landsleute, denen ähnliche Unternehmungen scheiterten, oder die durch uns sich beein-
trächtigt glaubten, streichen ihre feindlichen Flaggen und suchen
bei uns Brod und Unterkommen. . . . Lassen Sie sich durch Ge-
rüchte über hier stattgefundene Störungen nicht irre leiten; durch
Consequenz, Streben nach Wahrheit und vernünftiges Ausharren
wird auch das Schwierigste beseitigt und Alles arbeitet nun einig,
freudig vorwärts; die Lots gehen jetzt reissend ab und solche welche
gut gelegen sind, werden aus zweiter Hand für 150 Doll. gekauft
und steigen täglich an Werth. Wharf-Lots werden, nach Lage,
auf 4 bis 500 Doll. gehalten. — Häuschen von circa 200 Doll. an
Werth, vermiethen sich zu 5 Doll, per Monat und tragen also 30
Procent ein. Der Preis des Landes ist nun auf 2¼ Doll. im Durchschnitt festgesetzt, da eine Eintheilung in Classen unzweckmässig
erschien, eine Taxation nicht gut möglich und zu kostspielig war,
und so alle billig denkenden Interessenten zufrieden sein können.
Der Missouri war gestiegen, sieht aber seit einigen Tagen wieder
trüb aus. Drei Dampfböte landeten hier und brachten uns eine
Menge Fremde."

---

* *A. und N. W.* of April 6th, 1839.

Hermann, Mo. March 13, 1839

Our Settlement is progressing splendidly, daily new arrivals come in; more than 50 new houses will be erected soon and our misfortune-prophesying countrymen for whom similar undertakings went to ruin or who believed themselves placed at a disadvantage by us, lower their antagonistic banners and seek bread and hospitality from us. . . . Do not let yourselves be deceived by reports of disturbances here; through consistency, striving after truth and sensible persistence the greatest difficulties are overcome and everything now progresses harmoniously and joyfully; the lots are now in great demand and those which are well situated are bought at second hand for $150.00 and the price rises daily. Wharf lots are valued at from $400.00 to $500.00, depending on their location. Small houses of about $200.00 in valuation rent at $5.00 per month and so yield 30%. The price of the land has now been set at an average of 2¼ dollars, since a division into classes seemed not to the purpose; a taxation was unfeasible and too expensive, and so all right-thinking people interested can be satisfied. The Missouri had come up, but for several days has again apeared murky. Three steamboats landed here and brought us a host of strangers.

In an earlier part of this work, we called attention to the interest the Philadelphia Society aroused in Germany. Then we recorded an appeal which an editor made to his countrymen to support such a laudable undertaking. Now we are about to chronicle a tangible proof that the seed sown by the American society was about to bear fruit.

In May, 1839, the officers of the Philadelphia Society received a communication from one F. G. Sprewitz, a lawyer by profession, in Lauenburg, on the Elbe. It appears that the good reports of the Hermann colony had been heard beyond the Atlantic, and given an incentive for the organization of a "Neue deutsche Ansiedlungs-Gesellschaft." Mr. Sprewitz inclosed a copy of the constitution of this organization, in the name of the European body, he expressed the wish that this constitution be published in the official organ of the Philadelphia Society together with the overtures to consolidate the two societies into one grand and mighty body. Though the American Germans did not feel inclined to enter upon this proposition, it will be of interest, nevertheless, to read the article of the Lauenburger:

„Am 27. August 1836 ward in Philadelphia die sogenannte deutsche Ansiedlungs-Gesellschaft gestiftet, deren Zweck gleich Anfangs darin bestand, durch Aktien zu 25 Doll. ein Kapital zu gewinnen, um davon in einem der nordamerikanischen Freistaaten Land zur Ansiedlung und wo möglich zur Gründung einer Stadt ankaufen zu können. Der Erfolg war so überaus lohnend, dass die Actie schon vor Ablauf eines Jahres 50 Doll. galt, und dass im Frühjahr vorigen Jahres von den Capitalien der Gesellschaft die neue Stadt Hermann im Missouristaate mit 2200 Bauplätzen gegründet ward. Dies bei den günstigen Verhältnissen jenes schönen Landes ganz natürliche Gelingen brachte mehrere Actieninhaber auf die Idee, dass ein noch glänzenderes Resultat zu erwarten sein möchte, wenn in Deutschland selbst, einem der Hauptzuflüsse der Bevölkerung Nord-Amerika's, eine solche Niederlassungs-Gesellschaft gegründet würde. In der That scheint auch Auswanderungslustigen nichts willkommener sein zu können, als ein Vereinigungspunkt, den ihnen die zu stiftende Stadt, wo sie ein wohlfeiles und unverlierbares Eigenthum besitzen, darbieten würde, — ein Vereinigungspunkt, wo man deutsche Sprache und Sitte wieder vorfindet. Besonders wird den Aelteren, welche für die Zukunft ihrer Kinder im übervölkerten Geburtslande besorgt sind, und denjenigen, welche Beförderer des Gemeinnutzens sind, oder welche ihr Geld auf eine sichere und zugleich gewinnreiche Weise unterzubringen wünschen, eine neue deutsche Ansiedlungs-Gesellschaft am Herzen liegen. Dieses Alles berücksichtigend, hat Unterzeichneter nachstehende Statuten für eine „neue deutsche Niederlassungs-Gesellschaft" in Gemässheit einer an ihn ergangenen Aufforderung entworfen. Dieser Aufforderung lag vornehmlich zum Grunde, dass der gegenwärtige auf das Dreifache erhöhte Werth der Actien der alten Gesellschaft eine Vergrösserung des Gesellschaftsvermögens durch Hinzutreten neuer Mitglieder nicht mehr erwarten lässt, und zugleich die von der alten Gesellschaft, behufs Ermittelung passender Ansiedlungsörter, durch die kostspieligen Reisen eines bestimmten

Deputirtenausschusses erworbenen Localnotizen, zum besten der neuen Gesellschaft benutzt werden können."*

F. G. Sprewitz, Advokat.

Lauenburg, im März 1839.

"On August 27, 1836 was founded in Philadelphia the so-called German Settlement Society whose purpose at the very beginning was to raise capital from shares at $25.00 in order to be able to purchase therewith land in one of the North American states for settlement and, if possible, the founding of a City. The result was so overwhelmingly successful, that a share was worth $50.00 already before the end of the year, and that in the spring of last year the new City of Hermann in the State of Missouri with 2200 building sites was founded from the capital of the Society. This natural success, which could be expected from the favorable circumstances of that beautiful land, gave several shareholders the idea that an even more splendid result could be expected, if in Germany itself, one of the principal sources of the population of North America, such a Settlement Society would be founded. As a matter of fact, it would seem that nothing could be more welcome to those wishing to emigrate than a meeting point, the city which is to be founded for them, would offer them, where they would possess an inexpensive and inalienable property—a point of meeting where German language and customs would again be found. The older people especially who are concerned about the future of their children in the over-populated native land, and those who are promoters of community of goods, and those who wish to invest their money in a secure and at the same time remunerative manner, will be most interested in a new German Settlement Society. In consideration of all of this, the undersigned has formulated, in conformity with a petition sent to him, the following statutes for a "New German Settlement Society". The principal point of the petition consisted in this, that the present tripled value of a share of the old Society precludes the expansion of the property of the Society by the addition of new

---

* *A. und N. A.* of May 25, 1839.

members, and in addition that the local memoranda concerning the investigation of suitable sites for settlement obtained for the old Society by costly journeys by a designated Committee of Deputies, can be utilized best by the new Society."

F. G. Sprewitz, Lawyer

Lauenburg, March 1839

This shows how popular the movement had become even beyond the sea. The Philadelphians did not favor the proposition and it soon fell into forgetfulness without bearing any fruit whatsoever.

Among the many valuable accounts and suggestions found in the *"Alte und Neue Welt,"* we find a letter from Hermann signed by three members. It is the last communication of this nature from the colony during the régime, under which it was organized. We report it, because it gives an excellent picture of a prosperous, promising socialistic group.

Hermann, Mo., d. 15. Mai 1839.

„Wer jetzt das Gebiet der „deutschen Ansiedlungs-Gesellschaft" betritt, wer es bedenkt, dass erst ein Jahr verflossen, seit die ersten Mitglieder der Gesellschaft hier Hand an's Werk legten, und wer es weiss, mit wie vielen Schwierigkeiten eine neue Ansiedlung zu kämpfen hat, der kann es kaum glauben, dass in so kurzer Zeit und im Beginne durch so wenige Personen das bewirkt worden, was sich jetzt dem Blicke des aufmerksamen Beobachters darbietet. — Täglich kommen neue Ansiedler an, und man kann mit Bestimmtheit annehmen, dass in den letzten drei Monaten im Durchschnitt jede Woche ein Haus aufgerichtet wurde. Man baut hier nur Frame- oder steinerne Häuser, indem die Blockhäuser nicht mehr zu gefallen scheinen. Es sind jetzt gegen 90 Häuser erbaut und die Zahl der Bewohner beläuft sich auf 450.

Die Farmer, welche Land gekauft haben, eilen herbei und bearbeiten es. Wir haben hier fast alle Geschäftsleute; sie haben Arbeit und leben billig. Ein Mann, der sein Handwerk gut versteht, kann 12 Doll. die Woche verdienen. Es sind hier 5 Kaufläden, zwei grosse Gasthäuser und ein Postamt. Für eine katholische und eine evangelische Kirche sind die Lots ausgesucht und das Schulhaus ist im Bau begriffen. Zwei Jäger-Compagnien haben sich hier gebildet, jede 50 Mann stark, nebst einem Musik-Chor mit Blech-Instrumenten.

Man hat Eisenerz gefunden und nach mehreren Zeichen zu schliessen müssen auch Kohlenlager vorhanden sein. Der Missouri ist jetzt so hoch, dass die Dampfschiffe nahe an den Kaufläden am Wharf landen.

Alles ist hier guten Muthes und strebt freudig vorwärts.

> J. N. Stühlinger,
> Aug. Leonhard,
> F. W. Pommer.*

Hermann, Mo. May 15, 1839

"Whoever now visits the territory of the German Settlement Society, whoever considers that only one year has passed since the first members of the Society set to work here, and whoever knows with how many difficulties a new settlement must contend will hardly be able to believe that that which now presents itself to the view of the attentive observer has been wrought within such a short time and in the beginning by such few people. New settlers arrive daily, and it can definitely be asserted that in the last three months on the average a house has been erected every week. Only frame—or stone houses are built here as it seems that log houses are no longer in style. About 90 houses have been built now and the number of inhabitants is 450.

The farmers who have bought land do not delay to cultivate it. We have almost all kinds of trades people here; they have work and live cheaply. A man who understands his trade well can earn $12.00 a week. There are 5 stores, two large hotels and a post office here. Lots have been selected for a Catholic and an Evangelical Church and the building of the school-house has begun. Two sportsmen's societies have been formed here, each consisting of 50 men, as well as a chorus with brass band.

Iron ore has been found, and judging from various indica-

---

* *A. und N. W.* of June 15, 1839.

tions coal beds are also present. The Missouri is now so high that the steamboats land near the stores along the wharf.

Everyone here is of good cheer and striving joyfully forward."
G. N. Stühlinger
Aug. Leonhard
F. W. Pommer

The tone of this letter is hopeful, it is encouraging. Despite the petty protests offered by some of the participants, to existing conditions at Hermann, the colony grew apace. Fundamentally the society was sound. Though individual differences and personal opinions sometimes threw the settlers into hostile camps, after all the original plans were rather closely adhered to, for the accomplishment of the proposed end.

On July 23, 1838, an enterprise was begun at the colony, which, though it did not succeed in yielding the full measure of good expected of it, was nevertheless, an encouraging sign of the American help-yourself spirit. The growth of the colony was encumbered by the want of a grist and saw mill. It seemed impossible for the home society to render aid. Therefore a number of settlers bent on bringing about this commodity and at the same time introducing a lucrative business, organized a milling company. The nucleus of the new enterprise was formed by a group of men, who, with two exceptions, had hitherto been totally inactive in the management of affairs. The names appearing subjoined to the writ of incorporation are the following: Joseph Snyder, Henry Wiemann, D. Widersprecher, Geo. F. Bayer, Fried. Leupold, Fried. Mühlenbach. It was a stock company. Each share cost $25, payable in five equal payments, due during the period from Aug. 1, 1838, to Jan. 1, 1839. The maximum cost of the mill was set at $2,500.00. Although the changes that were soon to be made at Hermann prevented this company from actually going into operation, it is nevertheless a sign of progress not to be overlooked.

To facilitate and encourage the work of colonization, and to assist incoming colonists, a bureau of information was organized in St. Louis. One Neumann, residing on "lower Market Street," issued certificates of purchase, and instructed the travelers as to the most convenient ways of travel to Hermann. Branch offices were also established with Schachleiter, of Pittsburg; Charles Liebau, of Cincinnati, Ohio, and Hunn, of Louisville, Kentucky.

5. THE SEPARATION OF THE COLONY FROM THE PARENT SOCIETY.

It now becomes our duty to chronicle the closing scenes of the Philadelphia Society and the beginnings of independent activity at Hermann.

To the minds of the unselfish fathers of the German Settlement Society of Philadelphia it had never occurred that the spirit of ungratefulness, the desire for self aggrandizement, an apparent disregard of the rights of others would so soon dominate the settlers of that colony which their ardor, their devotion and self-sacrifice had succeeded in establishing—a colony that still stands, in a slightly altered form, as a monument to those noble sons of old Germany. Yet such were their bitter experiences. Such was to be their sore disappointment. The ideal heights could not be reached. The way was full of hindrances. They had overestimated the power, the determination and willingness of their followers to overcome them. Scarcely had the task of winning the wild tract for the abode of man begun, when here and there a voice was raised arguing the advantages of a severance from the home society. The occasional murmurs soon became frequent and bold. To the unbiased observer they now seem rather premature. If for no other reason than the prestige, which the undertaking derived from the connection with highly-esteemed Germans, residing at the very cradle of Germanism in America, the separation of the Colony from the home society should have been delayed. In proportion as the old fighters for the good cause were pushed into the background, in that proportion general interest waned. The great mass of argument produced to hasten the transfer of the governing body to the colony may very well be expressed in the language of the Jewish mob: "Wir wollen nicht dass diese (r) über uns herrsche (n)."* Some of their reasons were, of course, cogent and well-founded. This we shall see in the course of our discussion.

The home society had never entertained the intention of exercising continued supervision over the colony. Its primary purpose had always been the founding of a home for things German on the western continent, and it was deemed best to have this experiment centralized in a town where the beneficent influences of culture could work to the best advantage and to surround this town with colony farms from which should be derived the major portion of the means of subsistence. It had always been understood, as in the nature of things it was but rational to understand, that the colonists should govern themselves as soon as they were found strong enough to do so, and offered sufficient guarantee of the absolute safety of the interests of all stockholders. It so happened that many capable men went to the colony early—some of the best the society had on its roster. They were eager to have absolute self-government. And we can not blame them for that. The distance to Philadelphia was so great and communication so slow that many inconvenient delays occurred. Then too the home society could not appreciate in the fullest measure the conditions and pressing needs of the colony. But still we believe that a firm connection with the Philadelphia men, tried and not found wanting, would have, in itself, argued better and more convincingly than a thousand letters of promise, assurance and commendation on the part of the colonists. For the sake of the ultimate good, for a means of advertisement as well as advertising, for a positive guarantee of the good intention of the whole undertaking the old

---

*"We do not wish that these rule over us."

society should have been kept at the helm longer than it was permitted to stay.

The first concession of power, acquiescing to urgent requests from Hermann, was made on July 2nd, '38, when the Board of Managers, after learning positively that Bayer could not supervise the affairs alone, voted:

„So hält der Verwaltungs-Rath es für nothwendig die Gesetzgebung und Verwaltung den Mitgliedern in Hermann soweit zu übertragen, als es die Localität und die Bedürfnisse der Mitglieder erheischen."

"Therefore, the Board of Managers deems it necessary to transfer the legislative powers and management to the members in Hermann to the extent that the locality and the needs of the members require it.

This suggestion was favorably received, and the Board of Managers at once instructed to work out a definite plan pointing towards the transfer. The board was charged to submit their report within 5 days. This body promptly complied with the order, and on July 7th, the society accepted the report unmodified. The resolutions were prefaced by these reasons why a partial transfer was deemed advisable.

1. Because a large number of shareholders already resided at and around Hermann, they might be safely intrusted with a proportionate share of the management and responsibility. It was deemed especially desirable to do so, since they were most intimately acquainted with the local needs and possibilities.

2. Because the agent, G. F. Bayer, for unknown reasons, had failed to abide by his instructions and it was not known if he had even performed his first duty of appointing a controlling committee.

3. Because the affairs of the society were speedily approaching that period when a transfer of the entire management would become imperative, and a balancing of all accounts necessary.

Therefore, it was resolved that the following men, Julius Leupold, E. C. Staffhorst, W. Senn, M. Krauter and W. L. Henrich, should call a meeting of all the colonists for the purpose of effecting the permanent organization of an executive committee. The report continues thus:

„Die Versammlung hat alsdann einen Präsidenten, einen Vice-Präsidenten, einen Sekretair, einen Schatzmeister und fünf Trusties zu wählen. Der Präsident, Vice-Präsident und Sekretair der *executiven Committee,* nebst vier von der letzteren zu wählenden Mitglieder sollen eine *spezielle Committee* bilden, deren Pflicht es sein soll, unverzüglich den General-Agenten Herrn Bayer zur Abrechnung aufzufordern, welche letzterer vor der genannten speziellen Committe abzulegen hierdurch verpflichtet ist und zwar innerhalb vierzehn Tagen von dem Tage an gerechnet, an welchem diese Aufforderung an ihn gemacht wird.

Die besagte spezielle Committee soll ferner bewirken, dass alle in den Händen des General-Agenten befindlichen Gelder und sonstiges Eigenthum der Gesellschaft, welches von dem General-Agenten noch nicht an die Trusties der Gesellschaft überschrieben worden ist, von jenem an die von der executiven Committee gewählten fünf Trusties übergeben werde. Der General-Agent ist hierdurch verpflichtet, solche Uebergabe der vorhergehenden Bestimmung gemäss zu machen.

Die mehrgenannte spezielle Committee soll ferner das Amt und die Pflichten der in der Instruktion des General-Agenten angeordneten controlierenden Committee übernehmen. Dabei soll jedoch die Abänderung stattfinden, dass zur Suspension des General-Agenten die Uebereinstimmung von vier Mitgliedern der genannten speziellen Committee und die Mehrheit der executiven Committee erforderlich sein soll. Die spezielle Committee soll ferner die Pflicht haben wenigstens alle zwei Wochen an die executive Committee, sowohl als die Gesellschaft umständlich Bericht über den Fortgang ihrer Geschäfte zu erstatten.

Die executive Committee soll sich regelmässig wenigstens alle zwei Wochen versammeln und der Gesellschaft wenigstens alle vier Wochen Bericht über den Fortgang ihrer Geschäfte abstatten. Die executive Committee soll ferner die von ihr zu erwählenden fünf Trusties sowie den Schatzmeister unter passende Verbindlichkeiten legen, um die Gesellschaft vor Schaden zu hüten.

Ueberhaupt wird der executiven Committee empfohlen, ihre Geschäfte innerhalb der genannten Grenzen dahin zu leiten, dass

sobald als möglich, die Gesellschaft zu der Ueberzeugung kommen
möge, dass es mit ihrer Sicherheit und ihrem besten Gedeihen über-
einstimme die ganze Regierung der Gesellschaft nach der Stadt
Hermann zu verlegen.

Philadelphia, am 7ten Juli 1838.   Wilhelm Schmoele, Präs.

The assembly shall then elect a President, a Vice-President, a
Secretary, a Treasurer and 5 Trustees. The President, Vice President and Secretary of the Executive Committee in addition to
four of the latter members to be elected shall comprise a Special
Committee whose obligation shall be to immediately demand an
accounting from the General Agent, Mr. Bayer, which the latter is
obligated to present to the above-named Special Committee, and
indeed within fourteen days, counting from the day on which this
demand is made of him.

The above named Special Committee shall further see to it
that all monies and other property of the Society in the custody of
the General Agent, which has not yet been conveyed by the
General Agent to the Trustees of the Society, shall be conveyed by
him to the five Trustees appointed by the Executive Committee.
The General Agent is hereby obligated to make such a transfer in
accordance with the preceding decision.

The repeatedly mentioned Special Committee shall furthermore assume the offices and the duties delegated to the Controlling Committee as outlined in the instructions to the General
Agent. There shall, however, be made the alteration that for the
suspension of the General Agent the approval of four members of
the said Special Committee and the majority of the Executive
Committee shall be necessary. The Special Committee shall furthermore have the obligation to furnish a detailed report on the
progress of its affairs to the Executive Committee at least every
two weeks.

The Executive Committee shall meet in regular assembly at least every two weeks and submit a report of the progress of its affairs to the Society at least every four weeks. Furthermore, the Executive Committee shall require adequate security from the five trustees which it elects, as well as from the Treasurer, in order to give the Society protection from loss.

In general it is recommended to the Executive Committee that it conduct its affairs with the above mentioned limits to the end that as soon as possible the Society may arrive at the conviction that it may in the interest of its security and greater prosperity transfer the entire administration of the Society to the City of Hermann.

Wilh. Schmoele, President

Philadelphia, July 7, 1838

It is at once seen that by these resolutions the agent's duties were curtailed to such an extent that scarcely more than the name of the office remained. Obviously one of the purposes of the action was to have this officer supervised by a strong and vigorous and obedient body. From now on the agent appears only as a figure head, and early in October the unfortunate man was released from his position entirely. He had worked hard and self-sacrificingly for the company. He had left a good and peaceful employment and subjected himself and family to great hardship. There is no doubt whatsoever in our mind, that he did all within the power of one man and he did even more. Because of the extremely strenuous service to the colony, he contracted serious illness. The nervous strain, brought upon him, at this time, through evidences of distrust from selfish, ignorant, and even caluminious contemporaries, finally broke his strength and in March, 1839, he died. His remains now rest in a remote corner of the town cemetery, which he had laid out with his own hand.

A modest marble slab marks his final resting-place. The simple inscription bears little more than his name and the dates Sept. 27, 1800, and March 18, 1839.

As to the colony—the resolutions gave the members prospect of early self government. It now virtually depended upon the pioneers themselves, whether they would soon be independent or not. As soon as they could satisfy the home society beyond the least doubt that they were capable of managing the affairs judiciously and profitably and fairly for all stockholders, theirs was to be absolute freedom of action.

The home society remained firm in the opinion that the transfer would be productive of mutual good. At least this was their position for a long while. The letters of Bayer of June 25th and July 3rd, were read on Aug. 2. They seem to have made but a slight impression on the members. Certainly they did not place the agent in a more favorable light with them. They only repeated their demand for a settlement with that officer. The agent, by virtue of the power and authority vested in his office, had sold snares at Hermann. It was these sales that now worried the Philadelphians most of all. The agent had not reported the details of these transactions. This anxiety was quite natural, and even commendable, for the money represented the very life substance of the organization. They did not understand then why their representative had not reported the details of his business at stated intervals. But even when on Sept. 6th, Bayer's letter of Aug. 10th was read, in which he presented a plea for himself, even then they did not change their opinion of the affair. They only repeated for a third time their request for a speedy summing up of affairs, adding:

„Dass die General-Versammlung (wenn es die Muttergesellschaft für gut findet) von hier aus nach Hermann mit allen den Protokollen und Büchern der Gesellschaft u. s. w. verlegt werde."

"That the General Assembly (if the Mother Society approves) with all the minutes and books of the Society, etc., be transferred from here to Hermann."

On November 1st, the report of the special committee at Hermann was read. When on the 8th of October, Bayer's term of office came to a close, the special committee assumed control, binding the colony trustees—Senn, Henrich, Lehder, Widersprecher and Leupold by this contract:

I.

„Wir endesunterschriebenen Trustees der Deutschen Ansiedlungs-Gesellschaft in Hermann verpflichten uns hiedurch alle Einkäufe der Gesellschaft in unserem Namen, zum Besten der Gesellschaft zu machen.

II.

Wir wollen das von dem General-Agenten, Herrn G. F. Bayer für die Gesellschaft gekaufte noch nicht überschriebene Land sofort auf uns als Trustees, überschreiben und recordiren lassen.

III.

Alle welche Actien zu kaufen wünschen sollen eine Order von der Mehrzahl von uns, als Trustees bekommen, nach welcher die Kaufgelder an den zeitigen Schatzmeister zu bezahlen sind, welcher ermächtigt ist einen Empfangschein darüber auszustellen.

IV.

Wir verpflichten uns der speciellen Committee oder den zeitigen Beamten der Gesellschaft, oder im Fall die Stadt Hermann bis dahin incorporirt seyn sollte, den Trustees der Stadt Hermann sobald als für nöthig erachtet werden sollte, alles uns überschriebene und sonst anvertraute Eigenthum der Gesellschaft zurückschreiben zu lassen und abzuliefern.

V.

Wir wollen ein genaues Verzeichniss führen über die bereits verkauften und noch zu verkaufenden Actien und die zurückgegebenen Actienscheine wollen wir sorgfältig aufbewahren.

VI.

Alle in den Händen des General-Agenten befindlichen Gelder und sonstiges Eigenthum der Gesellschaft welches von dem General-Agenten noch nicht an die Trustees der Gesellschaft in Philadelphia überschrieben worden ist, soll von dem Agenten an die Trustees in Hermann übergeben und von denselben in Empfang genommen werden.

So geschehen — Hermann, 8. Oct. 1838."

(Signatures.)

I.

We, the undersigned Trustees of the German Settlement Society in Hermann, obligate ourselves herewith to make all purchases of the Society in our names, for the benefit of the Society.

II.

We wish to have all untransferred land bought for the Society by Mr. G. F. Bayer transferred to us as Trustee, and recorded.

III.

All who wish to purchase shares shall obtain a permit from the majority of us, as trustees, in accordance with which the monies from the purchases are to be paid to the contemporary treasurer, who is authorized to furnish a receipt therefor.

IV.

We obligate ourselves to convey and transfer to the Special Committee or to the contemporary officers of the Society, or in the case that the City of Hermann should be incorporated by then, to the Trustees of the City of Hermann as soon as it is deemed necessary, all the property of the Society conveyed and otherwise entrusted us.

V.

We wish to keep a detailed accounting of the already sold and the still to be sold shares and we wish to carefully preserve the returned shares.

VI.

All the monies and other property of the Society in the hands of the General Agent, which has not already been conveyed to the Trustees of the Society in Philadelphia by the General Agent, shall be transferred by the Agent to the Trustees in Hermann and taken into custody by the same.

(signatures)

So done—Hermann, Oct. 8, 1838

Under date of Nov. 3rd, the *"Alte und Neue Welt"* contains the following resolutions signed by the executive committee at Hermann:

„Dass die Mitglieder hiermit aufgefordert seien, sich mit den Trustees hieselbst über die in Beschlag genommenen Lots und Ländereien sofort zu berechnen, und zwar bei Verlust ihrer Ansprüche darauf."

That the members are hereby notified to come to a settlement of the lots and tracts of land under attachment with the Trustees here under penalty of the loss of their claims thereto.

From this, one can but conclude that some records had been loosely kept and that a readjustment was deemed necessary, and that vigorous measures were resorted to, to compel all concerned to come to a speedy settlement.

Up to this date the society had confidently looked forward to an early transfer. It was compelled to be conservative, however, and to proceed slowly, because too many interests were involved in the venture. They proceeded entirely too slowly for the colonists, however. This is evidenced by a letter of the special committee at Hermann, dated December 27th, which assumes more the tone of a demand than that of a petition. It appears that the parent society was negligent about forwarding the necessary authority. This they forced upon the Philadelphians' attention in terms none too delicate. We quote from this letter, for the reason that it, in itself, reflects better the *milieu* in which it arose, than any abstract or translation we could make of it.

„Die bisherigen Fortschritte dieser Ansiedlung sind wahrlich die Früchte Ihrer Fürsorge nicht, wohl aber gereicht der Gesellschaft in Philadelphia zum gerechten Vorwurf, dass die Ansiedlung den viel höheren Standpunkt noch nicht erreicht hat, den sie nun einnehmen möchte, hätten unverzeihliche Missgriffe und Vernachlässigungen von Philadelphia aus, ihren Fortschritt nicht entgegengewirkt. Diese sind insonderheit: die Absendung eines für seine Verpflichtungen unfähigen Agenten, *ohne alle specielle schriftliche Instruktion* von seiten der Trustees; und nach dessen Absetzung, das Vorenthalten jeglicher, rechtskräftiger Vollmacht, welche die, an des Agenten Stelle erwählte Committee nur ermächtigen konnte, an seiner Statt die Geschäfte der Gesellschaft wahrzunehmen. Die von dort gesandten Instruktionen für die hier erwählten Trustees waren nicht einmal nach der Verfassung unseres *Privat-Vereins* gültig, da sie nur von zweien der dasigen Trustees unterzeichnet waren, nicht einmal soweit schenkte man einer so wichtigen Sache Aufmerksamkeit.

Der hiesigen Verwaltung liegen unter anderen, die Pflichten ob: Deeds für Land und Stadt-Lots zu ertheilen — denn die in Philadelphia gedruckten Scheine können unmöglich als Deeds gelten, und viele der hiesigen Ansiedler haben auch diese nicht einmal — wo hat sie die Vollmacht dazu? Ferner, Ausstände für Land und Lots einzuziehen, wo ist Kraft dazu im Weigerungsfalle? Besonders drückend macht den Mangel an gerichtlicher Vollmacht, die Unrichtigkeit des von Herrn Bayer empfangenen Deeds, von Mrs. Phillips, über das Land worauf der östliche Theil der Stadt Hermann gelegen ist, und nach welchem uns dieses Land entschieden streitig gemacht werden kann, wird eine Berichtigung des Kaufbriefes *nicht sofort und mit Umsicht betrieben!* Wer hat gegenwärtig *ein Recht* hier die dazu nöthigen Schritte zu thun, zu verlangen? Die Stadt Hermann soll incorporirt werden, und wäre es schon, aber auf wessen Grund und Boden? Wer ist Eigenthümer oder Repräsentant?

Wer soll unter diesen und vielen anderen *unverhehlbaren Mängeln* sich entschliessen, Grundeigenthum von dieser Gesellschaft zu kaufen? und mancher Gutgewillte hat sich auf diesen Grund hin schon von uns zurückgezogen! Manche die da kauften, halten sich für hintergangen!!

Den General-Deed über das von Bayer gekaufte Land, fast das wichtigste Document welches die Gesellschaft besitzt, erachtete man für gut, anstatt der Verwaltung hier, einem benachbarten Individuum Behufs Recordirung einzusenden, für dessen Descretion und Sorgfalt sich keiner der Unterschriebenen zu verbürgen wünscht. Was ist aus dem Documente geworden? nach Philadelphia zurückgesandt ist es bis dato nicht! Doch dies ist Ihre Sorge, uns nächst liegt im Namen aller deren, für welche wir zu handeln verbunden sind die Aufforderung an Sie:

Die Deutsche Ansiedlungs-Gesellschaft in Hermann ohne ferneren unnöthigen Aufschub in juridischen Besitz aller der Rechte und Vortheile zu setzen, welche sie von Ihnen zu fordern hat, und worauf sie, vertrauensvoll auf die Weisheit und Fürsorge anderer nun schon zu lange verzichtet hat!

Die unterzeichnete Committee rechnet somit zuversichtlich auf die prompteste Erfüllung ihres Ansuchens, und zeichnet

Achtungsvoll,

Julius Leupold,
D. Widersprecher,
Lud. Henrich,
M. Krauter,
Georg Rieffenstahl,
Conrad Baer."

The past progress of the Settlement is indeed not the fruit of your precaution, but rather the justified reproach may be made against the Society in Philadelphia, that the Settlement has not attained a much higher standing, which it might have reached, had not unpardonable blunders and neglect on the part of Philadelphia hemmed its progress. These are in particular: the sending of an Agent incapable of performing his duties, *without any special written instruction on the part of the Trustees;* and after his suspension, the withholding of all effective authority, which only the Committee elected in place of the Agent could assume, to take over in his place the affairs of the Society. The instructions sent from there for the Trustees elected here were not even valid according to the Constitution of our private organization, since they had only been signed by two of the Trustees of that place; not even to such an important matter was attention given.

The Administration at this place has the duties, among others: to issue deeds for land and city lots—for those certificates printed in Philadelphia cannot possibly be valid as deeds, and many of the settlers here do not even have these—where has it received the authorization to do this? Furthermore, to collect debts for land and lots, where is the power to do it in case of default? The lack of legal authority is made especially oppressive by incorrect deeds given by Mrs. Phillips to Mr. Bayer for the land upon which the eastern part of the City of Hermann is situated, and because of which this land can definitely be contested unless a correction of the document of purchase is *immediately and carefully made.* Who, here at present, has the right to take or to demand the necessary steps? The City of Hermann is to be incorporated, and would already be so, but in whose authority or name? Who is owner or who is representative?

Who, in view of these and many other inconceivable defects, shall decide to purchase landed property from this Society? And many a well-disposed person has on this account already withdrawn himself from us! Many who have bought here have considered themselves cheated!!

It was deemed proper to send, for the purpose of recording, the General-Deed of the land purchased by Bayer, almost the most important document which the Society possesses, instead of to the Administration here to a neighboring individual for whose discretion and reliability not one of the undersigned would vouch. What has become of this document? To date it has not been returned to Philadelphia! But this is your worry; more important to us is the demand we make of you in the names of all those for whom we are obligated to negotiate:

To place the German Settlement Society in Hermann without any further unnecessary delay in legal possession of all the rights and privileges which it is justified in asking of you and of which, trusting to the wisdom and precaution of others, it has been denied far too long.

The undersigned Committee confidently expects the promptest fulfillment of its petition and signs"

> Respectfully,
> Julius Leupold
> D. Widersprecher
> Lud. Henrich
> M. Krauter
> George Riefenstahl
> Conrad Baer

There can be no doubt that some of the above statements are slightly magnified, in order to bring about a speedier decision and acquiescence on part of the officers at Philadelphia.

It is plainly to be seen that the colonists would accept but one term and that was absolute separation from the old society. Under these conditions the originators of the movement must have looked forward to a separation with a certain anticipation of relief.

Up to this point it had the appearance as if all the colonists desired the transfer. To the great surprise, as well as discomfort, it now came to light that the settlers entertained very different views concerning this question. In one of these hostile camps were grouped most of the towns folk, in the other all the agriculturists and a few of their town sympathizers. The former championed the cause of the transfer, the latter sought to check it. The views of the opposition took tangible form in a long article of protest, written at Hermann, Feb. 22, 1839, and signed by Daniel Trautwein.

It had been drawn up by these men, Fr. Husmann, Fr. Leupold and Daniel Trautwein, though only the latter affixed his signature to it. This committee had been appointed on Feb. 19th at a special meeting of the opponents to the idea of the transfer. The incorporation of the town of Hermann had been sought for at the same time that negotiations were entered into for the transfer. The case was unmistakably plain, that if this incorporation took effect, if the town of Hermann became the custodian of the society property, then in the nature of things the town was the society. To this very amalgamation the country-folk most vigorously objected. And why should they not? If the town-people carried their point, the farmers had been duped; they had promoted an undertaking for the good of others; they had failed to gain any return for a great outlay. No wonder then that the loyal Trautwein indignantly bursts out:

„Es handelt sich um Ausschliessung eines achtbaren, wichtigen und zahlreichen Theiles der Gesellschaftsmitglieder von allen Rechten und Vortheilen der Gesellschaft, um die Beraubung der Landbewohner zum Besten der Stadt. Soll der Grundsatz der Rechtsgleichheit aller unserer Mitglieder schon am ersten Morgen unseres jungen Lebens niedergetreten und von einem deutschen Whigismus verschlungen werden?“

"It concerns the exclusion of a respectable, important and numerous part of the members of the Society from the rights and privileges of the Society, of the deprivation of the country people for the advantage of the City. Shall the principle of equality of all our members be trodden down already on the first morning of our young life, to be devoured by a German Whiggery?"

Continuing, he points out, that it had not been the intention of the founders of the society to establish a town only, but "eine lebenvolle Deutsche Ansiedlung Landwirthe eben sowohl als Gewerbe teibende Städter." * Quite sensibly he remarks:

---

* "An active German Settlement of country people just as well as City inhabitants of tradesmen."

„Wie hätte auch eine deutsche Stadt inmitten einer amerikanischen Landbevölkerung eine Heimath für uns werden können? Eine Oase in der Wüste — bald überweht von deren austrocknenden Sande! Wir sollten ein Ganzes seyn, ein Ganzes bleiben, gleiche Rechte geniessen, ob wir es vorziehen sollten auf dem Lande oder in der Stadt zu leben."

"How could a German city surrounded by a country population of Americans have become a home for us? An oasis in the desert—soon to be buried under its dehydrating sands. We should be one body, remain one body, enjoy equal privileges, whether we prefer to live in the country or in the city."

He condemns the presumptuousness of the townsfolk to attempt to become sole beneficiaries. He strengthens his point by showing that the farmers have the same constitutional right as all others, and could as well claim exclusive recognition as their village friends.

The chief agitators urging an unconditional transfer, seem to have been D. Widersprecher and Julius Leupold. Both of them were rather eccentric and—selfish. They were forced to appear before the assembly of Feb. 19 at Hermann to explain their position and their action. They claimed to have acted upon the authority of a resolution of October 28th, 1838, according to which all the property of the society had been transferred to the town of Hermann. No one recalled such a resolution. An investigation was instigated. The books contained not a syllable of such an act. Under the minutes of the special committee, however, an unapproved resolution was found:

„Dass es die höchste Zeit sei, um Inkorporirung der Stadt Hermann bei der am 6ten des nächsten Monats sitzenden County Court nachzusuchen, zur Wahl von 5 Trustees der Stadt Hermann, wie das Gesetz sie vorschreibt, am nächsten Montag, als den 29ten October, Mittags 1 Uhr, in der Wohnung des Herrn Lehder geschritten werden soll. Diese Trustees werden sodann, sobald die Stadt Hermann incorporirt worden ist, das ganze Vermögen der Deutschen Ansiedlungs-Gesellschaft zum alleinigen Nutzen und Frommen der Stadt Hermann verwalten."

That it is highest time, in order to institute proceedings for incorporation of the City of Hermann with the County Court meeting on the 6th of next month, to proceed with the election of 5 trustees of the City of Hermann, as prescribed by law, next Monday, the 29th of October, at 1:00 o'clock noon, in the residence of Mr. Lehder. These trustees shall then, as soon as the City of Hermann has been incorporated, administer the entire property of the German Settlement Society for the sole use and benefit of the City of Hermann.

This was a rather well planned ruse, designed to dupe the unsophisticated farmers, who, however, were too keenly awake to their rights. This incident marks an ugly blot on the record of the usually square dealing townspeople. Finding his party thus defeated at this point, J. Leupold undertook to misinterpret paragraph 3 of the constitution, presenting it in such a light as if the land owning members were not entitled to the same privileges as other shareholders. Of course he was instantly corrected by the opposition, for they knew only too well what part of the basic laws contained their support.

In conclusion Trautwein pleads for the rights of the rural constituency. He does this in a number of interrogations, more forceful than a series of declarations:

„Worin beständen denn unter Herrn Leupolds und Widersprechers System die Vorzüge der landbewohnenden Mitglieder des Vereins vor anderen umherwohnenden Nichtmitgliedern? Etwa darin, dass wir unser Land theurer bezahlen dürfen als die vom Staate kaufenden Nichtmitglieder? Darin dass wir die Nachtheile zu tragen hätten, ohne die Vortheile geniessen zu dürfen? Welches Reizmittel wäre diess für Fremde unser Land um einen theureren Preis zu kaufen als sie es vom Staate haben können?"

"Where then, under the system of Messrs. Leupold and Widersprecher would be the advantages that a member of the organization who lives in the country would have over other non-members living hereabouts? Perhaps in this, that we must purchase our land at a higher price than non-members buying from the Government? Therein, that we must suffer the disadvantages without enjoying the advantages? What an incentive would this be for strangers forced to buy our land at a higher price than they could obtain it from the Government?"

As was to be expected, this communication caused the Muttergesellschaft to reflect, and to postpone the transfer indefinitely. Previous to the arrival of this letter, Wesselhoeft, Schmidt and Feuring had been appointed a committee to council as to the means and ways of transferring the management to Hermann without imperilling the rights of the shareholders. They were instructed to confer with the special committee in Missouri and to request them to submit suggestions. On February 14th, the committee was even directed to begin the legal steps towards this change. But Trautwein's appeal and a philippic from one Gentner caused the society to annul all these actions. It was now decided to abide a time when these disturbances might be amicably adjusted. In the meantime earnest investigation was conducted by the officers. Treasurer Schmidt was sent to the colony to enquire:

„Ob die Gesetze in Missouri es erlauben, dass die Landbewohner dasselbe Stimmrecht als die Stadtbewohner haben.“

"Whether the laws of Missouri permit, that the inhabitant of the country have the same voting privilege as the inhabitant of the city."

Though the matter was delayed, there was no question but that the change was bound to come. A new committee consisting of Klett, Gentner and Stockfleht, was appointed and instructed to see

„wie und auf welche Weise die Verlegung der Verwaltung auf die sicherste Art bewerkstelligt werden kann.“

"How and in what manner the transfer of the Administration can be made in the most effective way."

In June, Schmidt returned and urged the transfer without delay.

There was no longer any doubt that the end must soon come. Several meetings had been called at Philadelphia, but no quorum appeared. Interest had died out. To secure yet what funds they could, the treasurer was instructed:

„Eine Aufforderung ergehen zu lassen, um diejenigen Actionäre, welche ihre Actienscheine noch nicht abgeholt haben, zu veranlassen, dieses schleunigst zu thun."

"To publish a summons to induce those shareholders who have not yet obtained the Certificate of Shares, to do this without delay."

A great number of letters arrived from Hermann, some signed by individuals, some by a great number of persons; some favoring the change, others urging continuation of the old regime. The solution of the problem became extremely difficult.

In this extremity the committee on transfer, of which body the president of the society was ex-officio member, prepared a long report, addressed to the special committee at Hermann. This special committee consisted of the following five gentlemen:

> J. Leupold,
> M. Krauter,
> Ludw. Geis,
> Heinr. Heckmann,
> Peter Müller.

The report is headed by this request to the committee:

„Sie sind freundlichst ersucht so schnell als möglich, eine Versammlung aller, in der Ansiedlung wohnenden Mitglieder der Gesellschaft zu berufen und denselben den folgenden Bericht zur Verhandlung vorzulegen."

"You are most kindly requested to call, as soon as possible a meeting of all members of the Society living in Hermann and to present the following report to them for consideration."

This report, written July 1st, 1839, contains many interesting points hitherto unmentioned. It reiterates the intentions of the society in regard to the future control thus:

„Es ist der einstimmige Wunsch der Muttergesellschaft, dass die Verlegung der Verwaltung so bald als möglich geschehe, und nur das Streben, die Verlegung auf eine die Rechte aller Mitglieder sichernde und allgemein befriedigende Weise vorzunehmen, hat die Ausführung bisher verzögert." The obstacles to an absolute transfer when the request first became known are these:

„(1) Der damalige Mangel an Personen in der Ansiedlung welche zu gesetzlich gültigen Pfandhaltern (Trustees) gewählt werden konnten. (2) Der Mangel an Sicherstellung der Privatinteressen aller ihre Stadtlotten noch nicht gewählt habenden Mitglieder der Gesellschaft, indem die Wahl der Lotten für diese hätte können ungebührlich beschränkt oder erschwert werden."

"It is the unanimous wish of the Mother-Society that the transfer of the Administration take place as soon as possible, and only the endeavor to undertake the transfer in a manner which secures the rights of all members and affords universal satisfaction, has up to now delayed the fulfillment."

The obstacles to an absolute transfer when the request first became known are these:

"1) The lack of persons in the Settlement at that time who could legally be elected as Trustees.

2) The lack of protection of the private interests of those members of the Society who had not yet selected their city lots, as the selection of the lots could have been excessively limited or rendered more difficult for these."

It is conceded that this first hindrance had been removed, but it is emphatically impressed that the latter problem must yet be solved. It is further pointed out that the most varied and contradictory reports have arrived from Hermann.

1. It had been stated that a most threatening agitation existed at the colony. 2. Certain men at Hermann advised that all action be deferred until this difference was adjusted. 3. The landowners urged continuation of control by the home society. 4. Others proposed that the form of management remain unchanged, only the residence of the society be changed. 5. The people of the town Hermann demanded complete and unconditional yielding to their proposition to consolidate the town and the society. 6. It was not known whether the town Hermann was or was not incorporated, and, if so, how.

On this last point Schmidt, who had just been in Hermann, could not give accurate information. It was positively necessary to know whether Jarvis' land, which lay adjoining to the colony, had also been incorporated in the town. Certain concessions and restrictions hinged on this fact. As a matter of fact the land of several private individuals was included in the incorporation. This multiplied the difficulties in a great measure and protracted the negotiations greatly.

The committee on transference was given a most delicate task when they were asked to find an equitable settlement of the affair so variously judged. In their dilemma they finally hit upon a course which, though not altogether just, was nevertheless human. The beginning of their action was the giving of a definition of the original purpose of the society. In this opinion they took care to side with the stronger faction of the colonists. Though this may not accord with our interpretation of equity, yet it was a starting point towards a very difficult solution, though Sec. 3 of the constitution was recklessly overruled. This opinion they couched in these well-chosen words:

„Der ursprüngliche Zweck der Gesellschaft war die Gründung einer deutschen *Stadt,* welche durch vereinigtes Capital und sonstiges öffentliches Vermögen, Gleichheit des Strebens und harmonisches Zusammenleben schnell zu dem Grade der Blüthe in physischer, sowohl als geistiger Rücksicht emporwachsen sollte, dass sie dem deutschen Namen zur Ehre und den heimathlosen Stammgenossen zum glücklichen Asyl gereichen möchte. In diesem Sinne müssen die Constitution und alle Nebengesetze der Gesellschaft gedeutet werden. Dann ergiebt es sich von selbst, dass die Forderungen der Rechte der Mitgliedschaft für die, welche *alle* ihre Actien für gekauftes Land an die Gesellschaft zurückgegeben — mithin ihren Privatvortheil, durch die erhöhten Actienpreise, welche ihnen bei der Rückgabe berechnet wurden, bereits genossen haben — oder gar niemals Mitglieder gewesen sind, obgleich sie nun der Gesellschaft oder Privatpersonen Grundeigenthum gekauft haben mögen — gänzlich haltlos ist, und weder in der Constitution noch in irgend einem Gesetze der Gesellschaft auch nur einen Scheingrund für sich finden können.

Dieser genannte ursprüngliche Zweck der Gesellschaft macht es aber sehr wünschenswerth, dass die von den unternehmenden, und durch Muth und Fleiss sich auszeichnenden Mitgliedern der Gesellschaft in unglaublich kurzer Zeit gegründete und bereits vom Staate incorporirte Stadt Hermann als letztes Ziel des gesellschaftlichen Unternehmens, nunmehr so bald als möglich mit der Gesellschaft verschmelzen möge, so dass Stadt Hermann und Ansiedlungs-Gesellschaft in jeder Beziehung tautologisch seien."

"The original purpose of the Society was the founding of a German *City,* which through common capital, and other public' property, equality of effort and harmonious coexistence was to speedily attain to such a degree of prosperity, from the physical as well as the ethical standpoint, that it would be an honor to the German name and a happy refuge for the homeless countrymen. The Constitution and all by-laws of the Society must be interpreted within this context. From this it is self-evident that the demands for the privileges of membership for those, who return *all* their shares to the Society for purchased land—consequently having already benefited from their private advantages due to the increased value of the shares, which was accredited to them on the redemption—or even have never been members although they now may have bought landed property from the Society or private individuals—are entirely indefensible, and neither in the Constitution nor in any law of the Society can even as much as a pretext for such be found.

"This above named original purpose of the Society makes it very desirable that as a final goal of the undertaking of the Society, the City of Hermann, founded in an incredibly short time by venturous members of the Society, characterized by courage and industry, and now incorporated by the State might now merge with the Society so that the City of Hermann might be synonymous in every respect with the Settlement Society."

By this decision the difficulty was vastly minimized while the possible solution was proportionately facilitated. The farmers are entirely excluded from consideration. The problem is now wholly concentrated upon the town Hermann. The report continues by enumerating certain advantages which such a change would promote:

1. Such a consolidation of town and society would unify and centralize the various interests, would preserve order and promote public undertakings.

2. The property of the society would be more secure under State supervision.

3. The constitution and by-laws would be more effective if clad in the garb of State laws.

4. Such consolidation of town and society interests would bring about equality of rights and duties of all residents—a condition impossible under a separate existence of these bodies.

Although the consolidation appeared, on the whole, beneficent to a great number concerned, there were still very serious objections to be raised against it.

1. All inhabitants of Hermann would, by virtue of the laws of the State, become joint owners and beneficiaries of the society property whether they had contributed an equivalent or not.

2. The members living in various parts of the country would lose their vote in society matters, while such men as Jarvis would *eo-ipso* have a voice in the transactions of the society.

3. In making public improvements the society would be unduly burdened, while the non-members would reap the benefit without proportionate co-operation.

4. The estates of non-members would be exempt from taxation the same as the society property. The public improvements would increase the value of the property of non-members and practically make impossible the purchase of such property.

It was made plain that no consolidation was possible until these matters were satisfactorily settled. In making this last decision it was, however, clearly stated that a transfer of the offices of the society was much desired and recommended. But before this change could be positively granted answers to these questions were called for:

„1. Wie werden die Glieder der Gesellschaft, welche ihre Stadtlotten noch nicht aufgenommen haben, sicher gestellt, dass Ihnen nicht künftig die Wahl ihrer Lotten erschwert oder gar unmöglich gemacht werde?

2. Wie soll es mit der Besteuerung der von vielen Actienbesitzern noch nicht aufgenommenen Stadtlotten gehen, im Falle die Einkünfte des gesellschaftlichen Vermögens zu irgend einer Zeit nicht hinreichen sollten, um sämmtliche Taxen, die auf den gesellschaftlichen Theil der Stadt fallen, zu decken?

3. Wie steht es um die bisherige Geschäftsführung der executiven, sowohl als der speziellen Committee? Besonders wird eine definitive Rechnungs-Ablegung der Letzteren gewünscht.“

"1) How shall the members of the Society who have as yet not selected their City lots be given assurance that the choice of their lots shall not be made difficult or even impossible in the future?

2) How shall the imposition of taxes on the City lots not yet taken by the many shareholders be made, in case that the income from the Society's property shall at some time not suffice to cover the total taxes levied upon the Society's city property?

3) What is the condition of the business affairs of the Executive Committee up to the present, as well as of the Special Committee? A final accounting of the latter is especially desired."

The Philadelphia committee went so far as to suggest answers to these questions, which suggestions, however, fell upon deaf ears. The men at Hermann had their own solution for problems in hand, as will appear later.

Since the incorporation of the town Hermann, a very interesting and indeed unique state of affairs existed. The report, under discussion, expands somewhat on this point. An odd state of confusion had come about. And all this, too, at a time when it was thought impossible for any such thing to occur. The colony had existed a little over one year and already the town was no longer purely German.

„Die Gesellschaft hat seit der Incorporation der Stadt Hermann einen *höchst* beschrenkten Wirkungskreis," the report continues, „während das Stadt-Council beinahe unbedingte Gewalt besitzt. Das Council hat zu befehlen (natürlich innerhalb der Grenzen der Incorporations-Acte), die Gesellschaft zu gehorchen, soweit sich die Befehle auf den gesellschaftlichen Stadtgrund erstrecken."

"Since the incorporation of the City of Hermann the Society has a most restricted sphere of action", the report continues, "while the City-Council possesses almost unlimited authority. The Council may command (of course, within the limits of the Charter of Incorporation), the Society must obey, insofar as the orders affect the City property of the Society."

What then, really, was the relation of the town Hermann and the society? The committee defined thus:

„Die Stadt Hermann besteht aus Bürgern, welche theils Mitglieder der Ansiedlungs-Gesellschaft sind, theils nicht, die aber alle gleiches Stimmrecht in der Stadt-Verwaltung haben. Sie erstreckt sich über Land, das theils gesellschaftlich ist, theils nicht, aber alles im Stadtgebiete liegende Land, gleichviel ob gesellschaftliches oder fremdes der Stadtverwaltung (Council) unterworfen, besteuerbar für öffentliche Ausgaben, Verbesserungen, Stadtbauten, etc. Nur für den ganzen gesellschaftlichen Antheil (die von Mitgliedern aufgenommenen und bebauten Stadtlotten) zahlt die Gesellschafts-Kasse alle Grundsteuern, so lange die Einkünfte der Gesellschaft dazu hinreichen (welches aller Wahrscheinlichkeit nach immer der Fall sein wird) für das fremde Land aber, innerhalb des Stadtgebietes, müssen die respectiven Eigenthümer einen proportionellen Tax bezahlen. Die Ansiedlungs-Gesellschaft hat mithin mit der Stadt Hermann weiter nichts zu thun, als dass sie die dem gesellschaftlichen Stadttheile zufallenden Grundtaxen bezahlt, und die auf diesen Theil sich beziehenden Council-Verordnungen erfüllt; auf dieselbe Weise und in derselben Ordnung, als z. B. Herr Jarvis dasselbe in Proportion für den von ihm geeigneten Stadttheil thut. . . . . . Der Grund für die Schule so wie anderen öffentlichen Gebäuden muss von der Gesellschaft gekauft werden. . . . Die Gesellschaft eignet oder representirt einen grossen Theil der Stadt. Sollen auf diesem gesellschaftlichen Stadttheil Anlagen (z. B. Squares, Gärten, Promenaden etc. etc.) angelegt, öffentliche Gebäude gebaut, oder andere öffentliche Verbesserungen gemacht werden, so muss die Stadt den dazu nöthigen Grund von der Gesellschaft kaufen. Dieser Baupreis muss dann wieder durch Grundtaxen, theils von der Gesellschaft theils von den Eigenthümern des nicht gesellschaftlichen Stadtlandes aufgemacht werden. Jedenfalls würde es ungerecht sein, dass die Gesellschaft sollte gratis Land und Geld zu öffentlichen Verbesserungen abtreten, die zur Wertherhöhung *aller* Stadttheile dienen. . . . Die Stadt als *solche* besitzt *Nichts* als was sie kauft. Um zu kaufen schreibt sie Taxen aus, welche von der Gesellschaft, Jarvis, Schiefer und Schmidt proportionsmässig zu zahlen sind.''

"The City of Hermann consists of citizens who are in part members of the Settlement Society, and in part those who are not, but who all have an equal voting privilege in the administration of the City. It covers land which in part belongs to the Society, and in part not, but all land lying within the City limits is equally under the jurisdiction of the City Council, whether belonging to the Society or otherwise, is taxable for public expenditures, improvements, City buildings, etc. Only for the entire portion owned by the Society (the City lots acquired and improved by the members) does the Society pay the land tax, as long as the income of the Society is sufficient (which in all probability will always be the case); for the foreign land within the City limits, however, the respective owners must pay a proportional tax. The Settlement Society consequently has nothing more to do with the City of Hermann than to pay the land taxes on the part of the City owned by the Society and to observe the Council ordinances pertaining to this part in the same manner and in the same order as e.g., Mr. Jarvis does in proportion for that part of the City owned by him. ... The site for the school as well as other public buildings must be purchased from the Society. ... The Society owns or represents a large part of the City. If on this part of the City owned by the Society projects are initiated (e.g., squares, gardens, promenades, etc., etc.) public buildings erected, or other public improvements made, then the City must purchase the necessary land from the Society. This purchase price must then again be obtained from land taxes, in part from the Society and in part from the owners of City property not belonging to the Society. In any case it would be unjust for the Society to furnish land and money gratis for public improvements which serve to increase the valuation of *all* parts of the City. The City as such possesses nothing except that which it buys. In order to be able to buy, it levies taxes which are to be paid proportionately by the Society, Jarvis, Schiefer, and Schmidt."

From the foregoing it is difficult to state just what was meant by a consolidation of the company and the town Hermann. If, as was stated in the outset, company and town are identical, then, according to the later statements, the town would be buying from itself. The report continues:

„Sollten die letzteren drei Eigenthümer (Jarvis, Schiefer und

Schmidt) des fremden Stadtgrundes von der Gesellschaft ausge-
kauft werden, so würde die Bedeutung von Stadt und Gesellschaft
leicht zu verschmelzen sein, und dann könnte man in Wahrheit
sagen, die Stadt Hermann eignet das ganze gesellschaftliche Vermögen."

"If the latter three property owners (Jarvis, Schaefer and
Schmidt) would sell the part of the City belonging to them to the
Society, then the concept of City and Society could easily be
merged, and then one could say in truth the City of Hermann
owns the entire property of the Society."

The report is signed:

„Wilhelm Schmoele — im Namen der von der Muttergesellschaft niedergesetzten Committee, welche die Verlegung der Verwaltung der Gesellschaft zu beraten hatte.
Philadelphia, Juli 1, 1839."

"Wilhelm Schmoele—in the name of the Committee desig-
nated by the Mother Society to consider the transfer of the
Administration of the Society.
Philadelphia, July 1, 1839"

The society seal is affixed to the document to prove its
authenticity.

In response to this report an answer was punctiliously prepared and signed by 65 members at Hermann. The tenor of this
reply seems to have been entirely satisfactory. Attorneys-at-law
were at once employed to assist the committee on transference in
drawing up a general deed conveying the property into the hands
of the trustees at Hermann.

While this was doing in Philadelphia, a final, grand report
was being prepared and signed by 106 colonists. It was the ulti-
matum, so far as the colony was concerned. This report contains a reiteration of many of the points referred to in the letter
of the preceding paragraph. In it are found the answers to the
questions propounded by the Philadelphians. A part of this communication is appended here:

„Erstens

Ist es fortwährend unser Wunsch, dass die Verwaltung des gesellschaftlichen Vermögens sobald als möglich nach der Stadt Hermann verlegt werden möge, welches in Uebereinstimmung mit den Statuten der Gesellschaft und namentlich mit den Bestimmungen ist, nach welchen die Trustees der Stadt Hermann installirt worden.

Zweitens

Glauben die Unterzeichneten, dass kein Mangel an Personen vorhanden, welche zu gesetzgültigen Trustees der Stadt Hermann gewählt werden können.

Drittens

Erklären wir hiedurch, dass wir es niemals zugeben, vielmehr immer dagegen protestiren wollen, dass in dem jetzigen Werthe, so wie auch in der bestehenden Auswahl von Stadtlotten, zum Nachtheil derjenigen Mitglieder, welche ihre Stadtlotten noch nicht gewählt haben, irgend eine Beschränkung oder Veränderung stattfinden soll.

Viertens

Ist es unsere Meinung, dass von einer in dem Berichte erwähnten Aufregung der Gemüther in der Ansiedlung veranlasst durch entgegengesetzte Wünsche, Zwecke und Ansichten jetzt nicht mehr die Rede seyn kann, indem wir hiedurch nochmals erklären, dass es unser Wunsch ist, dass die ganze Verwaltung des gesellschaftlichen Vermögens sofort der Stadt Hermann übertragen werden möge.

Fünftens

Sehen wir nichts dabey zu erinnern, dass alle Bewohner der Stadt von ihrem gesetzlichen Stimmrecht nach Belieben Gebrauch machen, da solche doch nur durch Ankauf oder Benutzung von Grundeigenthum Bürger respective Bewohner der Stadt Hermann werden können.

Sechstens

Ist es unsere nicht beengte Ansicht, dass das Wohl der Stadt Hermann durchaus nicht dadurch gefährdet werden könnte wenn sich auch noch fremdes Grundeigenthum im Weichbild der Stadt befindet. Nur müssten die jedesmaligen Besitzer solchen Grundeigenthums von den Trustees der Stadt Hermann aufgefordert werden, einen Revers auszustellen, dass sie ausser ihrer eigenen Tax auch noch sobald solches nöthig seyn sollte, und verlangt wird, unweigerlich nach der gesetzlichen Norm die Taxen der Stadt pro rata mittragen wollen.

Siebentes

Ist es evident, dass nur die in der Folge von den Trustees der Stadt Hermann ausgeschriebene Taxe von den Bürgern zu bezahlen ist, indem die alten Grundtaxe von den angekauften Ländereyen, sobald das gesellschaftliche Vermögen der Stadt Hermann übertragen von besagter Stadt als Besitzerin dieses Grundeigenthums zu entrichten seyn wird, und solte jemals die Zeit herannahen, dass das jetzige Vermögen der Gesellschaft nicht mehr zu diesen Zwecken ausreicht, so werden allerdings sämmtliche Besitzer von Grundeigenthum im Weichbilde der Stadt Hermann nach dem üblichen Norm die Taxen der Corporation pro rata zu entrichten haben. Wollen sie das nicht so steht es ihnen schon jetzt oder dann und zu jeder Zeit frey aus der Incorporation herauszutreten.

Achtens.

Durch diese unsere bündige Erklärung müssen diejenigen Glieder der Gesellschaft, welche ihre Stadtlotten noch nicht aufgenommen haben, sich sicher gestellt fühlen, dass ihnen nicht künftig die Wahl ihrer Lots erschwert, oder gar unmöglich gemacht werde.

Neuntens.

Sobald das gesellschaftliche Vermögen der Stadt Hermann übertragen, kann, in so weit dies in Folge stattfinden wird, nur von einer Besteuerung derjenigen Stadtlotten die Rede seyn, welche bereits aufgenommen und mit Gebäuden versehen oder sonst cultivirt sind.

Zehntens.

Was eine Rechnungsablage über die Geschäftsführung in der Ansiedlung anbelangt so sind die früheren Rechnungsverhältnisse mit dem General-Agenten bereits eingesandt, die executive Committee hat weiter mit der Geschäftsführung nichts zu thun und ward durch die specielle Committee in dieser Hinsicht vertreten. Da aber eine specielle Committee, wie oben erwähnt, bey Empfang des Berichts nicht bestand, so werden die früheren Mitglieder gewiss eben so bereit seyn als willig, die verlangte Rechnungs-Ablegung sofort einzusenden und wird der Secretair sofort das Nöthige bewerkstelligen wollen.

Elftens

Ist es uns freylich tröstlich zu vernehmen, dass alle diejenigen welche Grundeigenthum von der Gesellschaft erworben und dasselbe zum vollen bezahlt haben, auf ein Certificat der speciellen Committee — soll wohl heissen ein Certificat der Trustees in Hermann — oder von beiden unverzüglich bekommen können.

Zwölftens

Haben wir uns endlich dahin noch ausdrücklich aussprechen wollen, dass wir des festen Glaubens sind, dass durch Uebertragung des gesellschaftlichen Vermögens an die Stadt Hermann dieses mit dem übrigen Vermögen der Stadt Hermann gänzlich verschmolzen wird und ist der raisonierende Theil des hier beantworteten Berichts durchaus auf falschen Prämissen basirt, denn was die Pflichten und Rechte der Stadt Hermann anbelangt, so wird solche durch die Corporationsacte bestimmt und vorgeschrieben und will die Stadt Hermann Schulhäuser etc. etc. bauen, so haben die Bürger und Trustees sich nach dem zu richten, was besagte Corporationsacte vermeldet.

Es findet sich auch nicht ein einziges mit den Verhältnissen bekanntes Mitglied in der Ansiedlung welches mit dem letzten raisonierenden Theil des Berichts einverstanden wäre. Dies wäre ja weiter nichts als das Geld von einer Tasche in die andere stecken, wenn die Stadt Hermann von der Stadt Hermann Hausplätze etc. zu Stadtzwecken kaufen sollte."

"First

It is continually our desire that the Administration of the property of the Society be transferred as soon as possible to the City of Hermann, which is in conformity with the statutes of the Society and in particular with the regulations according to which the Trustees of the City of Hermann were installed.

Second

The undersigned believe that there is no lack of individuals on hand who can be elected as legal Trustees of the City of Hermann.

Third

We hereby declare that we shall never approve of, but on the contrary will always protest any limitation or change in the present valuation or in the prevailing choice of the City lots, which could work to the disadvantage of those members who have as yet not selected their City lots.

Fourth

It is our opinion that there are no grounds whatever for the charge made in the report about agitation of the dispositions caused by conflicting desires, goals and views, as we hereby again declare that it is our desire that the entire administration of the property of the Society be transferred to the City of Hermann.

Fifth

We see it desirable thereby to indicate that all inhabitants of the City may avail themselves of their legal voting privilege since citizens can become inhabitants of the City of Hermann only through purchase or use of landed property.

Sixth

It is our broad view that the welfare of the City of Hermann cannot be endangered by the presence of foreign landed property within the precincts of the City. It would only be necessary that the actual owners of such landed property be required to furnish a counter-deed, that in addition to their own tax, they will unquestioningly be willing to assume pro-rata the taxes imposed by the City whenever these become necessary and are levied.

Seventh

It is evident that in the future the only tax to be paid by the citizens is that levied by the Trustees of the city, as the former land-tax of the purchased tracts is to be discharged by said City as possessor of this landed-property as soon as the property of the Society has been transferred to the City of Hermann, and if ever the time should come that the present assets of the Society should no longer be adequate to this purpose, then certainly all the owners of landed property within the precincts of the City of Hermann will be obligated to pay the taxes of the corporation pro-rata according to the customary norm. If they do not wish that, they are free to leave the Corporation even now, or later, and at any time.

Eighth

By this, our united declaration, those members of the Society who have not yet taken their city lots may be assured that in the future their selection of their lots will not be made more difficult or even rendered impossible.

Ninth

As soon as the property of the Society has been transferred to the City of Hermann, insofar as this shall occur in the future, there can be possible only one kind of tax levy for those lots which have already been taken and improved by buildings or otherwise cultivated.

Tenth

As concerns a settlement of accounts of the business affairs in the Settlement, the former statements of accounts with the General Agent have already been sent in; the Executive Committee has nothing further to do with the administration of business affairs and was represented for this purpose by the Special Committee. But since a Special Committee, as mentioned above, did not exist when the report was received, the earlier members will be just as prepared as they are willing to send in immediately the required settlement of accounts and the Secretary will then arrange whatever is necessary.

Eleventh

It is indeed comforting to us to hear that all those who have obtained landed property from the Society and have paid the same in full can obtain a certificate from the Special Committee, i.e., a Certificate from the Trustees in Hermann, or from both, without delay.

Twelfth

Finally, we have expressly wished hereby to state our opinion that we are of the firm belief, that through the transfer of the property of the Society to the City of Hermann, this will be fully merged with the remaining property of the City of Hermann; and the argumentative part of the report which we have herewith answered, has absolutely been based upon false assumptions, for as concerns the obligations and the rights of the City of Hermann, these will be designated and assigned by the Act of Corporation, and if the City of Hermann wishes to build schoolhouses, etc, etc., the citizens and Trustees must proceed in conformity with the said Act of Corporation.

There is not a single member in the Settlement acquainted with the circumstances who would agree with the last argumentative part of the report. This would mean nothing more than taking money from one pocket and placing it in another, if the City of Hermann should buy building sites from the City of Hermann for city purposes."

Here then follow the 106 signatures. We shall attach them here for a two-fold reason. First, it shows who were the separatists at Hermann, and, secondly, it gives a partial list, at least, of householders at that time. The names are written in the order found in the document:

Jacob Morloch	Friedrich Reinhardt
David Lang	Joseph Vogt
Ernst Meyer	Joh. Quandt
Silvest Weber	Adam Wagner
George Clauss	Christian Rohrbacher
Jacob Dormeyer	Martin Mausehund
Adam Nider	John C. Rice
Hermann Kemper	Cölestin Diebold
August Kläring	Phillipp Schneider
Hermann Rothert	Otto von Schrader
John Woern	Theodor Baer
J. L. Idemann	Conrad Baer

Georg Müller
Nikolas Welter
H. G. Finn
Chas. C. Albers
Amedi Brunet
Daniel Oelschlæger
August F. Kläring
Christoph Fr. Oelschlæger
Fredrick Semken
Anton Franz Hemme
Wilhelm Stöhr
Wm. E. Young
C. L. Schlömer
L. Sommerhalter
Pierre Brunet, Sr.
Johann Gräber
Johann Meyer
Anthony Miller
Benedickt Bleile
Ignatz Bleile
Heinrich Heckmann
J. G. Prager
Leonhard Schramm

Charles Asmus
John H. Witmann
August Roeske
Jacob Schiefer
D. W. Wohlein
John Battermann
Kasper Greis
George Pfautsch
F. Langendörfer
J. Leupold
M. Krauter
Jacob Klink
Ludwig Hisigas
Georg Schäfer
John Blust
Thomas Gawley
Florenz Ritter
Elizabeth Trautwein

Georg Rieffenstahl
John H. Miller
Karl Kneisel
F. Lehder
W. Ameling
Fr. Leupold
Phillipp Köller
Fred Husmann
E. C. Staffhorst
Nicolaus Bensing
Gottlieb Kreuchy
Johannes Abglanalp
Johannes Böhm
Adam Böhm
Silfester Döss
D. Widersprecher
Charles Naegelin
A. W. Friedrichs
Jacob Rommel
Adam Bezold
Edward Pommer
Theodor Vogt
Charles D. Eitzen

Michael Kroeber
Carl Kohl
August Leonhard
Peter Scheidt
Adam Scheidt
Johannes Sidler
Catharina Bayer
Aug. Leimer
Caroline Pommer
H. Heinrichs
H. Jahns
H. von Schlegel
Hermann Bock
A. Brickwede
Fk. Wm. Pommer
J. H. Vahrenhorst
Joseph Schweyer
C. C. Osterloh

This was done early in September. At an extra session of the home society on September 17th these promises evidently were joyfully received. A final and decisive resolution was then passed:

„Dass die hiesigen Trustees sowohl, als die Trustees in der Ansiedlung hierdurch angewiesen sind, von allen ihnen respectiv anvertrauten gesellschaftlichen Vermögen einen vollständigen Deed of Trust an den Stadt-Council der Stadt Hermann, Gasconade County, Missouri, zu übermachen, welcher künftig als Trustee der deutschen Ansiedlungs-Gesellschaft das Vermögen der Letzteren repräsentiren soll."

"That the Trustees here, as well as the Trustees in the Settlement, are hereby charged to furnish a complete Deed of Trust for all the property of the Society respectively entrusted to them, to the City Council of the City of Hermann, Gasconade County, Missouri, which as Trustee of the German Settlement Society shall in the future represent the property of the latter."

With the passage of this act the great decision had been reached. Everyone breathed more freely—even those who felt that the step was injudiciously made. The die was cast, and Hermann was thrown upon its own resources and its members upon their own ingenuity to make or mar the future of a German town. With this decision there went certain requirements to which the colony readily acceded and which they sought to carry out to the best of their ability. These conditions were:

„1. Dass die jetzt bestehende Bestimmung der Gesellschaft für die Wahl der Stadtlotten von Mitgliedern niemals soll geändert werden können, bis alle Ansprüche der einzelnen Mitglieder auf Privatvermögen, welches ihnen durch ihre Actienscheine zugesichert ist, befriedigt sein werden.

2. Dass die Trustees immer verbunden sein sollen, jedem Mitgliede welches den genannten Bedingungen nachgekommen ist, für jede Lotte zu welcher er durch solches Nachkommen berechtigt ist, oder sein wird, einen vollen Eigenthums-Deed zu geben, und dass der Preis der Actien nie unter Fünfzig Thaler herabgesetzt werden soll.

3. Dass endlich keine Stadtlotte von der Auswahl der Mitglieder soll ausgeschlossen sein, welche nicht schon gewählt, oder Pri-
vat-Vermögen oder zu specifischen öffentlichen Zwecken bestimmt
ist oder sind."

"1. That the resolution of the Society in force at present
concerning the selection of city lots by members shall never be
altered until all claims by the individual members for private
property, which are assured them by their Certificate of Shares,
have been satisfied.

2. That the trustees will always be obligated to furnish a
complete property-deed to every member who has met the
required conditions, for each lot to which he is or will be entitled
by his compliance, and that the price of the shares shall never be
set at less than $50.00.

3. That finally no city lot shall be excluded from the selection
of the members, unless it has already previously been chosen or is
private property, or has been designated for public purposes."

It was further decided to inform the authorities at Hermann
at once and to forward the power of attorney poste haste to the
proper officers. By virtue of this authority the Hermann officials
were charged to collect the sum of $1,300.00 which was due in
October. To facilitate the transfer the colonists had implied
previously that they would meet all obligations incumbent on the
society provided they were given full control of things. The
people at Hermann had no money to pay this debt. On the 25th
of September, 1839, they resolved to make a loan.

"That, as the Trustees of the Society are incapable of pro-
curing the 1,300 dollars necessary for the payment of the last
instalments due October 1, 1839, Mr. Julius Leupold be authorized and empowered to borrow the above sum, at the lowest possible interest; but in case he should not be able to raise the money,
all responsibility shall fall on those who have approved the trans-

ferring of the property of the society from Philadelphia to Hermann."

There must have been some difficulty in obtaining the money, for on January 22, 1840, another order was issued "requesting and authorizing Julius Leupold to contract a loan of $1,300 for the town of Hermann." At any rate, the home society was satisfied that this obligation would be met. So on December 12, 1839, the last meeting was held at the Penn Hotel, the same place where, three and a half years before, the organization sprang into being, full of promise, amid the keenest interest and wildest enthusiasm. At this meeting the president made his final address. Nothing of great interest or importance was transacted. The work had all been done. The minutes closed thus:

„Mit dieser Versammlung hörten die Funktionen der hiesigen Gesellschaft auf, und die Beamten wurden entlassen, wodurch die Gesellschaft sich auflöste.

A. J. Stockfleth, Sekretair."

"With this meeting the functions of the Society here ceased, and the officers were dismissed whereby the Society was dissolved.

A. J. Stockfleth, Secretary"

Nearly three score and seven years have passed since that last meeting of the Philadelphia society, but still the records of that final session make the reader sad. A deep pathos lies in the President's simple words of parting. A great thing had been accomplished it is true, but yet how far was it below the lofty ideals of the fathers; in how small a measure had their devoted services been rewarded.*

„Heute zum letzten Male sind wir hier versammelt (so spoke President Schmoele in opening his farewell address) um über das Wohl unserer Gesellschaft uns zu berathen. Unser letztes Geschäft besteht darin, die bisher von der Muttergesellschaft geübte Ver-

---

* *A. und N. W.* of January 18, 1840.

waltung unseres gesellschaftlichen Unternehmens auf die bereits selbstständig und mehr als grossjährig gewordene Tochter im fernen Westen zu übertragen."

"Today we are assembled here for the last time (so spoke President Schmoele in opening his farewell address) in order to consider the welfare of our Society. Our last business consists in this, to transfer the administration of our common undertaking, exercised up to now by the Mother-Society, to the now independent daughter in the far West who has more than become of age."

Then he reiterates the proceedings we have already discussed regarding the transfer. In closing he says:

„Werfen wir nun am Schlusse unserer Geschäftsleitung noch einen Blick auf die Vergangenheit unserer Gesellschaft zurück, so begegnen uns zwar manche Unannehmlichkeiten und Schwierigkeiten, mit denen wir zu kämpfen hatten, und denen besonders derjenige wackere Theil unserer Mitglieder ausgesetzt war, welcher nunmehr unsere blühende Colonie im fernen Westen bildet — dagegen finden wir aber auch Erfolge, welche nicht nur in der Geschichte ähnlicher Gesellschaften ungewöhnlich sind, sondern unsere schönsten Hoffnungen übertreffen und zu den angenehmsten Aussichten für die Zukunft berechtigen.

Wo vor anderthalb Jahren noch eine Wildniss war, da prangt nunmehr eine blühende Stadt, lebendig mit Handel und Gewerben, und umgeben von gedeihenden Landgütern — der Name der Stadt ist Hermann, und ihr Gebiet das der deutschen Ansiedlungs-Gesellschaft.

Mögen unsere Nachkommen Ursache haben, das Unternehmen ihrer Väter zu segnen!

Wilhelm Schmoele.

Philadelphia, den 12. Dec. 1839."

"If we now at the close of the Administration of our business take a look at the past of our Society we indeed meet with many annoyances and difficulties with which we had to contend and to which especially that brave part of our members was exposed, which now forms our flourishing Colony in the far West—on the other hand we also find results, which are not only unusual in the history of similar societies, but which exceed our fondest hopes and justify the pleasantest expectation for the future.

Where 1½ years ago there was still a wilderness, there a flourishing city now shows itself, active with trade and industries and surrounded by prosperous farms—the name of the city is Hermann and its territory that of the German Settlement Society.

May our descendants have reason to bless the undertaking of their ancestors!

Wilhelm Schmoele

Philadelphia, Dec. 12, 1839"

With this meeting the history of this undertaking, so far as Philadelphia was concerned, had come to a close. Its management was now intrusted into the hands of the men in Missouri. How well they succeeded in fulfiling this trust, we are yet to see. The attempt to unify the Germans on American soil had aroused the interest of all Germans in America, as well as of many in Germany. With all this enthusiasm it strikes the impartial observer as rather singular, that greater things were not accomplished. But a great number of causes united to mar the harmony of the participants and to hinder the execution of the plans, on the whole laudable as well as sound.

First among these causes we would place the financial crisis of 1837. All forms of business were wrecked. Public confidence stood at its lowest ebb. Most of the shareholders were limited in means, hoping for an amelioration through the proposed colony. Many prospective members found even the modest outlay too great a tax, since the possibilities for an income were curtailed by the lull in business. In Germany these conditions were known, and but few men would invest their small savings in a country whose monetary basis was so unstable. This stage of depression continued long enough to allow certain changes to occur in the management of the German Society which could not be altered when the years of plenty and public confidence returned.

A second cause was the lack of harmony among the Germans themselves. They came from a country where the word "Einheit"* was found written in books but not in hearts. Most of them had come here with no higher motives than to improve their economic conditions. But few of them had dreamed of a united Germany, how could they reaonably be expected to hope for a German union in this new land? The high ideals that were voiced in this attempt were those of the few leaders—unselfish, devoted, self-sacrificing men—of few faults and of many virtues—but they awakened no echo in the masses. To them the prime purpose was the betterment of their material condition. A depressing spirit of the Kleinelei peculiar to the sons of the Kleinstaatliche Deutschland of that day, dominates many of their actions. They were distrustful and often unjust and so increased the labors of their officers and retarded the progress of their undertaking. A blighting jealousy also made itself felt. Certain of the German newspapers criticised the whole attempt most scathingly. If they had been small local publications, their influence would not have been so baneful. But some of the strongest representatives of the German American press opened a most virulent attack upon the infant enterprise. Some of these editors indulged in this vituperation for no other reason than a personal enmity with the editor of the official organ of the society. Much of the strength of the society was thus spent in internal strife.

A third cause was the appointment of a man to the responsible position of General Agent who had but a very limited business education.

We have already stated that as a gentleman Bayer was beyond reproach. Also that he did do all he was capable of doing. A board of officers under a leader with clear judgment, undoubted integrity, and an indomitable will to stand up to his just decisions would have altered things materially. Under these conditions the cry for self-government would have been duly hushed. If this had been done the seat of power would have remained longer

---
*Oneness

at Philadelphia. The very retention of control at Philadelphia would have instilled confidence in the wavering ones. Then it might have been possible to bridge over the calamitous years following 1837 and to start in upon a newer and brighter era. As it was, a body of a few German pioneers settled in a howling wilderness could not be expected to live up to the high ideals of the founders of the society.

As a final cause must be mentioned the choice of location. Bayer, for unknown causes, succeeded in purchasing only a small part of the land specified by the three prospecting deputies. The land around Hermann is very broken and of little value except for horticultural purposes. The farming land was, as may be seen from the accompanying map, far away from the town, and then very much scattered. Communication was slow and soon the townspeople and the farmers became estranged from each other. The site of Hermann can boast of no great amount of potential wealth. There is no mineral or metal found in the vicinity. Hence, it was impossible for great manufacturing establishments to spring up. To execute the lofty plans of the society it was positively necessary, as Pfarrer Ginal pointed out in one of the very first meetings, that agriculture and manufacture should go hand in hand at the colony. Neither of these industries could prosper in or near Hermann. The only industry in which Hermann now excels all other towns of Missouri is the production of wine. If the colony had been laid in west Missouri, as a Low German settlement was laid, we might have a different history to chronicle.

Great must have been the disappointment of the sturdy promoters of the settlement scheme when the conviction forced itself upon them, that the cause for which they had sacrificed so much was to be abandoned. Again and again we meet with the sentiment "Es wär zu schön gewesen . . . es hat nicht sollen sein."*In after years J. G. Wesselhoeft, the boldest fighter of them all, wrote in his autobiographical account:

---

*"It had been too beautiful . . . . it was not to be."

„Was man bei der Gründung der „Deutschen Ansiedlungs-Gesellschaft" mit der Zeit zu realisiren hoffte, ist nur zum Theil ausgeführt worden. Wenngleich Vieles, was die Gründer beabsich-
tigten, und wofür sie uneigennützig gestrebt und gearbeitet haben,
nicht ins Leben getreten ist, so haben doch viele Deutsche in einer
gesunden hübschen Gegend eine trauliche Heimath gefunden und
für Schulen und deutsche Geselligkeit manches gethan."*

"What we hoped to realize in time at the founding of the
German Settlement Society has only been carried out in part.
Although much which the founders intended, and for which they
unselfishly have struggled and worked, has not materialized;
nevertheless, many Germans have found a congenial home in a
healthful picturesque region and have done much for schools and
German companionship."

Before we go over to a consideration of the colony after its
separation from the Philadelphia society, we shall mention the
names of the principal officers who represented the organization
in various capacities, then we shall append the complete list of the
members.

Julius Leupold was the first president of the society. He
was a promient business man of the firm of Hagedorn, Leupold
& Co. When he had fully decided to go to the colony he retired
from the office and Dr. Wm. Schmoele took the chair. This was
in January, 1838. Dr. Schmoele remained on the post until the
dissolution of the body.

J. G. Wesselhoelt served faithfully as secretary until the middle of February, 1838, when ill health, brought about by over-
work, compelled him to resign. The vice-secretary, Franz G.
Schreiber assumed the responsibilities of this office and continued
in its service until early in January, 1839. Then A. J. Stockfleth
was elected and remained to chronicle the memorable final minutes of the Philadelphia society.

---

* G. Körner, *"Das deutsche Element,"* p. 71.

Dr. Möhring, the first treasurer elected, seems to have served only for a short time. Adam Schmidt then assumed the trust and continued custodian of the wealth of the society until late in the autumn of 1839, when a trip abroad compelled him to lay down his office. J. G. Wesselhoeft then served as treasurer until the end of the organization.

The first board of managers consisted, to reiterate, of these gentlemen: Stark, Viereck, Ritter, Bayer, Kiderlen, Stollmeyer, Gentner, Pommer, Gebhard. As was to be expected this body underwent many changes. The following men served a longer or shorter period: W. H. Leupold, E. C. Staffhorst, Wm. Feuring, —— Bock, D. W. Woﬂlein, C. W. Gronau, —— Schrader, Jacob Hummel, H. Didrich, Georg Riefenstahl, F. Schreiber Adam Maag, Georg Herwig, F. W. C. Seelhorst, Daniel Stühlinger, —— Koch, Johann Christmann.

To give a fairly complete statement of the finances of the society while under the agent's management, we insert here the full ledger of Bayer accounts. The treasurer's record should be more desirable, but unfortunately that is not extant in full. But since the agent received and expended much of their money this will prove valuable.

G. F. BAYER, CONTO.

DR.   CR.

1837					1838				
July	25	An Cassa	$1000	00	Nov.	15	Ausgelegt für Congressland in Silber	$13568	68
Aug.	24	An Postnote	5000	00			Discount 5% $5500.00 U. S. N.		
Oct.	6	Durch Vollmacht auf Adam Schmidt bezogene Wechsel . . .	7000	00			$275.00. $5000 per Treasure Draft. Disconnt 7% $3343.57 Ill. N. $234.05	509 05	$14077 73
Sept.	20	Treasure Draft	5000	00			Ausgelegt für Private Land		1535 00
		Empfangen für verkaufte Actien	$675 00				Deponirt auf die Bank in St. Louis		1947 30
		Ausgezahlt an den Schatzmeister	497 97	177 03			Reisekosten nebst Begleitung und dergleichen Kosten und alte		
Nov.	15	An Cassa		350 00			Schreibereien eingeschlossen . .		459 50
Dec.	18	An Cassa (zugesand nach Pittsburg)		125 00			Für ein Pferd ausgelegt		60 00
							Extra Ausgaben gemacht		50 00
							An Schulhalter bezahlt		47 50
							Saldo		475 00
				$18652 03					$18652 03

G. F. Bayer Account

Debit
1837

July 25	On account		$1,000.00
Aug. 24	Post Office note		5,000.00
Oct. 6	By Power of Attorney Bill of Exchange drawn to Adam Schmidt		
Sept. 20	Treasurer Draft		5,000.00
	Received for shares sold	$ 675.00	
	Paid to the Treasurer	497.97	177.03
Nov. 15	On Account		350.00
Dec. 18	On Account (Sent to Pittsburg		125.00
	Cr.		$18,652.03

1838
Nov. 15

Paid for Congressland in Silver		$13,568.68
Discount 5% $5,500.00 U.S.N. $275.00		
$5000 per Treasure Draft. Discount 7%		
$3,343.57 Ill. N. $234.05		
		509.05
		$14,077.73
Expended for private land		1,535.00
Deposited on the Bank in St. Louis		1,947.30
Travelling Expenses in addition to		
Accompaniment and related costs and		
including old papers:		459.50
Expended for a horse		60.00
Additional Expenses		50.00
Paid to the School Teacher		47.50
		475.00
Balance		$18,652.03

It goes without saying that this does not represent the full amount received. The ledger, which by the way remained unclosed when the society disbanded, shows that up to February 12th, 1839, the sum of $30,464.51 had been received. After this date no entries are made in the ledger though we know that certain transactions took place.

The names of the participants in the settlement movement are here given. The addresses accompanying them are those which the shareholder claimed when they joined the society. As the source of our information we cite the ledger of the organization, yet found in Hermann.

Abglanalp, Joh., Hermann, Mo.
Abker, Joh. Phil., Philadelphia
Ackermann, Gottfried, Philadelphia
Albeck, J. Georg, Montreal, Canada
Albrecht, Joh. F., Philadelphia
Albers, Carl, Philadelphia
Ameling, W., Hermann, Mo.
Arnold, Ferdinand, Philadelphia
Arnsfeld, Heinrich, Philadelphia
Artemiews, E. D., Philadelphia
Arx, Samuel J. von, New York
Asmus, Charles, Hermann, Mo.
Austermell, Louis, Philadelphia

Bachmann, Heinrich, Lancaster, Ohio
Backhaus, Carl, Cincinnati, O.
Bader, Georg, Philadelphia
Baer, Carl F., Newark, O.
Baer, Conrad, Philadelphia
Baer, Theodor, Philadelphia
Bandel, Georg, New Orleans, La.
Bär, Karl, Philadelphia
Barthels, Friedrich, Philadelphia
Barthels, Heinrich, Philadelphia
Bartz, Johann G., Buffalo, N. Y.

Batheusen, Jacob, Philadelphia
Bauer, Adolf, Allentown, Pa.
Baumann, Joseph, Philadelphia
Bayer, Catharina, Philadelphia
Bayer, Geo. F., Philadelphia
Beck, Christian, Montreal, Can.
Beck, Georg, Montreal, Can.
Becker, Carl, Baltimore
Becker, Jacob, Baltimore
Beisswanger, Joh. G., Philadelphia
Benninghoff, Georg, Philalelphia
Bensing, Nicolaus, Hermann, Mo.
Berger, John, Baltimore
Berger, J. A., Baltimore
Bergmann, August, Philadelphia
Betz, Wilhelm, Philadelphia
Bezold, Adam, Hermann, Mo.
Binz, August, Hermann, Mo.
Birk, Matthias, Philadelphia
Bischoff, F. G., Baltimore
Blaschek, Franz, Philadelphia
Bleile, Benedickt, Hermann, Mo.
Bleile, Ignatz, Hermann, Mo.
Blust, John, Hermann, Mo.
Bock, Friedrich, Philadelphia
Bock, Hermann, Hermann, Mo.
Bock, Johann, Philadelphia

Bodenhoefer, Joseph, Philadelphia

Boehringer, Georg, Hermann, Mo.

Bohlen, Carl D., Philadelphia

Böhm, Adam, Hermann, Mo.

Böhm, Johann, Hermann, Mo.

Bonzano, N. A., New Orleans, La.

Bonzheimer,, Heinrich, New Orleans, La.

Borchers, Georg, Baltimore

Bottermann, John, Hermann, Mo.

Braue, Georg, New Orleans, La.

Braun, Valentin, Philadelphia

Breyer, Ludwig, Philadelphia

Brickwede, A., Hermann, Mo.

Brode, H., New Orleans, La.

Bröhmer, Friedrich, Albany, N. Y.

Bruder, Thadeus, Philadelphia

Brues, Dr. Thomas, Wheeling, Va.

Brügger, Ignatius, Skippacksville, Pa.

Brunet, Amedi, Hermann, Mo.

Brunet, Pierre Sr., Hermann, Mo.

Brunner, Joseph, New York

Bruno, C. C. F., New York

Bühler, J. Heinrich, Philadelphia

Bullmann, Caroline, Cleveland, Ohio

Bunker, Heinrich, New Orleans, La.

Bürger, Samuel, Zoar, O.

Burkhard, Phil. Jac., Reading, Pa.

Buss, Jacob, Cleveland, O.

Bute, Georg Heinr., Philadelphia

Campe, J. F. J., Pittsburg, Pa.

Carsten, H. A., Hermann, Mo.

Christern, Jac. Fried., Philadelphia

Christmann, Johann, Philadelphia

Circovich, Gabriel Kowitzky, Philadelphia

Clauss, George, Hermann, Mo.

Clemmer, Johann, Pittsburg, Pa.

Combernas, Albert, Philadelphia

Cullmann, Jacob, Philadelphia

Curtius, Hermann, New York

Decker, Christian, Albany, N. Y.

Decker, Philipp, Albany, N. Y.

Degenhardt, Philipp, Pittsburg, Pa.

Deutsch, Georg, Phœnixville, Pa.

Dikemann, Anna Maria, Philadelphia

Diebold, Cölestin, Springfield, Ohio

Diebold, Michael, Springfield, O.

Diedrich, Heinrich, Philadelphia

Dill, Johann, New Orleans, La.

Disteldorf, Christian, New York

Disteldorf, Wilhelm, New York

Dithmer, Carl, Philadelphia

Doeltner, Hannah, New York

Doeltner, Joh. Michael, New York

Dohrmann, Friedrich, New York

Dold, Andreas, Philadelphia

Döll, Joh. Michael, New York

Dormeyer, Caroline, Cleveland. O.

Dormeyer, Jacob, Cleveland, O.

Dormeyer, Philipp, Cleveland, O.

Döss, Silvester, Hermann, Mo.

Ducommon, Henry, Philadelphia

Duetz, Philipp, Saloma, Center Co., Pa.

Duhring, Dr. Georg, Philadelphia

Ebstadt, Louis, Philadelphia

Echternacht, Heinr. Wilh., Philadelphia
Eckhard, Leonard, Philadelphia
Egers, Eduard, Hermann, Mo.
Ehrmann, Benjamin, New Berlin
Eichinger, Jacob, New Orleans
Eickhoff, Carl Ludwig, Philadelphia
Eitzen, Chas. D., Hermann, Mo.
Engelbert, Benjamin, Philadelphia
Engelbert, Johann, Hermann, Mo.
Engelbert, Joseph, Philadelphia
Engelhardt, Wilhelm, Philadelphia
Eppelsheimer, Daniel, Philadelphia
Erler, Friedrich G., Zoar, O.
Ernst, J. G., New Orleans, La.
Eyer, J. Ph., Baltimore

Fegenbusch, Jacob, Philadelphia
Ferentheil, C. v., Philadelphia
Feuring, Eva M., Philadelphia
Feuring, Wilhelm, Philadelphia
Fickeisen, Daniel, Pittsburg, Pa.
Fiedler, Adam, Philadelphia
Finn, H. G., Hermann, Mo.
Finn, John G., Philadelphia
Fischer, George, Philadelphia
Fischer, Jacob, St. Francisville, La.
Franksen, Franke, Manayunk, Pa.
Frechmann, Sabinus, Philadelphia
Freyvogel, Christian, Hermann, Mo.
Friedrichs, Aug. Wilh., Philadelphia
Frommherr, J., New Orleans, La.
Fuchs, Nicholaus, Philadelphia

Fugger, Phil. Jacob, Columbia
Furch, Friedrich, Hermann, Mo.
Fuss, G. A., Philadelphia

Gabriel, Daniel, Reading, Pa.
Gabriel, Dominicus, Reading, Pa.
Gaebler, J. Friedr., Montreal, Canada
Gartmann, Heinrich, Philadelphia
Gawley, Thomas, Hermann, Mo.
Gebhard, F. L. C., Philadelphia
Gellert, Wilhelm, Philadelphia
Gemf, Friedrich, Hermann, Mo.
Gentner, Friedrich, Philadelphia
Gentner, Heinrich, Philadelphia
Gerber, Christian, Baltimore
Gerber, Dr. J., Lancaster, O.
Gerber, J., Newark, O.
Gerker, Heinrich, Philadelphia
Gerlach, Georg, New York
Gerssle, Heinrich, Philadelphia
Gessler, Christian, Philadelphia
Goelitz, Louis, Philadelphia
Goetz, Rudolph, Philadelphia
Gott, Bernard, Philadelphia
Gottlieb, Friedrich, Philadelphia
Gräber, Johann, Philadelphia
Graf, Anton, Philadelphia
Grahn, Carl M., Philadelphia
Grasseley, Eugen, Philadelphia
Greiner, Christoph, Philadelphia
Greis, Kaspar, Hermann, Mo.
Groh, Johann, New York
Gronau, C. W., Philadelphia
Gronhardt, Johann, Philadelphia
Gulden, Ferdinand, Philadelphia

Haas, Ernst, Philadelphia
Haas, Fried. Joh., Philadelphia
Haberstock, Daniel, Philadelphia
Hagel, Jacob, Philadelphia
Hagel, Michael, Philadelphia

Haggenmacher, Heinr., Philadelphia

Harig, Joh. Bernhardt, Baltimore

Harig, Johann, Philadelphia

Harnisch, Julius, Philadelphia

Hartmann, Jacob Christ., New York

Hartung, Jacob, Beaver Co., Pa.

Hasenpatt, Christian, Philadelphia

Heckmann, Heinrich, Pittsburg, Pa.

Heckmann, Mathias, Philadelphia

Heinlein, Jacob, Philadelphia

Heiner, Anna Maria, Philadelphia

Heinemann, Daniel, Philadelphia

Heirtz, Ferdinand, Philadelphia

Heitzmann, C. F., Reading, Pa.

Heitzmann, Gabriel, Reading, Pa.

Heitzmann, Maria, Reading, Pa.

Helffrich, Johann, Lehigh Co., Pa.

Hemme, Anton Franz, Philadelphia

Henning, Wilhelm, Philadelphia

Henrich, W. L., Columbus, O.

Herwig, Georg, Philadelphia

Herzog, Eduard, Philadelphia

Hesse, Caspar, Hermann, Mo.

Hetz, Joseph Friedr., Montreal, Canada

Heyl, Elizabeth, Jersey

Heywald, Charles, Philadelphia

Hildebrand, Jacob, Albany, N. Y.

Hiller, Joseph, Philadelphia

Hirschmann, Johann, Philadelphia

Hisigas, Ludwig, Hermann, Mo.

Hitz, Joseph, Philadelphia

Hoch, Heinrich, Reading, Pa.

Hoehling, Adolph, Philadelphia

Hoesel, Ferdinand, Philadelphia

Hoffmann, Christoph, Pittsburg, Pa.

Hoffmann, H., Pittsburg, Pa.

Hoffman, Johann, Mantau Village

Hoffmeister, Fried., Philadelphia

Hoffstätter, Michael, Pittsburg, Pa.

Höfle, Johann, New York

Hoge, Jacob, Hermann, Mo.

Horn, August, Philadelphia

Horn, Johann, Philadelphia

Hornmeyer, Francisca, New Orleans, La.

Horstmann, W. H., Philadelphia

Hostätter, Christian, Philadelphia

Hubeli, Jacob, Philadelphia

Huber, H., Lancaster, O.

Hummel, Jacob, Philadelphia

Hussmann, Joh. Heinr. M., Philadelphia

Hussmann, Friedr., Philadelphia

Hussmann, J. F. M., Philadelphia

Hütz, M. J., Philadelphia

Idemann, J. L., Hermann, Mo.

Idler, Ernst, Montreal, Canada

Inderrieden, Joseph, Baltimore

Israng, David, New Orleans, La.

Iversen, Anton, Augusta, Ga.

Jacobus, Margaretha, Philadelphia

Jaeger, Friedrich, New Orleans, La.

Jaeger, Leupold Georg, Philadelphia

Jahn, F. G., New Orleans, La.

Jahns, Heinrich, Philadelphia

Jarton, Maria Louisa, Philadelphia
Jenny, Abraham, Philadelphia
Jenny, Johann, Philadelphia
John, F. G., New Orleans, La.
Jordan, Johann, New Orleans, La.
Jung, Hermann, Hermann, Mo.
Jung, Leonhard, Philadelphia
Jungandreas, Carl, Hermann, Mo.

Kaercher, Conrad M., Philadelphia
Kaiser, Friedrich, Philadelphia
Kaltner, F. G., Baltimore
Kayser, Alexander, Hermann, Mo.
Kehr, Joh. Andreas, Philadelphia
Kehrer, Martin, Philadelphia
Keller, Adam, Philadelphia
Kemper, Hermann, Hermann, Mo.
Kerchner, Mich. Anton. New York
Kersch, Ferdinand, New York
Kerschenbach, Fried., Philadelphia
Kessler, Joseph, Cincinnati, O.
Kiderlen & Stollmeyer, Philadelphia
Kiefer, Jacob, Albany, N. Y.
Kielmann, Wilhelm, Philadelphia
Kinkelin, A., Philadelphia
Klaering, August, Hermann, Mo.
Klaering, A. F., Hermann, Mo.
Klapp, Jacob, Albany, N. Y.
Kleber, Heinrich, Pittsburg, Pa.
Klein, Christian, Philadelphia
Klett, Friedrich, Philadelphia
Klingling, Richard, Dayton, O.
Klink, Jacob, Hermann, Mo.

Kloth, J. H., Phœnixville, Pa.
Klotter, Georg, Philadelphia
Klumpp, Johann, Philadelphia
Kneisel, Carl Aug., Cleveland, Ohio
Knodel, Casper, Philadelphia
Knoll, Jacob, Philadelphia
Knoll, Johann, Philadelphia
Knop, Hermann, Philadelphia
Koch, Eduard, Philadelphia
Koch, Georg, Albany, N. Y.
Koch, Joh. Heinr., Philadelphia
Koch, Georg Mich., Albany, N. Y.
Koenig, Lorenz, New Orleans, La.
Koepf, Reinhold, Philadelphia
Koepken, Heinr., Philadelphia
Kohl Carl, Hermann, Mo.
Kohlenberg, Eduard, Albany, N. Y.
Köller, Philipp, Hermann, Mo.
Koos, Eugen, Newark, O.
Korkhauss, Heinr., Philadelphia
Körner, Christian, Dayton, O.
Kormeyer, Franzisco, New Orleans, La.
Kranz, Johann, Albany, N. Y.
Kraug, Christian, Philadelphia
Krauss, Gottfried, Philadelphia
Krauter, Mathäus, Philadelphia
Kreikemeyer, Christ., Philadelphia
Kreuchy, Gottlieb, Hermann, Mo.
Kripplebert, Michael, Albany, N. Y.
Kroeber, Michael, Cleveland, O.
Kroecker, Margaretha, Philadelphia
Krueger, Ludwig, Germantown
Kruse, Heinrich, Philadelphia
Kühn, John, York, Pa.
Kühne, Carl Ludwig, Philadelphia

Kühne, Conrad Fried., Philadelphia
Kühne, Franz Heinr., Philadelphia
Kühnholtz, Friedrich, Philadelphia
Kurz, Joh. Jacob, Baltimore

Laackmann, Ferdinand, Philadelphia
Lahring, Heinrich, Philadelphia
Lahring, Jno. H., Philadelphia
Laib, Friedrich, Philadelphia
Laib, Gottlieb, Philadelphia
Lambers, Rebecca, Baltimore
Lampartee, Heinrich, Hermann, Mo.
Lang, David, Hermann, Mo.
Langendörfer, Franz, Philadelphia
Langguth, Christ. Aug., Philadelphia
Lauer, Friedrich, Hermann, Mo.
Ledermann, J., New Orleans, La.
Lehder, F., New Orleans, La.
Leibrock, Fritz, Reading, Pa.
Leichmann, Wilh., Hermann, Mo.
Leidorff, Philipp, Philadelphia
Leimer, Alexander, Philadelphia
Leimer, August, Philadelphia
Lemberger, Johann, Philadelphia
Lemberger, Wilh., Philadelphia
Lenke, Friedrich, Philadelphia
Lensing, Gerhart, Hermann, Mo.
Leonhard, August, Philadelphia
Leonhard, Friedrich, Philadelphia
Leser, Andreas, New Orleans, La.
Leupold, Friedrich, Philadelphia
Leupold, Julius, Philadelphia
Leupold, W. H., Philadelphia

Liebach, Konrad, Hermann, Mo.
Liebau, Charles, Cincinnati, O.
Liebermann, Alphonse, Philadelphia
Liebrich, Conrad, Philadelphia
Lindauer, Christian, New Orleans, La.
Lion, Peter, Philadelphia
Lipsz, Johann, Hermann, Mo.
Loewen, John, Cleveland, O.
Loos, Ferdinand, Pittsburg, Pa.
Lötterle, Gottlieb, Philadelphia
Lüdeking, Friedrich, Philadelphia
Ludolph, Justus, Pittsburg, Pa.
Lutz, Friedrich, Phœnixville, Pa.
Lutz, Joseph, Phœnixville, Pa.
Lutz, Johann, Georg, Albany, N. Y.

Maag, Adam, Philadelphia
Maag, Friedrich, Philadelphia
Maag, Mathias, Philadelphia
Magens, Christoph, Montreal, Canada
Manercke, Joh. Heinr., Philadelphia
Mann, Theodor, Philadelphia
Manss, Georg, Philadelphia
Martin, Adam, Philadelphia
Matthiä, A., New York
Mausehund, Martin, Hermann, Mo.
May, Johann, Philadelphia
Mayer, C. L., Philadelphia
Mayer, Johann, Hermann, Mo.
Mayer, W. F., Philadelphia
Mecke, Georg Heinr., Philadelphia
Medinger, Christoph A., Baltimore
Melcheor, Carl, Philadelphia
Mendenhall, Philipp, Philadelphia
Mersinger, Jacob, Philadelphia

Metzger, Karl, Philadelphia
Metzger, Christopher, Philadelphia
Meyer, Bernhard Martin, Philadelphia
Meyer, Ernst, Hermann, Mo.
Meyer, Johann, Philadelphia
Meyer, Wilh. F., Lancaster, O.
Miller, Anthony, Hermann, Mo.
Miller, Joh. H., Hermann, Mo.
Mitthoff, Hecktor A., Schuylkill Co., Pa.
Mittnacht, G. H., Baltimore
Moedinger, Gottl. F., Baltimore
Moehring, Dr. G., Philadelphia
Moersinger, Georg, New Orleans, La.
Mohl, Wilhelm, Philadelphia
Molidor, Franz, Philadelphia
Molidor, Joseph, Philadelphia
Molidor, Wilhelm, New York
Moroth, M., Newark, O.
Morloch, Jacob, Pittsburg, Pa.
Morsfelder, S., Baltimore
Muermann, Heinr., New York
Mühlenbach, F., Hermann, Mo.
Müller, Caspar, Philadelphia
Müller, Georg, Hermann, Mo.
Müller, Peter, Cleveland, O.
Müller, Wilhelm, New Orleans, La.
Müller, Wilhelm, Philadelphia
Müntzke, Anton, Newark, O.
Müssig, Anton, Philadelphia
Müssig, David, Philadelphia

Naegelin, Chas., Philadelphia
Neitzmann, C. L., Hermann, Mo.
Nestler, Martin, Philadelphia
Netz, J. F., Hermann, Mo.
Neufeldt, Capt., Hermann, Mo.
Neumeyer, Herm. F., Hermann, Mo.

Nider, Adam, Hermann, Mo.
Niekerke, Ludw. Friedr., Philadelphia
Nock, Joseph, Philadelphia
Noe, Carl Friedrich, Philadelphia
Noessel, Georg, New Orleans, La.
Nuys, W. van, Pittsburg, Pa.

Oelschlaeger, Catherine, Hermann, Mo.
Oelschlaeger, Christoph Fr., Hermann, Mo.
Oelschlaeger, Daniel, Philadelphia
Oesterle, Johann, Baltimore
Oesternacht, Heinr. Wilh., Philadelphia
Oestreicher, Johann, Philadelphia
Orth, Alexander, Philadelphia
Osterloh, C. C., Hermann, Mo.
Ott, Georg, Hermann, Mo.
Ottoh, Franz Herm., New York

Petri, Martin, Philadelphia
Pfautsch, Georg Herm., Hermann, Mo.
Pfeiffer, Wilhelm, Pittsburg, Pa.
Pfeil, P., Baltimore
Pfister, Philipp, Philadelphia
Pfoi, Sylverius, New Orleans, La.
Pinker, H. J. C., New Orleans, La.
Plank, Friedrich, New Orleans, La.
Pollart, Joh. Friedr., Philadelphia
Pommer, Carl, Philadelphia
Pommer, Caroline Dorothea, Philadelphia
Pommer, Edward, Hermann, Mo.

Pommer, Heinrich, Philadelphia
Pommer, Wilhelm F., Philadelphia
Pommer, Wilhelm, Cincinnati, O.
Pond, Daniel, Philadelphia
Prager, J. G., Hermann, Mo.
Presser, C. Valentine, Philadelphia
Pulte, Carl Anton, Skippacksville, Pa.

Quandt, Johann, Hermann, Mo.

Rammelsberg, Friedrich, Cincinnati, O.
Rasche, F., Philadelphia
Rasche, Heinrich, Philadelphia
Rau, Peter, Philadelphia
Rauschlager, Johann, Cleveland, Ohio
Rebhun, Friedrich, Philadelphia
Reichenbach, Friedrich, Philadelphia
Reiger, Louis, Hermann, Mo.
Reinhardt, Friedrich, Hermann, Mo.
Reinhardt, Gottlieb, Montreal, Canada
Rice, J. C., Hermann, Mo.
Richter, Joh. Gottfr. Carl, Philadelphia
Rickle, Jacob, Newark, O.
Rickle, John, Newark, O.
Rickenbock, H., Lancaster, O.
Ried, Jacob J., Philadelphia
Rieffenstahl, Georg, Philadelphia
Riemann, Ferdinand, Philadelphia
Rietze, Heinrich, Hermann, Mo.
Ripperger, Conrad, Philadelphia
Ripperger, Heinr. J., Philadelphia
Ritter, C. G., Philadelphia

Ritter, Florenz, Hermann, Mo.
Roemer, Heinrich, Philadelphia
Roesle, Gottfried, Hermann, Mo.
Roessler, J., New Orleans, La.
Rohe, Michael, Philadelphia
Rohrbacher, Christian, Hermann, Mo.
Roller, Joseph, Philadelphia
Rollhaus, Daniel, Albany, N. Y.
Rollhaus, Philipp, Albany, N. Y.
Rommel, Jacob, Philadelphia
Roos, Conrad, Philadelphia
Rösche, Heinrich, Philadelphia
Rosenberger, Michael, Cleveland, Ohio
Rosenberger, Nicholaus, Cleveland, Ohio
Rosienkiwiez, Martin, Philadelphia
Roeske, August, Philadelphia
Roeske, Caroline, Philadelphia
Rösle, Gottfried, New Orleans, La.
Rothert, Hermann, Hermann, Mo.
Rothrang, Michael, Philadelphia
Ruff, Johann Georg, Philadelphia
Runkele, Daniel Fr., Philadelphia
Rutschmann, Siegmund, Philadelphia

Sandermann, Johann, New Orleans, La.
Sattler, Magdalena, Philadelphia
Schachtberger, Johann, New Orleans, La.
Schachtleiter, F. Anton, Pittsburg, Pa.
Schäfer, Christian, Philadelphia
Schäfer, Georg, Hermann, Mo.
Schaefer, Christopher, Philadelphia

Schaefer, Jacob Friedr., Philadelphia
Schaeffer, Friedr. Georg, Philadelphia
Schaeffer, Joh. G., Philadelphia
Scheide, Wilhelm, Philadelphia
Scheidemantel, Charles, Columbia, Texas
Scheidt, Adam, Hermann, Mo.
Scheidt, Peter, Hermann, Mo.
Schellenberg, Franz, Philadelphia
Scherff, J., Baltimore
Schernicke, Marie Louise, Cleveland, O.
Scherr, Christian, Philadelphia
Scherr, Ludwig, Philadelphia
Schiedel, Jacob, Philadelphia
Schiefer, Jacob, Philadelphia
Schierholz, Emil, Cincinnati, O.
Schild, Conrad, Philadelphia
Schindler, Joseph, Philadelphia
Schlachtberger, Joseph, New Orleans, La.
Schlegel, H. von, Hermann, Mo.
Schlömer, C. L., Hermann, Mo.
Schmid, Emanuel Fried., Cincinnati, O.
Schmid, Wilhelm, New Orleans, La.
Schmidt, Adam, Philadelphia
Schmidt, Adam, Newark, Ohio
Schmidt, Joh. Fried., Philadelphia
Schmidt, Johann, Albany, N. Y.
Schmidt, Josef, Philadelphia
Schmidt, P. Wilhelm, Philadelphia
Schmitz, Bernhard, Newtown, Pa.
Schmoele, Heinrich, Philadelphia
Schmoele, Dr. Wilh., Philadelphia
Schneider, Adam, Philadelphia

Schneider, Friedrich, Philadelphia
Schneider, Georg Jacob, Philadelphia
Schneider, Philipp, Hermann, Mo.
Schniedewind, Hermann, Philadelphia
Schock, Georg, Philadelphia
Schock, John J., Philadelphia
Schönthaler, Gottfr., Hermann, Mo.
Schönthaler, Joh. Christ., Philadelphia
Schotten, Georg, Hermann, Mo.
Schrader, August, Philadelphia
Schrader, Franz von, Philadelphia
Schrader, Heinr. Christ., Philadelphia
Schrader, Otto von, Philadelphia
Schramm, Leonhard, Hermann, Mo.
Schreiber, Franz G., Philadelphia
Schreiber, Johann, Hermann, Mo.
Schuatz, Friedrich, Philadelphia
Schubert, Wilhelm, Philadelphia
Schuele, Joh. Georg, Philadelphia
Schultz, Joseph, New York
Schurmacher, Conrad, Baltimore
Schütze, Gottfried, Hermann, Mo.
Schwacke, Joh. Heinr., Philadelphia
Schwartze, Friedrich, Baltimore
Schweikert, Bernhard, Philadelphia
Schweitzer, Conrad, Albany, N. Y.
Schweitzer, Hermann, Philadelphia

Schweyer, Joseph, Hermann, Mo.

Seelhorst, F. W. C., Philadelphia

Seffert, John, Philadelphia

Seiler, Johannes, Hermann, Mo.

Seilheimer, Heinrich, Philadelphia

Seitz, Adam, Philadelphia

Seitz, Johann, Philadelphia

Selter, Andreas, New York

Seltzer, Eduard, Philadelphia

Semken, Fr., Hermann, Mo.

Sengenberger, Adam, Philadelphia

Senn, Wilhelm, Philadelphia

Seybold, Joh. Philipp, Montreal, Canada

Sidler, Johann, Hermann, Mo.

Siedler, Adam, Philadelphia

Sigrist, Ludwig, Philadelphia

Soller, Georg M., Philadelphia

Sommerhalter, Ludwig, Philadelphia

Spererer, Fried. Carl, Pittsburg, Pa.

Spindler, Matthias, Baltimore

Staffhorst, Erhard C., Philadelphia

Stark, Ferdinand, Philadelphia

Stephan, Martin, Philadelphia

Stieweg, H. C., Fairfield, Pa.

Stietenroth, Heinr., Evansville, Ind.

Stirnemann, Ulrich, Philadelphia

Stockfleth, Adolf Fr., Philadelphia

Stoecklein, Martin, Philadelphia

Stoehr, Wilhelm, Hermann, Mo.

Storb, Theodor, Montgomery Co., Pa.

Stottmeyer, C. F., Hermann, Mo.

Stübgen, Gustav, Philadelphia

Stühlinger, Daniel, Philadelphia

Stumm, Carl Wilh., Pittsburg, Pa.

Summ, Jacob, Philadelphia

Supper, Georg, Philadelphia

Supper, Johann, Philadelphia

Talmann, Johann, New Orleans, La.

Thaldorf, ——, Baltimore

Theiss, Johann, Philadelphia

Tiemann, Christian, Philadelphia

Tilg, Wilhelm, Philadelphia

Trautwein, Carl, Hermann, Mo.

Trautwein, Daniel, Hermann, Mo.

Trautwein, Elizabeth, Hermann, Mo.

Triebler, Friedrich, Philadelphia

Vahrenhorst, J. H., Hermann, Mo.

Valet, Adam, Philadelphia

Valet, Christoph, Philadelphia

Valet, Jacob, Philadelphia

Veit, Heinr. Ludw., Columbus, Ohio

Viereck, Catharine, Philadelphia

Viereck, Friedrich, Philadelphia

Viereck, Johann C., Philadelphia

Viereck, Marie Elizabeth, Philadelphia

Vieth, Joseph, New Orleans, La.

Voegtly, Nicholaus, Pittsburg, Pa.

Vogt, Joseph, Hermann, Mo.

Vogt, Theodor, Hermann, Mo.

Wagenschwanz, V., Cleveland, O.

Wagner, Adam, Hermann, Mo.

Wagner, Conrad, Philadelphia

Wagner, Jacob, Pittsburg, Pa.

Wallrapp, Wilhelm, Philadelphia

Walther, Georg, Manayunk, Pa.

Wandel, Adam, Philadelphia

Wandel, Peter, Russetville, Ky.

Wangelin, Adolf von, Cleveland, Ohio
Wangelin, Friderika von, Cleveland, Ohio
Weber, Albert, New Orleans, La.
Weber, Sylvester, Philadelphia
Weigel, Heinrich, New Orleans, La.
Weller, Jonas, Philadelphia
Welter, Nikolas, Hermann, Mo.
Wendel, J. Peter, Russetville, Ky.
Werkloe, Heinrich, Philadelphia
Werkner, Carl, New Orleans, La.
Wesselhoeft, J. G., Philadelphia
Wesselhoeft, C. F., Philadelphia
Wesselhoeft, Dr. W., Bath, Pa.
Westerfeldt, Heinrich, New Orleans, La.
Wetzel, August, New Orleans, La.
Wetzel, Jacob, New Orleans, La.
Wetzstein, John O., New York
Widersprecher, D., St. Louis, Mo.
Widmann, Fr. Wilh., Philadelphia
Wilcke, F. W., Philadelphia
Will, Georg, Albany, N. Y.
Willing, Nick., New Orleans, La.
Wirth, Franz, New Orleans,La.
Wittmann, David, Philadelphia.

Witmann, John H., Philadelphia
Woellner, Carl, Ciincinnati, O.
Woern, John, Hermann, Mo.
Wohlein, D. W., Philadelphia
Wolf, Moritz Leo, Piladelphia
Wollenscheider, Jacob, Newark, O.
Wollensack, Andreas, Albany, N. Y.
Wollensack, Johann, Albany, N. Y.
Wollenweber, L. A. Philadelphia
Wolsieffer, Johann, New York
Wörnweg, Wilhelm, Hermann, Mo.

Yeager, Jacob, Cleveland, O.
Young, Wm. E., Hermann, Mo.

Zaiser, August, Philadelphia
Zeller, Jno. A., Newark, O.
Ziegler, Georg, Philadelphia
Ziegler, August, Hermann, Mo.
Zimmermann, Christ, Philadelphia
Zimmermann, Gottlieb, Philadelphia
Zipperer, Johann Georg, Philadelphia
Zoller, Johann Georg, Philadelphia
Zorn, Joseph, New Orleans, La.
Zorn, Peter, New Orleans, La.

Thus we have a grand total of 678 participants in the affair.

The last share which the officials at Philadelphia disposed of was sold on Dec. 1, 1839, or a few days before the dissolution of the organization.

ENTERPRISE MILITARY BAND—1909

L to R: First Row: Hugo Wagner, Monroe Riek, Frank Huxol, Fritz Baumgaertner, Otto Gross, Billy Baumgaertner Middle Row: Alvin Rulle, Eugene Siedler, Robert Huxol, Gephart Gauss, Armin Eberlin Top Row: Richard Hirsch, John Schroeder, Alex Riek, Henry Stonner, Oscar Riek, Fred Hirschfeld, Philip Kolb

HERMANN ROLLERS—1890

L to R: Front Row: William Eberlin, William Herzog, Henry Bock, Billy Boeing, Ed Clark, Robert Robyn, (?) Land, (?) Fleemann, Phillip Kuhn Back Row: Hugo Kropp, M. P. Bensing, Theodore Stork, August Begemann, Sr., Conrad Gauss, George Kraettly, (?), Adolph Prudot, (?), (?), (?)

MÄNNERCHOR AT FOERSTER'S CAVE 1890

TURNVEREIN (Gymnasts) 1885

L to R: First Row: Oscar Beckmann, Louis Begemann, Robert Baumgaertner Second Row: Joe Pfautsch, Charles Hansen, Eugene Rippstein, Fred Fluhr, John Schwartz, Theo. Dilthey Top Row: John Helmers, Hugo Scherer, Henry Bock, Ed Clark, Julius Hasenritter

SCHUETZENVEREIN (Sharpshooters) 1895

Schuetzenverein Identification

L to R: Front Row: Louis Begemann, August Begemann, Jr., John Ochsner, Henry Ochsner, (?), (?), (?) Second Row: (?), (?), Christian Danuser, Christ Eberlin, William Eberlin, (?), (?), (?), Willie Walker, Gustav Eberlin. Third Row: Charles Kimmel, (?), George Eberlin, (?), Fritz Ochsner, William Poeschel II, Ed Ruediger, Bill Beckmann, (?), Louis Willmann, Julius Moebus, (?), Henry Drusch, (?), Eugene Eberlin

VIEW UPTOWN FROM WHARF STREET

WHARF ST. HERMANN, (BEFORE 1900)

HERMANN FIRE COMPANY NO. 1, 1909 — Fiftieth Anniversary

Fire Co. No. 1 Identification

L to R: First Row: August Wohlt, Julius Moebus, Jacob Strahsner, Charles Eberlin, William Haeffner, Sr., Brisca Siedler, Jacob Buehler, John Reiff, Fritz Siedler, Lebrecht Woest Second Row: Albert Naegelin, Louis Wittmann, Ernst Kuhfus, Henry Schuch, Gottfried Bay, Louis Haberstock, Charles Bentz, Julius Bauer, Albert Schubert, Gustav Fischer, Gustav Meyer Third Row: William Haeffner, Jr., George Ochsner, Charles Baumstark, Mike Newmann, Ed Ruediger, Touissant Schnell, George Hoessli, Fred Hansen, Henry Dickgraefe, (?), George Ruediger Fourth Row: Hermann Meyer, Otto Eberlin, George Eberlin, Henry Bruner, Frank Baumstark, Oscar Staude, Alex Riek, Charlie Fahrner, (?), Bill Fluetsch, Jackson Kurrelmeyer. Fifth Row: Henry Sohn, Arthur Gust, Billy Baumgaertner, Fritz Dickgraefe, Charles Hansen, August Drusch, Harry Ruediger, Emil Schuch, Ed Rebsamen,— Pfautsch, Harry Eberlin, Armin Eberlin

The Fire Company maintains a fine museum of antique fire equipment at the new Fire Station on Highway 100 and Gasconade St.

**The
Consiquence
First Handpumper**

CHAPTER II.

THE COLONY HERMANN.

1. GENERAL VIEW.

In 1858 the venerable Friedrich Münch gave this picture of Hermann, which was then twenty years old.

„Hermann, südlich am Missouri in Gasconade County mit 1400 teutschen Einwohnern, einem Hauptdepot der Pacific-Eisenbahn, zwei Kirchen, einem teutschen Gesellschaftshaus; Hauptgewerbe ist der Weinbau; hat eine teutsche Zeitung. Hermann ist auf der Südseite amphitheatralisch von Hügelreihen umgeben, auf welchen erst in den letzten Jahren der Urwald ausgetilgt wurde, um für die jährlich sich mehrenden Rebenanlagen Platz zu machen. Ist auch der Boden landeinwärts nicht besonders fruchtbar, so ist er doch mit grossem Fleisse angebaut und der nicht bebaute Theil gut beholzt. Gegenüber auf der Nordseite des Stromes erstreckt sich weithin ein Strich der fruchtbarsten Missouri-Niederung. Der Strom ist hier sehr breit, und gerade vor der Stadt liegt eine grosse aber unbewohnte Insel. In Hermann vergisst man dass man sich in einem nicht teutschen Lande befindet. Zwei öffentliche Schulen (von welchen die eine für immer eine teutsche bleiben muss) sorgen für die Unterweisung der Jugend.‟*

"Hermann, on the south bank of the Missouri in Gasconade County with 1400 German inhabitants, a principal depot of the Pacific Railroad, two churches, a German meeting house; principal industry is wine-growing; has a German newspaper. On the south side Hermann is amphitheatrically surrounded by chains of hills, from which the primeval forest has been cleared first in the last years in order to make room for vineyards which are increasing every year. Even though the soil towards the interior is not especially fertile, it is nevertheless cultivated very intensively and the part not cultivated is well wooded. Opposite on the north side of the river a strip of the most fertile Missouri bottom extends far off.

---

* Münch, *"Der Staat Missouri,"* p. 204.

The river is very broad here and just opposite the City lies a large but uninhabited island. In Hermann a person forgets that he is not in a German land. Two public schools (of which one must always remain a German school) take care of the instruction of the youth."

This rather general picture is supplemented by Gert Goebel who touches upon a few more details. His account dates almost twenty years after Münch's:

„Der eigentliche Geschäftstheil der Stadt liegt in der Nähe des Flusses und der Eisenbahn; dort ist das Terrain ganz eben, die Häuser stehen dicht beisammen und die Strassen sind gut gepflastert und mit breiten Trottoirs versehen, aber sobald man sich von diesem Stadttheil etwas entfernt, nimmt der Ort einen ländlicheren Anstrich an; die Wohnungen stehen einzelner und sind von einer einfacheren Bauart, und das ganze Grundstück um die Häuser herum ist mit Gemüse, Obstbäumen und Reben bepflanzt. Ein Spaziergang durch die Stadt, womöglich zur Zeit der Obstblüthe, heimelt einen alten Deutschen sehr an, denn er kann sich einbilden, plötzlich in eines der grossen, wohlhabenden Dörfer in der alten Heimath versetzt worden zu sein, und ich habe sogar schon manchen Amerikaner, den ich während eines solchen Ganges auf die einfachen und natürlichen Schönheiten aufmerksam machte, ganz gemüthlich werden sehen, besonders wenn wir erst in den Weinkellern der Herrn Georg Hussmann oder Michael Pöschel Weinprobe gehalten hatten."*

"The actual business section of the City lies in the neighborhood of the river and the railroad; there the terrain is quite level, the houses stand close together and the streets are well paved and provided with broad sidewalks; but as soon as one leaves this part of the City, the place assumes a more agrarian aspect, the dwelling places stand singly and are of a simpler style of architecture and the entire yard surrounding the houses is planted in vegetables, fruit trees and flowers. A walk through the City, if possible at the time of the blooming of the fruit tees, reminds an old German very much of his home, for he can imagine himself suddenly trans-

---

* Goebel, *"Länger als ein Menschenleben in Missouri,"* p. 140.

planted into one of the large prosperous villages of the old native country; and I have even seen many an American, to whom I pointed out the simple and natural attractions in the course of such a walk, become quite cheerful, especially if we had previously sampled some wines in the wine-cellars of Mr. George Hussmann or Michael Poeschel."

These quotations give indeed a very fair picture of Hermann as it appears even to-day. Only we do not really see how well the streets are kept, nor the touch of modern life in electric illumination, modern, tasteful, quite up-to-date business houses, nor the typical tall church steeples, nor the quaint old buildings, showing a strange architecture, their roofs dripping on the sidewalk, against which they are closely pressed, as if building space were indeed scarce: If one adds these facts to the above description the picture of peaceful Hermann is practically complete.

In previous chapters we have from time to time obtained an insight into the growth of the colony Hermann, while it was yet subject to the Philadelphia society. We shall now see how the settlement prospered, after the separation, how far it has remained true to its traditions and what it has contributed to the commonwealth in which it exists. In order to understand and appreciate the accomplishments of the colony, we are compelled to pursue the method of reverting constantly to the beginning, when rifle and axe prepare the way for civilization, and then lead up, gradually, to present day conditions. In this way, it is believed, a rather complete perspective will be obtained.

Throughout the State of Missouri, Hermann is familiarly known as Little Germany. According to the census of 1900 its population is only 1,575, most of whom are German, and the county in which it is found, Gasconade, has, according to the same census, 1,453 foreign born Germans. These last figures by no means represent the numerical strength of the Germans of the county, since all those born here are classed as natives. The settlement being old, most of those included in the report are American born. When Fr. Münch wrote the passage quoted at the beginning of this chapter, Hermann had 1,400 inhabitants. It was then no longer held, as was formerly the case, that Hermann would outstrip every town in the state save St. Louis. Still it was confidently expected that it would continue to grow consistantly. The reasons for this failure to grow have been previously enumerated and scarcely need reiteration here. In a word the geographical and topographical conditions of the location determined its growth. Though small, the town and its environs bear the unmistakable stamp of things German.

It is now seen clearly that the members of the Ansiedlungs-Gesellschaft, when they pleaded for, urged and then demanded the transfer of power, entertained but little intention of continuing in the spirit of the fathers of the movement. They wisely enough foresaw a continual struggle against insurmountable odds ahead of them, should they strive to carry out the plans to the letter. Consequently they early contented themselves with a modified interpretation of the plans, as in the nature of things they were compelled to do. But the way in which they have, after all, succeeded in fostering and upholding things German, after the curtailment of so many apparent possibilities, must elicit from all sides the heartiest plaudits. Their accomplishments still stand, and will long stand, as a worthy monument to their and their predecessors' zeal. They have in innumerable ways contributed their measure to the success of the Missouri Germans.

When it had become unmistakably clear that the times, conditions and surroundings absolutely compelled an abandonment of original intentions and hopes the town found itself in possession of thousands of acres of land, for which it had no practical use, and which on the other hand was a severe burden and a handicap to its progress. It was accordingly decided to dispose of the land at public sale. "That the lands of the German Settlement Society be sold to the highest bidder, in 40 acre tracts, on a credit of two, four, and six years, by giving notes with approved security and mortgage on the purchased land or other real estate, 6 per cent. interest, until maturity, 10 per cent. interest, after maturity." So read the trustee's minutes of April 28, '43. The minimum price per acre was set at $2.25. The announcement of the sale was made public through the St. Louis papers. Evidently not all land was disposed of at that time, for one year later the minimum price per acre was reduced to $1.25, which was the exact cost price. Apparently a speedy disposal of the land was desired.

In February of '43 a grievous misstep was made by the custodians of the old society lands when it was voted "that holders of certificates (Actien Scheine) of the German Settlement Society shall in future not be entitled to return the same as payment for land, but that said certificates shall entitle the owner only to a Town lot for each, expressed thereon." This showed a serious breach of trust and rudely overrode the old constitution, faith in which had really induced the purchaser to enter the body at all. It was also an open disregard of the promises made at the time of the transfer. What magnifies the wrong is that it remained unrectified until December of '45, when a more equitable board decreed: "That shares of the German Settlement Society, or sufficient vouchers for the payment of such, shall again be received at the rate of $50.00 a piece, at all payments for lots and lands belonging to this town, the land to be rated at $2.25 per acre and the resolution No. 1, passed on the 8th of February, 1843, be and the same is hereby repealed."

Ten years had passed and yet Hermann had not cleared up all the affairs of the old society. To bring the whole matter to an end it was resolved on May 6th, 1848: "That all shareholders of the German Settlement Society in Hermann, State of Missouri, are hereby requested to exhibit their claims, thereby granted to them, before the first day of May, A. D. 1849, otherwise they may be precluded from any benefit thereof. That the foregoing paragraph be published three times in seven of the most popular German newspapers printed in the different States of the Union."

First Courthouse at Hermann.
Used from 1842 to 1896.

Gasconade County Courthouse built in 1896-1898. Fire damaged the building in February 1905. The present dome was rebuilt to somewhat different specifications than the original.

As a matter of fact the land question gave the town serious concern for many years, even after this announcement. Hermann indeed still has some land whose owners never saw their possessions. Other portions have been sold for taxes.

When the Hermann settlement was made, the County of Gasconade was but sparsely settled. The county seat had for short periods existed at three different hamlets—Bartonville, Gasconade City, and Mount Sterling. When the settlement society chose Hermann as its site, population became massed in the northern part of the county. It is usually the custom to have the county seat located near the centre of the county. If, however, the centre of population is somewhere else the site for the public buildings goes to that centre. So it happens that Hermann though on the extreme northern border of the county now has the court house. As early as 1841 the settlement realized the advantages of having the county seat in their midst. They proposed to erect a brick courthouse instead of an old log hut 20 feet by 24 feet costing $303, as Mount Sterling then had. They also offered Mount Sterling, then an insignificant hamlet, certain material returns to permit the change. In 1842 the change was effected and Hermann began the erection of a new public building. This old building answered all the purposes of the county until a few years ago, when it was supplanted by a magnificent structure, modernly equipped. It is the magnanimous gift to the county by one person, the late C. D. Eitzen. We believe it would be difficult to find another instance of such altruism in the state. This public benefactor came as a young man to Hermann when it was still in its pioneer days. From the humble position of a penniless clerk in a store, he arose through individual effort, strictly adhering to the principles of equity and justice, until he became the wealthiest man of the county. Despite his wealth he ever remained humble. His voice was heard in every deliberation for the good of his town and county, and his counsel was ever just. He had the honor of serving in two constitutional conventions in his state.

He was ever a blessing to his contemporaries and his munificent gifts to the town school, the churches, the town, the lodge of Free Masons, the county and various other organizations make all men of Hermann and Gasconade County his lasting debtors. In these gifts he has erected for himself a memorial that will outlive bronze and marble. He was the largest hearted German the little town has ever had. In the splendid little park, the trees of which he planted himself, which his generosity prompted him

Bust of Charles Eitzen in the City Park

to bequeath to the comfort of his town, in this park his grateful beneficiaries have erected as a memorial, his bust in heroic size. On the supporting base there are inscribed the brief but fitting words: "A tribute to the memory of Charles D. Eitzen whose life was a record of Generous Deeds and Public Usefulness."

Politically most of the voters at Hermann are of Republican persuasion. During the Civil War they were avowed Unionists and furnished their share of soldiers. Some were detailed to do guard duty in the state while many others joined the troops that fought on southern battlefields.

A very amusing incident occurred at Hermann towards the close of the war. That loose conglomerate of men, 25,000 in number, known popularly as Price's army, who sided with the south, traversed Missouri from the Arkansas border to the Missouri river and on their way hit upon Hermann. This was in October of 1864. Most of the able-bodied men of the town were enlisted in the service of the nation. Only a few old men and the women and children remained. When the reckless cohort approached, a half dozen of the old resolute men who had seen service in the German army, could not resist the temptation to play a trick on the invaders despite the probable consequences. They took a small cannon which the town owned, mounted it on one of the many hills that overlook the town and when the vanguard of Price's army appeared in sight, they discharged a well directed shot at them and then beat a hasty retreat, tugging their cannon with them. The troops halted and opened fire on the unseen foe. After a short time the attack came from a second hill and soon from a third one. The troops were unmistakably bewildered. They believed that unexpectedly a strong enemy had been encountered. Detachments of troops were detailed to reconnoiter. They ascended the three hills successively and on the last hill found the old cannon, alone, and spiked. Angered at this prank the old cannon was rolled down the bluff and into the muddy Missouri. In later years the citizens extracted it from the river bed and it is now mounted in front of the court house at Hermann. The troops seeing that they had only been played with, passed on without molesting the town. The Germans had given the impression that several cannon were concealed among the trees, by transporting their gun rapidly from one hill to another.*

But where did the town get the cannon? Goebel explains it thus:

„Vor langen Jahren hatte sich in Hermann eine freiwillige Schützen-Compagnie organisirt und ihre Dienste für den Fall der Noth dem Staat zur Verfügung gestellt, als. Anerkennung dafür oder zur Uebung hatten sie einen Sechspfünder mit einiger Munition zum Geschenk erhalten."**

"Many years ago a voluntary rifle brigade organized itself and placed its services at the disposal of the state in case of necessity; as recognition therefor, or for practice, they had received a six-pounder with some munition as a gift."

This old cannon has added much to many a celebration at Hermann. Many a festive occasion has it announced, many a political and other victory. When in 1886 the town so beautifully celebrated its fiftieth anniversary, it was intended that the old cannon should boom once for every year of the town's existence.

For forty some rounds all went well when an extra heavy charge tore a great section out of its side and so put the old weapon out of commission.

The celebration of the fiftieth anniversary of Hermann, above alluded to, was a great event for the little town. The exercises extending over three days and judging from accounts that have come down to us, it must have been a memorable occasion. In July, 1886, this invitation was sent to various German communities far and near.

---

* Goebel, *"Länger als ein Menschenleben in Missouri,"* p. 213.
** *Ibid*, p. 214.

„Den früheren Einwohnern Hermann's, unsern Nachbarn, und allen Freunden deutschen Geistes und deutscher Gesittung senden wir unsern Gruss und laden sie zur Theilnahme an der Feier des 50jährigen Jubiläums unseres Städtchens freundlichst ein.

Die Bürger Hermann's."

"To the former inhabitants of Hermann, to our neighbors and to all friends of German spirit and German civilization, we send our greeting and invite them most heartily to participate in the celebration of the fiftieth anniversary of our little City.

The Citizens of Hermann"

The program for the occasion was as follows:

„Freitag, den 27sten August, Salut von 50 Kanonenschüssen. Samstag, den 28sten August, Abends halb acht Uhr, Illumination der Stadt; Fackelzug. Die Aufstellung erfolgt am Spritzenhaus.

Marschall, Hugo Kropp.

Nach dem Fackelzuge, Commérs in der Conzert-Halle. Ansprache von Gustav Ettmüller.

Sonntag, den 29sten August, Morgens 8 Uhr, Festzug. Die Aufstellung erfolgt vor der Conzert-Halle.

Marschall, Wm. Herzog. Nach der Ankunft auf dem Fairplatze, Begrüssung der Theilnehmer durch Hon. Rudolph Hirzel, von Washington, Mo. Nachmittags 3 Uhr, Festrede, gehalten von Dr. Hugo Starkloff, von St. Louis, Mo. Hierauf Vorträge des Gesangvereins „Harmonie", Conzert der Hermann „Apostel Band" und des Musikcorps von Rheinland, Mo."

"Friday, Aug. 27, Salute of 50 cannon shots.

Saturday, Aug. 28, Evening, 7:30, Illumination of City, Torchlight parade. The arrangement will take place at the fire engine house.

Marshall, Hugo Kropp.

After the Torchlight Parade, convivial gathering in the Concert Hall.

Address by Gustav Ettmüller.

Sunday, Aug. 29, 8:00 A.M. Anniversary Parade. The arranging takes place at the Concert Hall. Marshal, Wm. Herzog. After the arrival on the fairgrounds, greetings to the participants by Rudolph Hirzel of Washington, Mo. Afternoon, 3:00 P.M. Anniversary Address, given by Dr. Hugo Starkloff of St. Louis, Missouri. Following—selections by the "Harmonie" Chorus, Concert by the Hermann "Apostle Band" and the Band from Rhineland, Mo."

For this occasion the railroad company offered reduced rates and the steam boats made extra trips.

To the credit of the people of Hermann let it redound that most of them are proud of their German descent. They cling to their language tenaciously and lovingly, as will be verified by the Chapter on Education. On the streets and in the business houses German is quite generally spoken. This is not to imply that these people are ignorant of the language of their country. By no means. Only a limited number of very old people fail to respond in English when so addressed. This, however, should be said that with but few exceptions all of them have a striking peculiarity of accent and intonation. This peculiarity of speech can hardly be disposed of by stating that it is the common German-English. It is not the consonants that trouble these people. It is not so much the length of the vowels either but their quality, and then a most striking intonation. We believe some interesting problems for a dialectician and phonetician could be found here.

The few English speaking persons of Hermann have almost without exception acquired some knowledge of the German. While some of them cannot speak it well, all of them are practically, for business purposes, compelled to understand it when spoken. Their children take the German course in the schools without modification. Interestingly enough, the few negroes in the town are masters of a beautiful Hermann German. A German-speaking negro is indeed an exception in Missouri.

Most of the Germans of Hermann are descended from south or midland German stock, and naturally employ the dialect prevalent in those sections. Near Hermann is found quite a large colony of Swiss people.

HERE GERMAN AND ENGLISH ARE TAUGHT IN EQUAL PROPORTIONS.

2. EDUCATION.

The people of Hermann have ever been adherers to the motto *"juventus spes mundi."* Many of the early settlers were well educated men and quite naturally emphasized the absolute need of educating the young. In the nature of things they were seriously hampered by existing primitive conditions. Nevertheless from a humble beginning a laudable institution has arisen. In the face of almost insurmountable difficulties a school has developed which, from its incipiency to the present day, has stood and stands unique among the schools of Missouri. So far as it carries out the wish of the founders of the colony, in keeping alive their native tongue, it may indeed be called exemplary. An examination of the course of study of the Hermann Public School reveals the fact that German is being taught in every grade from that of the wee dimpled little ones, to the most advanced grade of the high school. This fact is known only locally even in Missouri. The reason perhaps lies in the fact that, barring one industry, the town is unimportant commercially. It is indeed remarkable how firmly the Hermannites have clung to their desire to perpetuate their language. And that too despite the external non-German influence and the sporadic deserters from the ways of the fathers within their own midst. That the system does not work hardship or become a hindrance to the young men so educated, is attested by the great number of highly successful business men that have gone to St. Louis, as well as those who do a flourishing business at home. On the contrary it works towards the betterment of its subjects equipping them with two most powerful tools for business purposes. As far as stimulating its students to advanced work it is a success also. Hermann has always had its quota of students at the Missouri University and other institutions of advanced learning.

To understand this system thoroughly we must study it from its beginning. In those early years the foundation was laid upon which the superstructure of to-day rests. We follow it, therefore, from its first beginnings.

During the summer of 1838 the colonists were too much occupied with the clearing of forests, building of houses and laying out of roads to even consider the intellectual welfare of their children. With the following summer came a little more ease and the education of the youth was earnestly considered. In the spring of 1839 a room was rented of one Oelschlaeger and rudely equipped for school purposes, Mr. Bayer administering instruction when his other numerous duties permitted him to do so. On the second day of July it was decided that a school house should be erected. Mr. Krauter agreed to build it for the consideration of $680.

The Philadelphia society assisted the colony in this important work. In the autumn of this same year the building seems to have been ready for occupancy. We conclude this from the minutes of the Board of Trustees of the town—which body, among a multitude of other executive duties, also had charge of school matters. The item under consideration appears under the date of August 7th, 1839. (In quoting from the town record, we are compelled to resort to the English version, the German copy being misplaced, stolen, or destroyed. The language of these records is not always faultless. We make no apologies, however, for using it, since an un-Americanized people wrote them. Their idiosyncrasies and errors will prove interesting in themselves, and may even be valuable.) At the meeting under the date above quoted, the serious problem of engaging a teacher confronted the trustees. The primitive mode of procedure is a pertinent relic of the pioneer days of a frontier State. And yet it was, under the circumstances, the best and most expeditious method at hand. That trans-Mississippi country had at that time not yet developed the closely knit educational system it now boasts of. The minutes read thus: "That a committee to consist of Wm. Pommer, J. Leupold, D. Widersprecher, is hereby requested to examine Mr. F. A. Hemme in regard to his knowledge of the German as well as the English languages." A lively examination these business men may have subjected this pedagogue to. They must have been satisfied with the proficiency shown, for upon their recommendation the colonists voted in favor of the candidate. Five days later this record was inserted:

"That Mr. Hemme is hereby appointed as teacher of the town school under the following conditions:

That he obey the instructions of the Trustees of the Town.

That his salary for the present shall not be less than $300 per annum.

That he shall attend school for the first year from 9 to 12 o'clock A. M. and from 2 to 4 o'clock P. M. in winter; and from 6 to 10 o'clock A. M. and from 2 to 4 o'clock P. M. in summer. Wednesday and Saturday afternoon no school to be held.

That we give instruction in Reading and Writing the German and English languages, Grammatic, Arithmetic, History, Geography and Drawing.

That school commence on the 26th of August, 1839."

Under what trying conditions this poor pedagogue entered upon his labors can be more easily imagined than described. School opened without any provision having been made for school-supplies. Two days after the date set for the opening, the Board resolved:

"That the necessary school books be furnished by the Town and sold to the parents of the children at cost price. There shall be bought 100 copies of Wilmsen's "Kinderfreund," 50 copies of Webster's "Spelling Books," $10.00 worth of common writing paper, quills, ink and inkstands. Mr. J. Leupold is to undertake the purchase of the "Kinderfrenud," and the other articles to be provided by Mr. F. A. Hemme." No mention is made of aids for the study of History, Geography, Drawing and Arithmetic until years after this date. Presumably the instructor was to furnish this information from the stock of his knowledge.

Despite all these difficulties and hindrances, the interest in the school was very much alive. The Trustees voted upon themselves the task: "That every week two of the Trustees together shall visit the School of the Town to ascertain the progress of the children and to further the same." Of course it was not an easy matter to find competent teachers at the price that was offered and with the requirements that the instruction should be in two languages. So we are not surprised to learn that Mr. Hemme did not remain in the graces of his patrons indefinitely. Every one having a voice in the man's election and retention, it was difficult to please all, for we all know the truth of "Viele Köpfe, viele Sinne."* It was then decided: "That a teacher be sought for the school of the town who has been educated in Germany for the business of teaching, and who understands the English language thoroughly." The nature of things caused a centralization of power. The Board of Trustees assumed more absolute control. To oppose hindering forces to mar the progress of the school they decided: "That (the teacher) continue in the mode of teaching adopted by him, pay no regard to individuals, and that in case of disobedience of his scholars he have to give notice to the Trustees thereof."

The manner of paying for services rendered the town was novel. Money was scarce in those days. Land was plentiful since the transfer of power to Hermann, so many payments were made in land grants. In the "Tagelöhner Buch"*at Hermann we find these entries:

„Carl Baer, für die Lotte No. 6 Ost zweite Strasse — $50.00 bezahlt durch Verfertigung eines flatboats — $50.00. Somit die Lotte frey und sein Eigenthum." And another: „F. Mühlenbach für die Lotte No. 7 Ost dritte Strasse $50.00. Derselbe hat zu gut für Arbeit $60.50, daran baar empfangen $10.50. Somit die Lotte frey und sein Eigenthum."

"Carl Baer, for Lot No. 6, East Second Street—$50.00 paid for by completion of a flat boat—$50.00; consequently, the lot is paid and becomes his property." And another: "F. Mühlenbach for Lot 7 East Third Street $50.00. The same is credited with $60.50 for labor; received cash $10.50; consequently, the lot is paid and becomes his property."

---

*"*Many heads, many opinions.*"

*"*Workmen's Book.*"

Even the village schoolmaster did not escape this method. The record of August 23, 1847, states that the teachers salary is $300.00, $150.00, to be paid in cash, $100.00 in notes "due on the Treasurer" and $50.00 in an order on lot and land.

On the 31st of March, 1841, a custom was inaugurated which has prevailed, in a modified form, until this day. On this day it was decided: "That the Secretary be directed to invite Messrs. Jno. C. Haufler, W. Franke, Francis Kuhne and Daniel Trautwein to be examined in the school of this town in the third week of April, Mr. W. Franke on the 19th, Mr. Fr. Kuhne on the 20th, Mr. D. Trautwein on the 21st."

This examination was for the purpose of ascertaining these gentlemen's knowledge of the common branches of learning and their method of instructing. We stated that this custom still prevails. The knowledge of the English and German languages being required, such a test is next to imperative. Every candidate is subjected to the test. Be his credentials and recommendations ever so good, he must undergo an examination as to his knowledge of the branches taught. This examination is administered by the superintendent of the school in the presence of the board of directors. A class of school children is present, and with them the candidate demonstrates his methods of developing and presenting certain phases of work called for by his examiner. This is a unique but highly successful method of procedure. It might be stated here that the Hermann school board is unlike any other similar body in the state, known to us. It consists of eleven members. Six of them are chosen in conformity with the School Law of Missouri, and five of them have for their specific task the supervision of the German instruction.

For three years all affairs of the Hermann school had been instigated and supported by the Germans of the colony. Quite naturally the German side of the instruction was especially emphasized. In the spring of 1842 the school district of Hermann was defined. This gave the colonists certain rights, as it also imposed certain obligations. Under this new régime *all* the residents within the limits of the village were entitled to benefits from the school. Taxes must defray the expenses. School houses must be built by *all* the people's money. Since the majority of the patrons were Germans, no difficulty was experienced in maintaining control. A new school house was erected and was known as the district school. For many years the two schools existed side by side.

It became quite apparent to the men at Hermann that for the German school to exist, it would be compelled to look to its own resources, as no support could be expected from the hands of the state. Through the generosity of J. H. Koch a beginning had been made towards the establishment of a German school fund. In December, 1839, he issued this grant:

„Geschenk für die deutsche Ansiedlungs-Gesellschaft.

Ich, Johann Heinrich Koch, aus Hamfeldt, Amt Alten Bruchhausen, Königreich Hannover, erkläre hierdurch für mich und meine Erben, dass ich eine Actie obiger Gesellschaft, Share Book, No. 932, Running No. 576, ausgestellt in Philadelphia, den 18. September 1839 der Stadt Hermann im Staate Missouri *zum Besten einer deutschen Schule* geschenkt habe und ermächtige durch diese meine öffentliche Anzeige die Trustees der Stadt Hermann, denen ich nächstens den Actienschein schicken werde, nach diesem meinen Willen zum wahren Wohle der deutschen Jugend zu verfahren und die Einkünfte des zu wählenden Bauplatzes oder Landes zum Besten einer deutschen Schule in Hermann anzuwenden, wie sie es für eine gute und gediegene Bildung der dortigen Jugend am zweckmässigsten halten.

Philadelphia, den 19. December 1839.*

Johann Heinrich Koch."

J. G. Wesselhoeft,
A. J. Stockfleth,
Zeugen.

"Donation for the German Settlement Society. I, Johann Heinrich Koch, from Hamfeldt, district Alten Brockhausen, Kingdom of Hannover, declare hereby for myself and my heirs

---

* *A. und N. W.* of December 21, 1839.

that I have donated a share of the above named Society Share Book 932, Running No. 576, issued in Philadelphia, Sept. 18, 1839, to the City of Hermann in the State of Missouri, for the benefit of a German School and through this public notice authorize the Trustees of the City of Hermann to whom I shall shortly send the Certificate of the Share, to proceed for the true welfare of the German youth in conformity with my intentions and to use the income of the building site or tract to be selected for the benefit of a German School in Hermann, as they deem most suitable for the promotion of a good and genuine education of the youth there.

Philadelphia, Dec. 19, 1839. Johann Heinrich Koch"
I. G. Wesselhoeft
A. J. Stockfelth
    Witnesses

This donation became the nucleus around which accumulated a permanent fund. The leaders at Hermann were far-sighted men. They realized the possibilities of the wealth that was intrusted into their keeping after the relinquishment of control by the Philadelphians. They appreciated the opportunity that through the sale of certain tracts of land a handsome fund would accrue, the income of which would insure a school revenue for all future time. In doing this, they would conform to the idealistic plans of the founders of the society. When the Hermann School District was organized the citizens appreciating the vast good that would arise from it, and also realizing that only a few non-German residents would profit by it, they voted, on the 8th of August, 1842, to grant a portion of land to this purpose: "That the following lands, belonging to the German Settlement Society, now the inhabitants of Hermann, shall be deeded over as "A Donation" to the Hermann School District, in fee simple." Then follows the stipulation of the land so donated, amounting to 1,170.63 acres. On the 6th of June, 1847, another grant was made for the support of education: "That the reserve lands of the Town be layed off in Town-blocks in conformity with the plot of the Town and thereupon so many of said blocks shall be sold at public auction until a sufficient sum is realized to establish an independent Town-school fund." It appears that on March 10, 1849, there existed a German school fund of $5,000.00. On the 5th of June, 1855, another step was taken to increase the funds for educational purposes, and that in the adoption of this resolution: "That a public sale of 300 or 400 Town lots and of the Island in (the) Missouri River, belonging to the Town of Hermann, be held on the first Monday of September, 1855, for the amelioration of the town school of Hermann, and this be published in the German newspapers." This fund has been contributed to by benevolent, big hearted citizens, until to-day it amounts to more than $10,000.00. It is securely invested in real estate and high interest bearing bonds. Its income goes towards defraying the expenses of the German School. The District School also has an endowment of several thousand dollars. Since the two schools are curiously welded into one, as the population is almost wholly German, the distinction exists practically only in the name. Previous to 1871 two buildings were used for educational purposes, as has been pointed out. At that time, however, a more commodious building became a necessity. Since then this unique school is conducted under one roof, each teacher instructing in both the German and the English languages.

To conduct a school thus uniqely, it reqires more than the will of the people concerned. The school laws provide for and sanction instruction in the English language only, in the lower grades. It required a legislative act to overstep these bounds. This privilege was granted by the General Assembly of Missouri in 1849. It reads as follows:

"Charter of the German School at Hermann."

Be it enacted by the General Assembly of the State of Missouri as follows:—

Section 1. A school for males and females is hereby established in the town of Hermann, which shall be known by the name of "The German School of Hermann."

Sec. 2. Friedrich Hundhausen, Julius Leupold, Joseph Lessel, August Wasser and H. Burkhardt are hereby appointed trustees of said school, and they and their successors in office are hereby created and constituted a body politic and corporate, to be known by the name and style of "The Trustees of the German School of Hermann," and by that name shall have perpetual succession in office, shall have a common seal, may change, alter and break the same at pleasure, may sue and be sued, plead and be impleaded, answer and be answered unto in all Courts of this State or of the United States.

Sec. 3. On the first Monday of April next there shall be held an election in the town of Hermann for the election of five trustees to manage the affairs of said school. They shall hold their office for one year and until their successors are elected and qualified; on the same day every year an election for trustees shall be held.

Sec. 4. At the first meeting of the Board, which shall be held one week after the election, the members shall elect a chairman, who shall preside at all their meetings during the term for which he is elected trustee; but in case of his absence, a chairman *pro tempore* shall be appointed. The Board shall hold their stated meetings, but may be convened by the chairman or any quorum whenever occasion may require it. They shall keep a journal of their proceedings, and all their meetings shall be public.

SEC. 5. The trustees shall have power to receive by gift or otherwise and hold to them and their successors forever any land, tenements, moneys, goods or chattels of what kind soever, which may be purchased, devised or given to them for said school, and to lease, rent, put out on interest or otherwise dispose of the same in such manner as shall seem most conducive to the advantage of the school; but shall never have power to sell, mortgage or in any way encumber with debt any real estate belonging to said school.

SEC. 6. The Board of Trustees shall have power, and it shall be their duty, to superintend said school, to appoint one or more teachers, treasurer, and such other officers and servants as may be necessary, to remove the same for good cause, to stipulate their salary, to direct and determine what branches of education shall be taught in said school, and to make such by-laws, rules and regulations as they shall deem necessary for the management of said school, but not contrary to the laws of this State; and they shall never permit any professional religious doctrines to be taught in said school.

SEC. 7. The trustees and the treasurer shall, before entering upon their respective duties, take an oath to discharge the duties assigned to them as trustees or treasurer.

SEC. 8. The treasurer shall receive all moneys, etc., accruing to said school and pay or deliver the same to the order of the Board of Trustees. Before he shall enter upon the discharge of his duty he shall give bond and security in such sum as the Board of Trustees shall direct, payable to them and their successors, conditioned for the faithful performance of his duties, under such rules and regulations as the Board may adopt, and it shall be lawful for said Board to obtain judgment for the amount thereof, or for any special delinquencies incurred by him under the same, "on motion" in any Court of record in this State against the treasurer and his securities, his or their executors or administrators, upon giving ten days' notice of such motion.

SEC. 9. The interest of a capital stock of five thousand dollars ($5000) donated by the inhabitants of Hermann to said school shall annually be appropriated to the payment of a teacher or teachers and other necessary expenditures in the management of said school; but the principal shall forever be and remain inviolate. Should said interest prove insufficient to defray the necessary expenses of said school, then the trustees shall be empowered to make up the deficiency by issuing rate bills, as allowed to the common schools in this State.

SEC. 10. Every free white householder of the town of Hermann, who has been a resident of said town for at least twelve months preceding an election, shall be eligible and entitled to vote for trustees of this school, and all elections for trustees of this school shall be held and conducted in the same manner as elections for trustees at the town of Hermann, at least as near as practical. Should any election fail, the chairman of its Board of Trustees, or any quorum thereof (three) shall appoint judges and issue orders to hold an election without delay. Vacancies in said Board shall be filled by special election ordered as above.

SEC. 11. The Board of Trustees shall call at least one meeting a year of all the inhabitants of the town of Hermann, lay before them the situation of the school, and there shall be at least one public examination every year.

SEC. 12. The chairman of the trustees shall, on the first Monday of March of every year, publish handbills, or in a Hermann paper, an exhibit of its affairs and conditions of said school, stating the number of teachers employed, the number of scholars that have been attending the school during the preceding year, males and females; what branches of education have been taught. what languages, etc.; what money received and expended.

SEC. 13. The trustees shall receive no pay for any ordinary services rendered.

SEC. 14. This school shall be and forever remain a German school, in which all branches of science and education shall be taught in the German language.

This Act to take effect from and after its passage.
Approved March 10, 1849."

Under this charter the school prospered until 1870 without any revocation or amendment being made to the writ. At that time, however, it was felt that a more spacious and better equipped building was needed. The General Assembly had introduced into it a bill providing for an amendment to the Act of Incorporation of the German School at Hermann, which bill became a law on Feb. 25th, 1870.* The amendment, which is known as Section 15 of the charter, reads thus:

"The trustees of the German School at Hermann are hereby authorized to lay a tax on all taxable property in the town of Hermann, not to exceed one-half of one per cent. annually, for the purpose of erecting a school house in Hermann and for other school purposes, which tax shall be collected by the officer who collects the municipal taxes of said town, and be governed by the laws regulating the collection of the municipal taxes of Hermann, and when collected, the same shall be paid over to such persons as may be authorized to receive the same by trustees of said school."

It soon became evident that this process of securing the necessary money would require too long a time. For this reason an act, approved March 17, 1871, amended this amendment by adding:

"If the tax of one per cent. be inadequate for the purposes herein specified, the trustees are authorized to issue bonds, not to exceed the amount of $8000, said bonds to be of one hundred dollars each, bearing 8 per cent. annual interest, and payable at the

---

* *Laws of Missouri,* 1870, p. 315.

option of said trustees, within ten years from their respective dates, out of the proceeds of said tax one-half of one per cent."*

In this manner the German School has been placed on a solid foundation, and its future is securely provided for until the people shall desire a change.

The instruction given in the Hermann School is first-class, and quite up to date, as we can testify from personal observation. We have already emphasized the fact that German is taught in all the grades. It will doubtless be interesting to know what is being done in the High School. Three years of German are offered there, as Principal F. O. Spohrer writes me. We quote his course of study:

"First Year.—Grammar, supplemented by the reading of Storm's 'Immensee,' Volkmann's 'Kleine Geschichten,' Baumbach's 'Waldnovellen,' Schiller's 'Der Neffe als Onkel,' or the equivalent.

"Second Year.—First half of Harris' Prose Composition; the reading of Arnold's 'Fritz auf Ferien,' 'Auf der Sonnenseite,' Wildenbruch's 'Das edle Blut,' Chamissos' 'Peter Schlemihl,' or an equivalent amount, and sight translation.

"Third Year.—Second half of Harris' Prose Composition, sight translation and the reading of Freytag's 'Die Journalisten,' Schiller's 'Das Lied von der Glocke,' 'Wilhelm Tell,' 'Die Jungfrau von Orleans,' 'Maria Stuart,' Lessing's 'Minna von Barnhelm,' or an equivalent amount."

The term of school always extends over ten months.

The school has a library of some 1300 volumes. Of this number 705 are German publications. The greater part of this number are "Jugendschriften," to the number of 463. Other books appear classified under the rubrics: Geography, Stories of Travel, Agriculture and Natural Science, Biography, History, Philosophy, and Mythology. Under the caption, "Literatur,

---

* *Laws of Missouri,* 1871, p. 93.

Poesie, etc.," we find 145 volumes. Among this list we find the
following:

Auerbach, Berthold:

„Das Landhaus am Rhein."
„Auf der Höhe."
„Schwarzwälder Dorfgeschichten."

Brown, Chas. Brockden:

„Edgar Huntley, oder der Nachtwandler" (translator not
given).

Chamisso, A. von, complete in two volumes.

Carlyle, Thomas:

„Ausgewählte Schriften" (translated by A. Kretzschmar
1855).

Daumer, G. Fr.:

„Hafis, eine Sammlung persischer Gedichte."

„Deutscher Novellenschatz", compiled by P. Heyse and H. Kurz.

Freytag, Gustav:

„Die Ahnen."

An old volume bearing the title „Erste und Merkwürdige Reisen
eines Europäers — Ludwig Fontaine etc.", dated 1792.

Gerstäcker, Fr.:

„Tahiti."

Goethe's works complete in 15 volumes with introduction by Karl
Goedeke.

Goethe & Schiller Xenien — Aus dem Schillerschen Musenalmanach
für das Jahr 1797, with introduction by A. Stern.

Hackländer, F. W.:

„Das Soldatenleben im Frieden."
„Wachtstuben-Abenteuer."
„Humoristische Erzählungen."
„Bilder aus dem Leben."

Hartmann, Moritz — „Novellen."

Hauff, Wilhelm:
> „Gedichte."
> „Novellen."
> „Mittheilungen aus den Memoiren des Satan."
> „Othello."
> „Der Mann im Monde."
> „Märchen für Söhne und Töchter gebildeter Stände."
> „Lichtenstein."

Heine, Heinrich:
> „Reisebilder", pub. by Schaefer & Koradi, Philadelphia.

Herder, Joh. Gottfr.:
> Werke in IV volumes compiled by H. Kurz.

Herbert, Lucian:
> „Das Testament Peter des Grossen."

Heyse, Paul:
> Vols. III and IV of his „Novellen."

Körner, Theodor:
> Complete Works.

Lessing:
> „Minna von Barnhelm."
> „Emilia Galotti."
> „Nathan der Weise."

The writings of the next twenty-one authors were published in Philadelphia by *Morwitz & Co.,* in a series named *"Heimath und Fremde."* The dates are not to be found—apparently, however, they date from the middle of the last century.

Armand:
> „Die alte spanische Urkunde."

Betzold, M.:
> „Um Ehre und Leben."

Brachvogel, A. E.:
> „Der Fels von Erz."

Dedenroth, E. H. von:
> „Die Baronin."
> „Das Gespenst."

Fischer, Wilhelm:
„Vier Blüthen und eine Frucht."

Frenzel, Karl:
„Herodias."

Friedrich, Friedrich:
„Nemesis."
„Zwei Söhne."

Gaborian, Emil:
„Herr Lecog."

Gerstäcker, Friedrich:
„Die Franctireurs."
„Im Eckfenster."

Guseck, Bernd von:
„Deutschlands Ehre."

Hahn, B. Edmund:
„Die Sklaverei der Liebe."

Hiltl, George:
„Die Schlossdiebe."

Müntzelberg, Adolph:
„Zwei heitere Geschwister."

Pierce, Etta:
„Die Töchter des Millionärs", translated by Alfred Mü-
renberg.

Pitawall, Ernst:
„Gabriel, das Weib des Spielers."

Prosper, Merrimé:
„Colomba."

Samarow, Gregor:
„Kreuz und Schwert."
„Um Scepter und Krone."
„Zwei Kaiserkronen."
„Europäische Mienen und Gegenmienen."
„Held und Kaiser."

Schmidt-Weisenfels:
„Die Söhne Barnevelts."

Streckfuss, Adolf:
„Der tolle Hans."
„Der verlorene Sohn."

Wachenhusen, Hans:
„Salon und Werkstatt."

Winterfeld, A. von:
„Der Elephant."

As will be observed, it is a class of the lesser literary lights. The library also contains the following books:

Mügge, Theodor:
„Die Vendeerin."
„Der Vogt von Sylt."
„Toussaint."
„Erich Randal."
„Der Prophet."
„Der Cavalier."
„Spang."
„Tänzerin und Gräfin."
„Verloren und Gefunden."

Paul, Jean:
„Siebenkäs."
„Dr. Katzenberg's Bad-Reise."
„Flegeljahre."

Reuter, Fritz:
„Woans ik tau 'ne Frau kamm."
„Ut de Franzosentid."
„Ut mine Stromtid."

Ruppius, Otto. Found in „Gesammelte Erzählungen aus dem Deutsch-Amerikanischen Volksleben":
„Der Pedlar."
„Ein Stück deutschen Bauernlebens."
„Drei Tage aus dem Leben eines Schullehrers."
„Traumkönig und Schneider."
„Das Vermächtniss des Pedlars."
„Das Heimchen."
„Eine Karriere in Amerika."

„Prairieteufel."
„Ein Deutscher."
„Bill Hammer."
„Eine Speculation."
„Waldspinne.'
„Zwei Welten."
„Drei Vagabunden."
„Aus dem Schullehrerleben im Westen."
„Mary Kreuzer."
„Auf Regierungsland."
„Buschlerche."
„Vermisst."
„Unter Freunden."
„Die Nachbarn."
„Geld und Geist."
„Schlamm und fester Boden."
„Priester und Bauer."
„Eine Weberfamilie."

Steiger, E. Compiler of:
„Erstlingsblüthen deutscher Lyrik in Amerika."

Schiller's complete works edited by H. Kurz.

Scheffel's „Ekkehardt."
„Der Trompeter von Säkkingen."

Tiek, Ludwig:
„Vittoria Accorombona."

Witter, C. Compiler of:
„Neuestes Taschenliederbuch für Deutsche in Amerika."

Wieland's „Ausgewählte Werke" by H. Kurz.

Zschokke, Heinrich:
„Die Rose von Disentis", pub. by N. R. Cormany, Main
and Walnut Sts., St. Louis, Mo., 1846.

The following publications are also found in the Hermann
library:

„Die Gegenwart" for 1875.
„Globus-Zeitschrift für Länder und Volkskunde" for 1874.

„Gaea — Natur und Leben" for 1875.
„Unsere Zeit" for 1874—5.
„Deutsche Rundschau", 7 volumes.

Among the Jungendschriften are found a number of books which originally belonged to the library at Turnverein.

In closing this chapter on Education at Hermann, it should be stated that the Catholic Church supports a strong parochial school.

3. GOVERNMENT.

In dealing with the question of the government of Hermann, we must begin with transactions that took place during the colony days.

It will be recalled that the problem of transfer of power hinged largely upon the assurance of the incorporation of the town, for the society wisely declined to submit its rights and responsibilities to anything but a corporate body, accepted and recognized by, and responsible to the laws of the State. The colonists, eager to share certain privileges which incorporated towns enjoyed, had taken cognizance of this matter as early as the spring of 1838, or from the very incipiency of the settlement. On the 29th of October, 1838, a petition was addressed to the County Court of Gasconade County, which, under an act passed March 11, 1825, possessed the power to incorporate towns in its jurisdiction. This petition was passed upon favorably on February 4th, 1839. The limits of the new body politic were the following: "Beginning at a point in the middle of the main channel of the Missouri River; the west boundary line beginning north at the half-mile open line in Section 26, and running south 5060 feet through Sections 26 and 35; the east boundary line beginning at the quarter-section line in Section 25 and running south 5620 feet through Sections 25 and 36; the south boundary line beginning at the point where the above-mentioned 5620 feet cease and running west until it strikes the west boundary line at the end of the aforementioned 5060 feet, Township 46 South of Missouri

River, north of the base line range No. 5 west of Fifth Principal Meridian."

The executive functions of this corporation were vested in five trustees elected by the people for the period of one year. In order to expedite matters, as is customary, the County Court appointed a temporary Board of Trustees to serve until the regular election could be held. This appointed Board consisted of five men—Wilhelm Senn, Veit Ludwig Henrich, Friederich Lehder, Dedlev Widersprecher and Julius Leupold. The choice of the people, expressed about the middle of May, 1839, was the following, for the first trustees: Friedrich Lehder, Heinrich Heckmann, Hermann Bock, Julius Leupold, Silvester Doess.

For five years Hermann existed under this Act of Incorporation. In the winter of 1844-5 the legislature was petitioned for a special charter, and on February 4th, 1845, it was granted. Before the present Constitution of Missouri was adopted, that is to say, prior to 1875, the inhabitants of a particular settlement desiring to organize into a town, applied to the legislature for a special charter of incorporation, which defined its powers and described its territorial boundaries.* Since that date no special charters are granted. Cities are classified according to their population into first, second, third and fourth-class cities. The old charters could not be revoked except by a surrender of the same by the people incorporated under them. Most of the towns early voted themselves into the new order of things. Hermann, in its own peculiar way, clung to the old régime until April 4, 1905, when by a vote of 196 to 98 the people decided to abandon the old and come under the new rule. On the 16th of May, 1905, an election was held to choose the officers which the new régime calls for namely: Mayor, collector, aldermen, marshal, etc. August Wohlt has the distinction of being the first Mayor of Hermann, while its first aldermen are Gaus, Moebus, Schuch and Bohlken.

---

* Cf. Perry S. Rader, *"Civil Government and Hist. of Missouri,* p. 115.

At the first meeting of the trustees, May 18th, 1839, there was inaugurated a practice which, while the old charter was in vogue, was faithfully adhered to, namely, "That the Journal of the Proceedings of the Board of Trustees shall be kept both in the German and English languages." Whether this method still prevails since the change of 1905, we are not prepared to say.

The charter of 1845 defines the territorial limits more accurately, and also shows some changes in the boundary as recorded in the first Act of Incorporation. "That the district of country known by the name of the town of Hermann, shall be and continue a body politic and corporate lying within the following limits, to wit.: Beginning at a point in the middle of the channel of the Missouri River, due north from the quarter-section corner between Sections twenty-six (26) and thirty-five (35), Township forty-six (46), north, range five (5). west of the Fifth Principal Meridian; then running due south to the northwest corner of the southwest quarter of the northeast quarter of Section thirty-five (35), Township forty-six north, range 5, west of the 5th Principal Meridian; thence due east forty chains; thence due south twenty chains; thence due west forty chains; thence due south twenty chains; thence due east eighty chains; thence due north twenty chains; thence due east twenty chains; thence due north to the middle of the channel of the Missouri River, and along the channel back to the beginning."

The sketch for the accompanying drawing was sent to us by J. C. Danuser, County Surveyor of Gasconade County. Mr. E. B. Smith, Instructor of Mechanical Drawing at Drexel Institute, Philadelphia, had the kindness to make the drawing.

In comparing the charter of 1845 with the Act of Incorporation of 1839, we find that the two, barring only a few points, are identically the same in language and substance. Under the first act only the five trustees were elected by the people. The other officers: assessor, collector, constables, were appointed by this Board. The new writ prescribed that they be also elected by the people. The power of the trustees under the new charter was extensive and their duties legion. It must be stated here, however, that as time passed and new demands came, these powers were vested in special bodies, as, for instance, the matter of education, although the town continued to exist under the letter of the old document. To give a clear idea of the powers and duties of the Board, we quote from the old charter. Certain provisions were made which have no place in the charter of a city of the fourth class. This can only be accounted for by the fact that the idea of Hermann as a "Grossstadt" had not yet vanished. We quote from paragraphs 4 and 8 of the charter:

"Said Board of Trustees shall have power to pass by-laws and ordinances to prevent and remove nuisances, to prohibit gambling and gaming houses, to license, regulate and prohibit theatrical and other amusements, to license merchants, grocers, pedlars, auctioneers, inn, tavern and coffee-house keepers and all taxes raised from such licenses shall be paid to said Board and applied to the improvement of said town; to prevent or restrain the meeting of slaves, the firing of firearms, to regulate and establish markets, to erect and repair bridges, to open, establish, widen, extend and repair streets, avenues, lanes, alleys, public squares, to drain sewers and to keep the same clear, to graduate, pave and improve the streets of said town, to erect, repair wharves by the inhabitants thereof; and if any of them shall fail or refuse to perform the part assigned to them, the trustees may hire the same to be done, and levy and collect the price thereof on the persons so failing or refusing, and they shall also have power to cause the proportionate part of such erecting or clearing to be done for the account of non-resident lot owners, and the price thereof to be levied and collected as aforesaid, and, if it cannot be otherwise recovered, the trustees may have such lot or lots, or any part thereof, sold to defray the expenses of such improvements in such manner as said Board may by ordinance provide: to prevent the furious and unnecessary running, galloping, riding or driving any horse or mule within said town, or such part thereof as they may think proper; to prohibit the running of hogs at large, and other stock within the incorporated limits of the town, or such parts thereof as the Board of Trustees may think proper; to establish night watches and patrols; to suppress bawdy and other disorderly houses within the limits of said town; to erect and maintain hospitals; to prevent the introduction of contagious diseases, and to secure the general health of the town; to provide for the extinguishing of fire; to erect school houses, to keep the same in good repair and to provide for the education of children in said town; to levy and collect taxes upon real and personal property in said town, but shall not impose a tax at a higher rate than one-half of one per centum on the assessed value of the property; to fix the rate of wharfage; to regulate the landing and stationing of steamboats, rafts and water-crafts; to provide for the inspection of lumber, building materials and provisions to be used or offered for sale in said town, to be exported therefrom; to borrow money, if it be necessary, for paving or grading the streets, erecting warehouses, supplying water or making other public improvements in said town; to pass such ordinances for the regulation and police of said town as said trustees may think necessary, not contrary to the laws of this land, and said Board of Trustees shall have power to pass all ordinances to carry into effect the object of this act and the powers herein granted, as the good of the inhabitants may require and to impose fines and penalties for the breach of their ordinances; to regulate the clearing and cleaning of chimneys and fix the fees thereof; to regulate and order partition and parapet walls and partition fences; to have the footways and sidewalks of the streets paved at the expense of the owners and occupiers of the lots fronting on such paved sidewalks, and if said owner or occupier fail to pave the same as directed by ordinance, said trustees shall pave the same and recover the full expense thereof from such owner or occupier, by action of debt, before any Court of competent jurisdiction, and if any tenant be required to pave in front of the property occupied by him, the expense thereof shall be a good offset against so much rent due the owner; but no tenant shall be required to expend more than the rent for the term for which he occupied the property. If any person who is a non-resident fail to pave in front of his property in the manner and time prescribed by the ordinance, or if any person who is a resident fail to pave as aforesaid, and the expense of paving cannot be otherwise recovered from him, the trustees may have such lot, or any part thereof, sold to pay expenses of said improvement in such manner as said Board may by ordinance prescribe; provided, that such person, whether resident or non-resident, whose property has been sold under the provisions of this act, shall have the right to redeem the same within two years from the date of such sale, by paying the full amount of the taxes and cost due thereon, together with the interest, at the rate of fifteen per cent. per annum."

To a provision in these rigid regulations the good sidewalks of Hermann are in a great measure attributable. They are exceptionally wide and substantial. A board sidewalk is positively unknown in the town.

On February 3, 1870, the old charter was supplemented by an act providing for the macadamizing of the streets. This work has been done, and Hermann can boast of streets and sidewalks far above those of any other town of its size in the State.

Hermann is a very peaceful town. Until 1906 there was no holdover within its limits. But rarely disorderly conduct is seen on her streets, and then the transgressors are usually non-residents of Hermann, who do not know how to curb their appetites in this wine-town as those to the manor born have learned to do. The occasional cases were formerly cared for in the county jail, which is located here.

4. INDUSTRIES AT HERMANN.

Small as Hermann is, it nevertheless stands in a class by itself among the towns of Missouri in at least one industry, namely, the production of wine. The Missouri State Labor Bureau issued this statement: "Missouri for 1904 shipped a twelfth of the wine placed on the market by all States."* According to this same report, the surplus number of gallons of wine Missouri produced is 3,068,780 gallons. Of this quantity Gasconade County alone furnished 2,971,576 gallons. Almost all of this amount was produced at Hermann, or its immediate surrounding country districts.

This industry is by no means a recent venture. On the contrary, it is the legitimate outcome of many years of intelligent application, its beginning dating back to the strenuous days of Hermann's beginning. Gert Goebel comments upon this fact in his valuable book on the Missouri Germans: "Hermann kann mit Recht die Wiege des Weinbaues in Missouri genannt werden."** And as the statistics above quoted indicate, it maintains its birthright with dignity. Many causes for this centralization of the wine industry have been cited, many conjectures have been made to account for it. First of all, it is always stated that northern Gasconade County is almost wholly German. Most persons find this to be sufficient explanation. But when it is remembered that Putnam County, with only 53 foreign-born Germans, ranks second in this business, and that other German settlements produce no wine at all, the value of such an explanation is diminished. Of course, the aptitude the German has acquired for the wine culture played a great rôle in this matter. But it must be shown what class of Germans they were to make the statement really of value. This is done by Goebel, whom we quote here:

**Hermann can rightfuly be named the cradle of the Missouri vine growing.*

* Annual Report of the Bureau of Labor of Missouri for year ending November 5, 1905, p. 21.

** Gert Goebel, *"Länger als ein Menschenleben in Missouri,"* p. 141.

„Es ist sehr begreiflich, dass die ersten deutschen Ansiedler im Frain Thale sehr bald nach ihrer Niederlassung auf die Idee kamen, Versuche mit der Veredlung des Rebstocks zu machen; denn überall im Walde und selbst an den steinigsten Bergwänden wuchsen wilde, sehr rauhe Trauben in Menge, und da die allermeisten dieser frühen Ankömmlinge Süd-Deutsche und Schweizer waren, so mochten sie leicht an die Weinberge in ihrer alten Heimath am Rhein, Neckar und Main erinnert worden sein, und somit ward der erste Anstoss gegeben.*

"It is very probable that the first German settlers in Frene Valley soon after their arrival came upon the idea of making attempts to improve the grapes; for everywhere in the woods and even on the stoniest hillsides wild, very tart grapes grew in abundance, and since most of these early settlers were of South German or Swiss stock they were no doubt readily reminded of the vineyards in their old native country along the Rhine, Neckar and Main and thereby the first incentive was given."

Experiments with the wild grape were early made; but, proving unsatisfactory, the cultivated vine was introduced. Though no great yields are mentioned for the first years, yet the trial must have promised generous returns. As early as November 25th, 1844, the trustees of Hermann took an action which expresses the manifest intent to encourage the cultivation of the vine: "That those persons who reside here be allowed to take up vacant lots, belonging to the town, for the purpose of cultivating the vine, upon the following conditions, to wit.: (a) The lots are to be paid for, without interest, after a lapse of five years; that is to say, one-fifth of the purchase money to be due each year, without interest. (b) That no applicant can be allowed to have more than five lots, in the manner aforesaid, and that the persons so taking up lots, be required to pay all taxes resting upon the same from the time of the taking up of such lots. (c) That each person so taking up lots pledge himself within the space of two years to plant two-fifths of the lots taken up with the vine, so that in five

---

* Gert Goebel, *"Länger als ein Menschenleben in Missouri,"* pp. 141-2.

years the whole of said lots be planted; otherwise to forfeit his claim or title thereto and be liable to the payment of ten per cent. annual interest on the purchase money."

This was, indeed, a liberal offer. But, generous as this was, the town fairly outdid itself when it extended the time limit to ten years, making the first payment due five years after the taking up of the land. How eagerly this opportunity was accepted is manifested by the fact that by exact count just 600 "wine lots" were bought from the society. Selling at the uniform rate of $50.00 per lot, the coffers of the town must have been liberally replenished. In the "Verzeichniss der unter der zehnjährigen Kaufbedingung aufgenommen Weinlotten nebst Noten—Register A,"*it appears that John Sidler has the distinction of acquiring the first "wine lot." The simple record kept is this:

JOHN SIDLER.

Jan. 2, 1845		wherefore his notes					
Lots Nos. 106 W. 4 & 105 W. 5 St. 102, 104 W. 4, 101, 103 W. 5th St.		1851	1852	1853	1854	1855	Total
	Jan. 2	50	50	50	50	50	250

These incentives did not fail to arouse interest and bring results. Less than four years after the passage of the above-quoted resolutions, the brilliant success of the first yield was becomingly celebrated. At this point Goebel again furnishes us a most interesting account of Hermann's first "Weinfest."

„Ich kann mich des ersten Weinfestes in Hermann im Herbst 1848 noch sehr gut erinnern. Dr. Gerling und ich ritten mit einander zu diesem Feste nach Hermann und als wir gegen Abend dort ankamen, donnerte ein Sechspfünder seine Grüsse und Glückwünsche über Berg und Thal. Die Kunde von diesem Erfolg war in Missouri so weit gedrungen, wie damals deutsch gesprochen wurde; und es waren sogar Besucher von St. Louis, Damen und Herren, auf Dampfbooten angekommen. Am nächsten Morgen machte sich eine ganze Cavalcade auf den Weg zu dem Weinberg des Herrn Michael Pöschel, und ich habe es in der That nicht be-

---

*"*Register with Data of Winelots taken up under the Ten Years Conditional Purchase—Register A."*

reut, den weiten Weg von zwanzig Meilen gemacht zu haben, als ich dort die Traubenpracht mit eigenen Augen sah. Sein tragender Weinberg hatte kaum den Flächenraum von einem einzigen Acker, aber die Spaliere schienen dort eine Wand von Nichts als Trauben zu sein und darunter war keine einzige faule Beere zu bemerken. Der Ertrag aus der Lese von diesem kleinen Weinberg war ein sehr hoher, denn guter Catawba, der, wenn er richtig behandelt wird, dem Rheinwein sehr nahe kommt, war damals sehr gesucht und wurde gut bezahlt."*

"I can still remember very well the first Weinfest in Hermann in the fall of 1848. Dr. Gerling and I rode together to this festival in Hermann and as we arrived there towards evening a six-pounder thundered its greeting and welcome over the hills and valleys. The reports of this success had penetrated into all parts of Missouri where German was spoken at that time, and even visitors from St. Louis, ladies and gentlemen had come on steamboats. The next morning an entire cavalcade made its way to the vineyard of Mr. Michael Poeschel, and as a matter of fact, I didn't regret having traveled the long distance of twenty miles, when I beheld the splendid grapes there with my own eyes. His bearing vineyard covered hardly the area of a single acre, but the rows of posts seemed to consist of nothing but a wall of grapes and among them not a single rotten berry was to be found. The product of the vintage of this small vineyard was a very expensive but good Catawba, which, when it is treated right, resembles Rhinewine very closely, and was at times in great demand and brought a good price."

In striking upon this industry, Hermann had found the true sphere in which it could excel. The land, while not adapted to general agriculture, is admirably suited to fruit raising. To remove all hindrances to this industry, as well as to encourage the work, the trustees granted the "Western Fruit, Grape and Horticultural Society" the use of four lots, "for the purpose of a nursery, for the term of twenty years which, after ten years, may be sold to this society for $50.00 per lot."

---

*Goebel, *"Länger als ein Menschenleben in Missouri,"* p. 142.

From these small, determined beginnings the wine industry rapidly grew, outstripping all similar undertakings, not only in Missouri, but in the entire stretches of the great Missouri Valley, reaching the proportions we depicted in the beginning of this chapter. The golden age of Hermann's great industry began in the year 1865. By this time many of the best kinds of grapes had become acclimated. The Virginia Seedling, the Concord and the Delaware and other kinds had proven their hardiness to withstand Missouri's changeful climate.

Among the pioneers in this lucrative business at Hermann belong the brothers, Michael Wilhelm and Melchior Poeschel, Franz Langendoerfer, Jacob Rommel, Sr., Geo. Hussmann, Strecker, Vallet, Grein and others. Among the later and present promoters of the work may be named Fleisch, Eberlin, Vogt, Hundhausen, Henze, Franz and Jacob Kuhn, Mueller, Petrus, Weydemeyer, Puchta, Loehring, Rhodius, Sobbe, Jacob Rommel Jr., Sperry, and others.* Besides this long list of producers, there exists in Hermann an old wine company under a comparatively new name. The firm is now known as the Stone Hill Wine Company. It does the lion's share of Missouri's wine business. Its famous wine cellars are said to be the largest east of California.**

Other products of Hermann are beer, whiskey and shoes. In the palmy days of steamboating on the Missouri, Hermann was a widely-known shipping point. Many of the boats plying Missouri's dark waters were owned by men in Hermann. Even now the little town claims the distinction of ownig more boats than any other town along the river. When the many lines of railroad were constructed in the valley, steamboating became impracticable and ceased almost completely. Aside from the products already enumerated, Hermann furnishes nothing beyond the usual contributions peculiar to the average country town.

---

* *"Hermanner Volksblatt"* for Oct. 27, 1905.
** Walter Williams *"The State of Missouri,"* p. 388.

We cannot conclude the chapter pertaining to Hermann's business enterprises without considering briefly the quaint old market house, once the scene of hustle and bustle, but now almost deserted. It will be remembered that in an early part of our story reference was made to the broad street and the market houses that should be built in this street. As a matter of fact, only one such building was erected. It still stands—a two-story brick building, just in the middle of the broad street, below Fourth Street.

We believe it would be a difficult task to find another Missouri town of Hermann's population provided with such a building. We are at once reminded that we are dealing with a peculiar settlement—different from all its neighbors. It furthermore stands as an undeniable proof that the people once entertained the loftiest hopes of their creation. The fact also suggests itself that the founders of the settlement were of foreign extraction, to whom such institutions were familiar and apparently a necessity, even in smaller towns.

The first suggestion of such a centralization of the market business came on May 1st, 1854. We read in the minutes of the trustees of that day: "That the petition about a market house will be considered, and that the trustees will view the locality." It is remarkable that such a request should come as late as this in the history of the colony. By this time it was clearly understood that Hermann would not be a great city. It must have been due to the fact that many of the residents were formerly Grossstädter and of foreign birth. On the 14th of August of the same year quoted, the contract for the work was let. The building was completed early in March, 1856. The lower floor was provided with eight stalls for butchers and provisioners. The upper story consisted of one large hall and served as city hall and for public meetings of various kinds. The stalls were sold to the highest bidders. The regulations restricting the sale of meat and provisions to the market house made it imperative for provisioners to secure rooms

THE MARKET HOUSE AT HERMANN.

here. The stalls sold at various prices. The first occupants paid from $3.80 to $5.00 per stall per annum. A market master had supervision of the house, and was held responsible for the execution of the market regulations. Some of these rules bear insertion here. In drawing them up, the trustees admitted they were modeled after the regulations of the St. Louis market houses, but how close the resemblance is, we are unable to say:

"Each stall purchaser is bound to offer meat for sale 3 times a week, at least.

No stall shall be used for any other purpose than for selling provisions.

Each stallholder shall, within half an hour after the market time, sweep and clean his stall, if not, the Market master shall do it at the expense of the renter.

The market hours shall be from daybreak until 12 o'clock.

During market hours no meat shall be sold by pound without the market house, but it shall be permitted to sell meat at quarter.

Any person who will bring meat from sick or starved animals to the market, sell or offer for sale, shall be fined no less than $25.00 and no more than $100.00.

Butter, eggs, poultry, vegetables, etc., are not permitted to be offered for sale during the market hours at any place in town, without the market place. All persons acting against said ordinance, shall pay a fine of no less than one and no more than five dollars.

It is not permitted to sell sausages, hashed meat, ham, bacon, salt and dried meat during the market hours at any place in the town without the stalls in the market house, by pounds, but it shall not be forbidden to sell by wholesale without the stalls at the market place. All persons disregarding this ordinance shall be fined for $3.00.

No person is allowed to buy more provisions than necessary for his family use at the market, with the purpose of selling again.

All persons buying provisions with the purpose of selling again shall be considered as hucksters, and shall be obliged to rent a place from the Market master, for which the sum of $2.00 for 6 months shall be paid, payable in advance, for having the privilege to sell at the market place.

All self-produced articles, suitable for a provision market, can be sold during the market time at the market place without paying any particular tax.

Unwholesome or rotten articles, carried to the market, shall be confiscated and destroyed by the Market master, and the guilty shall be fined for not less than one and not more than $25.00.

The Market master shall be authorized to drive away from the market every drunken person or disturber, and if in such a case obedience is refused to him, the guilty shall be fined for not less than one and not more than five dollars.

It is forbidden to sell liquor at the market place during the market hours.''

Such were the regulations governing the Hermann Market. Long ago they have become void. But the old building still stands—a monument of a period of Hermann's history. The lower floor is now practically unused. In the upper room the

Town Fathers, until 1906, deliberated for the good of the town, and various town organizations and clubs convened here. Now their meetings are held at the elegant new city hall.

City Hall

Hermann, Missouri - City Hall - 1906

5. Religion, Social Life and Literary Activity.

It can hardly be asserted that Hermann is predominently religious in its inclinations. Many of the early settlers were "Freisinnige," and their views have been transmitted to the present generation. While there is no open opposition to things religious, yet a manifest indifference to the tenets of any church prevails. It must not be inferred from this, however, that the moral tone of the town is below the average. On the contrary, it compares quite favorably with the average Missouri town.

There are many things that would shock the newcomer, unacquainted with the customs that have prevailed, and some that still prevail among the people at Hermann. Among these was the custom by which all the places of business were open until noon on Sundays. The country folk came to town to purchase, as well as to pray. Such had been the custom since Hermann's pioneer days. And all this notwithstanding the Sunday Closing Law on the statute books of the State. They saw no wrong in this practice. They held that Sunday was made for them, and not they for the day. No wonder they regarded it as an infringement on their rights when Governor Folk proceeded to enforce the laws of the State relating to Sunday closing. But, to the credit of the good people be it said, they respected the law when it was brought to their attention. Governor Folk himself paid the Germans a fine compliment in his address before the Alumni of the University of Missouri, on June 7, 1905, when he said: "They are the most law-abiding and law-respecting people in the world. When they find the enforcement of Sunday closing means simply upholding the majesty of the law, and not the whim of the executive, I believe they will support it. They may not agree with me as to the wisdom of the law; but so long as it is the law, the expression of the sovereign will of the people of Missouri, they will uphold its enforcement until it is repealed."

The people of Hermann believe in a joyful Sabbath. It is their fête day. Public opinion outside of their community deters them not a whit. The "Maifest" of the public school, when young and old wander to the pretty park, always falls on Sunday. The gala-day of the Gasconade County Fair is Sunday. Lodges and societies hold their festivities and dances on Sunday. The "Schützenfest" and baseball games fall on this day. Every summer from six to eight Sunday railroad and boat excursions bring throngs of pleasure seekers from St. Louis and other places to "Little Germany." Most of the visitors are Germans who wish to spend a typically German Sunday. Music and song and wine lend their share towards a pleasant day, whose evening comes only too soon.

The three religious denominations represented are the Catholic, the Evangelical and the Methodist, which range numerically in the order here given. All of them draw their following from the town, as well as the surrounding country. Each of them owns its own house of worship, a parsonage, and, in the case of the Catholic, a spacious school building, in which Sisters instruct the youth of the parish. The architecture is that so commonly found in German churches of this country—a long rectangular structure, with a tall, slender spire with bell or bells directly in front of it. The ritualistic and all the other ministerial work of the Evangelical and Catholic Churches is conducted exclusively in the German language. The Methodist Church, in order to accommodate certain non-German residents, employs both the English and the German languages in its services.

While educational matters had received earnest consideration from the very first, religious affairs remained long in the background. Indeed, no mention whatsoever appears on the records regarding religion until the spring of 1841, when the trustees resolved: "That the request of the trustees of the General German Church to be allowed to hold their meetings in the school house be granted." Just what the nature of the teachings of this church was, is not known. Most probably, it was quite liberal, in conformity with the views of many of the settlers.

The Town Fathers were far less liberal towards the churches than they had been to other institutions. They, who had more land than they could well manage, felt unable to promote the growth of churches. So they voted: "That the town is willing to sell to the General German Church lots Nos. 5 and 6 at a price of $112.50 each, on ten years' credit, with 6 per cent. yearly interest; but that no donation of lots in favor the Church can be granted." These terms were, indeed, less advantageous than those which were offered to the vintagers. Later their former resolution was emphasized by the decree: "That all further petition for donations of lots by religious denominations be dismissed without deliberation by the trustees." On October 20th, 1841, all religious denominations were precluded from the use of the school house for religious services. A year later, however, it became plain to the trustees that such an antagonistic attitude towards the church must react on themselves, and prove detrimental to the growth of the town. They therefore hastened to make amends for their narrowness and rectify the impression that Hermann was altogether worldly. They revoked the action taken, and saw to it that this revocation should become public. "That the school house of this town shall be open to all religious persuasions for the purpose of holding their congregations therein, and that this ordinance be published in the *Anzeiger des Westens* at St. Louis and in the *Alte und Neue Welt* in Philadelphia."

The General German Church, with its liberal interpretation of the rules of conduct, did not prosper long. After a few years of unsuccessful existence it disappeared. The text which its minister (whose name we are unable to learn) used at the last meeting was: "Ist das Werk aus Gott, so wirds bestehen, ist es nicht aus Gott, so wirds untergehen."*

Simultaneously with this General Church, the Evangelical and Roman Catholic Churches took their rise. The trustees acted more liberally towards these bodies than was generally expected. The terms of purchase of land were generous, and permission was willingly granted to cut the necessary timber from the reserve lands of the town.

The Evangelical Church was not established under the auspices of the Evangelical Synod, but simply by Evangelical Protestants. During the first years it was ministered to by pastors unattached to any of the great church bodies. In 1851 it was for the first time provided with an adherent to the Evangelical Synod. But the body was still known as "Freie Gemeinde," and remained so, even until 1902, when it chose to come into the corporate religious body known as the "Deutsche Evangelische Synode von Nord Amerika," even though disciples of this body had administered to its spiritual needs for half a century.

---

*"If the work is of God, it will endure; if it is not of God, it will perish."

This unwavering adherence to existing conditions, this hesitancy to accept new things, though they be well tried, is a characteristic of Hermann. We have seen it in its municipal government, in its educational system, and, in the case of this one organization, in its religion.

The Hermannites have ever been a pleasure-loving people. We pointed out in the beginning of this work that the Germans desired to unite the advantages of America and the pleasures of Germany in the colony. To this principle they have ever adhered. The opposition to the interpretation of Americans of what is meant by keeping the Sabbath holy has ever now and again found expression. Never, perhaps, more sarcastically than in the second edition of the *Licht-Freund,* published by Mühl (of whom more later), on August 30, 1843. The editor had just discussed certain phases of social life at Cincinnati, his former home, and then continued to depict scenes of a Sunday at Hermann in the early days :

„Wenn der Sabbathsmissionar an uns in Hermann, eine ähnliche Anfrage wie an die Doctoren in Cincinnati hätte ergehen lassen, so würden wir ihm die ganz einfache Antwort, ohne alle Doctorweisheit freilich, gegeben haben : Herr Sabbathsmissionar, wir meinen allerdings auch, dass Mensch und Thier nicht zur Quälerei da sind, desshalb eine der Natur angemessene Ruhe und Erholung haben müssen ; auch halten wir unsern Sonntag allhier, aber nun freilich nicht nach englischer, sondern deutscher Weise, d. h. wir bringen ihn nicht grade ausschliesslich in der Kirche und dem Wiegestuhl zu, sondern so, wie wir es unserm Geiste und Körper angemessen halten ; deshalb hören wir wohl auch einen religiösen Vortrag an, oder lesen in einem Buche, das uns zusagt ; dann aber gehen wir wohl auf die Jagd oder fischen, plaudern so recht gemüthlich in Gesellschaft, und alle vier Wochen gehen wir einmal Sonntags Abends, in unser kleines Theater, wie z. B. letzten Sonntag, wo „Hedwig" von Körner aufgeführt und am Schlusse ein Tänzchen, in Anstand und Ehre, gehalten wurde. Uebrigens lassen wir einen Jeden seinen Tag feiern, wie er will, und wie seine religiöse Ansicht immer sein mag, ist er Jude, Muhamedaner, Heide u. s. w., denn sehen Sie, Herr Missionair, das nennen wir religiöse Duldsamkeit, gegen die ganze Welt, der wir keineswegs in irgend einer Art in religiöser Beziehung Vorschriften geben wollen. Das ist nun so unsere einfältige Meinung, drum kommen Sie lieber nicht nach Hermann, um den Sonntag hier zu verleben, denn Sie würden sich am Ende ärgern, weil Sie nichts als heitere Sonntagsgesichter sehen, und keine langen, trauerklöthigen, englischen Kirchenphysiognomien, die Sie, gestehen Sie es einmal recht ehrlich, gewiss zu Ihrer Sabbathfeier nothwendig halten."

"If the Sabbathmissionary had put a similar question to us in Hermann as he had to the Doctors in Cincinnati, we would have given him the very simple answer, without any doctoral wisdom, to be sure; Mr. Sabbathmissionary, we to be sure, also believe, that people and animals are here not for the purpose of slavery, therefore they require rest and refreshment in conformity to the demands of nature; we also observe our Sunday here, but of course not according to the English, but according to the German custom, i.e., not exclusively in Church or in the rocking chair, but in such a manner as our spirit and body find wholesome,; therefore, we also listen to a religious dissertation or read a book which appeals to us; but then we perhaps go hunting or fishing, converse quite amiably with each other in company, and every four weeks on one Sunday evening we go to our little Theater, as e.g., last Sunday when "Hedwig" by Koerner was presented after which a dance was sensibly and honorably held. For the rest, we let everyone celebrate his day as he wishes, be he Jew, Mohammedan, heathen, etc. for you see, Mr. Missionary, we call that religious toleration towards the whole world to which we by no means wish to dictate in any way in religious matters. This then is our simple opinion, so it would be better for you not to come to Hermann in order to spend your Sunday here, as you would in the end have regrets, because here you would see only cheerful Sunday faces and no long, mournful English Church physiognomies, which you, admit it quite honestly certainly consider necessary to your Sabbath celebration."

Such statements furnish us with the clearest pictures of things at old Hermann, and give us the only rational basis for accounting for the peculiar views now held.

In the autumn of 1847, there was organized at Hermann a society which was appropriately called "Erholung." It was the direct outgrowth of a "Theaterverein" which dates its beginning to the very early days of the colony, and to which Mühl referred in the quotation above given. Under the auspices of the "Erholung" every diversion was permitted that tended towards the amelioration, the enlivenment and cheer of its members, after the burdens of the week had been borne. On Washington's Birthday of 1848, this society presented its first drama. Curiously enough, it was Kotzebue's *Armuth und Edelstein*. Indeed, quite a fondness was shown for this author's plays. This, on the surface, does not argue well for the standards of this "Leibhabertheater." Still, it must be remembered that Kotzebue was once a very popular playwright, even in Germany. More pretentious efforts were made as the society grew older. On August 9, 1852, the *Hermanner Wochenblatt* announced the presentation of Schiller's *Die Räuber*. The society owned its own meeting place, and had it well furnished. Most of the citizens of Hermann were active members of the organization. For fourteen years it was the centre of social activity. During the disturbances of the Civil War the meetings were interrupted. When order was again restored, it appears that the interest and enthusiasm for the cause had waned. Despite the strenuous efforts to arouse the members again, this society ceased to exist in the year 1866.

The interest for dramatic performances is still alive, although a regular "Theaterverein" no longer exists. Every now and then a play is presented, and that quite creditably.

From the very beginning Hermann has had musical organizations, that have contributed to the enjoyment and edification of its inhabitants. In the letter previously quoted from the *Alte und*

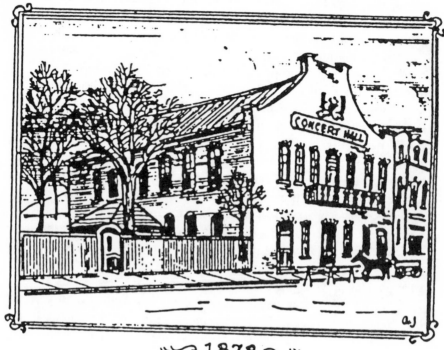

~~> 1878 ~~

THE CONCERT HALL 1878

The Concert Hall was built in 1878 by John Pfautsch and Phillip Kuhn. It contained a tavern and dining room on the first floor and a concert hall, in which four concerts were presented each year, on the second floor. It is still in use as a tavern, the oldest tavern in continuous use west of the Mississippi.

The above picture shows the open beer garden to the east of the building. In 1916 this lot was sold to the bank.

This two-story building originally had an iron balcony, now replaced by a porch over the sidewalk.

When Congress passed the 18th amendment the Concert Hall became an Ice Cream Parlor. The back room still dispensed beer and "booze." One of the former owners said, "The Concert Hall was never without beer at anytime— even during prohibition. I made the home-brew in 50 gallon crocks and I could mention 50 stills operating in Gasconade County then that made whiskey."

The building also housed Hermann's first two-lane bowling alley and from 1915 to 1923 was the only motion picture theatre in Hermann.

Großes Konzert

— veranstaltet vom —

Gesangverein Harmonie

— unter Leitung von —

Prof. Ernst Buddemeyer

— am —

Mittwoch, den 26. Dezember, 1906

— in der —

Conzert Halle.

Programm

1. Hochzeitsmarsch ....von Mendelsohn.
   (Streich-Orchester.)
2. Schön Rothtraut...........................von P. Feil.
   (Harmonie Männerchor.)
3. Lorbeer und Rose, Vocal-Duet ....von Grell.
   (Fräulein E. Leisner und L. Ochsner)
4. Grüße an die Heimath ....von Kromer.
   (Harmonie Gemischter Chor.)
5. Hoch der Wein, Trio für 3 Männerstimmen ......von Kuntze.
   Die Herren E. Kimmel A. Naegelin Theo. Graf.
6. Die Post im Walde ....von Schäfer.
   (Harmonie Männerchor, Cornet Solo Herr F. Reuße.)
7. „Selection aus" Mascot ....von Andran.
   (Streich-Orchester.)

Pause.

8. Lucrezia Borgia ....von Donizetti.
   (Streich-Orchester.)
6. Heda, Wein Her!...........................von Zöllner.
   (Harmonie Männerchor.)
10. Ein musikalischer Kaffeeklatsch...............von Schäffel.
    (Die Fräul. Juanita Graf u Martha Kient.)
11. „Ballade", Die 3 Liebchen; Bass Solo.
    (Herr Julius Moebus)
12. Mailied ....von Mendelsohn.
    (Gemischter Chor.)
13. O Schöner Wald.......................von Engelskirchen.
    (Harmonie Männerchor)
14. Violin Solo 6. Aria und Variation Dankla.
    [Prof. Ernst Buddemeier.]
15. Eine gemischte Gesellschaft, komische Scene für 5 Personen..
    von Simon.
    Handwerksburſche ....Herr E. F. Rippstein
    Sachſe ....Herr W. Mundwiller.
    Engländer..........................Theo. Graf
    Adele reiſende Dame ....Geo. Kient.
    Rattenfallen Händler ....Julius Moebus.
16. „On to Panama Marsch." ....von Armstrong.
    (Streich-Orchester.)

Nach dem Konzert findet ein Tanzkränzchen statt.

CONCERT PROGRAM.

Neue Welt for June 15, 1839, we saw that Hermann, even then, had a "Musik-Chor mit Blech Instrumenten." In 1844 a musical organization existed, which has, under one name or another, perpetuated itself until this very day. Proof of the existence of such a body is found in the minutes of the trustees of the town, who, on March 11th, 1844, voted "That the society for vocal music, existing and known by the name of 'Hermann Männerchor,' be allowed to have the use of the school house for their vocal exercises." At present such an organization of thirty members exists under the name of "Harmonie." To our question as to whether the club still continued its work, Mr. Glatte, the director, wrote: "Jawohl und erst am 10. d. M. (March, 1906) hat der Verein ein recht schönes Konzert gegeben."* At different times we have heard some delightful orchestra concerts at Hermann. It is, of course, impossible to hold an orchestra together the year around in such a small place. Mr. Glatte says concerning it:

> „Ein Orchester trommle ich gewöhnlich zusammen für unser jährliches Harmonie-Konzert. Wir beginnen unsere regelmässigen Uebungen ein paar Monate vor dem Konzert, und das Konzert selbst markirt den Tag der Auflösung der Vereinigung. „Der Mohr hat seine Arbeit gethan, der Mohr kann gehen."

"I usually drum together an orchestra for our annual Harmonie Concert. We begin our regular practices several months preceding the concert, the concert itself marks the day of the dissolution of the organization. The "Moor has done his work; the Moor can go."

A brass band, passing under the pious name of "Apostel Band," contributes to the enjoyment of all public gatherings at the park.

Some twenty-five years ago, a Turnverein was organized at Hermann, and for some time flourished. To our question as to its present condition and activity, Mr. Glatte writes, in the letter above referred to:

---

*"Yes, indeed, and just on March 10, 1906, the organization presented a very fine concert."

„Finanziel in vorzüglicher Verfassung, aber schon seit ca. einem Jahre suspendirt. Es ist nicht möglich gewesen genügend Leute dafür zu interessieren und regelrechte Turnabende abzuhalten."

"Financially in excellent condition, but has been suspended about a year. It was not possible to interest sufficient people in it and to conduct regular Turn-evenings."

Of fraternal organizations, Hermann has three, viz.: the "Masonic," the "Independent Order of Odd Fellows" and the "Knights of Pythias." Of these, the lodge of Odd Fellows needs special mention, in that all their ritualistic work is conducted in German. There are ten other such lodges in Missouri working in German—seven in St. Louis, one in St. Joseph, one in Kansas City, and one in Lexington. The lodge at Hermann is named Robert Blum Lodge, No. 46. It was organized on April 27th, 1850, and named after the German patriot, Robert Blum, who was executed November 9th, 1848. It goes almost without saying that the founders of this lodge belonged to that renowned class of immigrants known as the Forty-eighters, or, at least, were ardent sympathizers with the radical movement that sought to liberate and unify the Fatherland. To commemorate the events of those years, they erected the martyr Blum a monument in the name of their lodge.*

In the days of the independent thinker and fearless opponent to every form of slavery—Eduard Mühl—many of the wide-awake residents of Hermann were united into a unique society, known as "Der Verein Freier Männer." As we learn from the *Hermanner Wochenblatt* of April 9, 1852,* this body had then

---

* For the information regarding the Lodge of I. O. O. F., we are indebted to Mr. L. E. Robyn, of Hermann, who communicated with the Grand Lodge of St. Louis for us.

* For volumes of valuable newspapers edited by Mr. Mühl, I am indebted to his kindhearted widow, still living in Hermann.

just been organized. We read there: "Am vergangenen Sonntag, als am 4ten, fand die Eröffnung des Vereines 'Freier Männer' allhier statt."* Mühl delivered an address at the opening. This

EDUARD MÜHL.—1800-1854.

*"The Organization of Free Men".

*"The past Sunday, on the 4th, the opening session of the Organization of Free Men took place here."

address was introduced and interspersed with original poetic snatches, as was Mühl's pleasure when he addressed a body of men. We insert here some of these verses. They breathe the purpose of the organization:

Gesang bei Eröffnung des Vereins Freier Männer, dem Verein gewidmet von E. Mühl.

(Mel.: Freiheit, die ich meine.)

Reicht die Hand zum Bunde,
Freie Männer euch,
Ernst ist diese Stunde,
An Bedeutung reich:
Denn es gilt das Ringen
Nach Freiheit und Licht,
Muthig durchzudringen,
Dass der Tag anbricht.

Ja wir sind die Kinder
Einer neuen Zeit,
Weih'n uns als Verkünder,
(Und das ungescheut)
Eines freiern Lebens,
Frei von Glaubenswahn,
Eines höhern Strebens
Auf der Menschheit Bahn.

Nicht was Priester lehrten
Gilt uns Gottes Wort,
Die die Welt bethörten,
Uebten Geistesmord:
Wenn sie blinden Glauben,
Der Vernunft zum Hohn,
Forderten, und rauben
So Selbstdenkens Lohn.

Was einst Weise dachten,
Dankbar sei's erkannt,
Wenn an's Licht sie brachten,
Was noch unbekannt;
Doch nicht sklavisch binden
Möge uns ihr Wort,
Wir selbst müssen finden
Prüfend fort und fort.

So nur sind wir Freie,
Kinder der Vernunft,
Unserm Glauben Weihe
Giebt nicht Priesterzunft;

Unser höchstes Streben
Ist nur Sittlichkeit,
Das ist göttlich Leben,
Wahre Frömmigkeit.

Ja lasst Hass uns schwören
Jeder Tyrannei,
Jedem Unrecht wehren
Ohne Menschenscheu.
So, zum heil'gen Bunde,
Reicht die Hände euch;
Drum ist ernst die Stunde
An Bedeutung reich."*

Song at the opening of the Organization of Free Men, dedicated to the Organization by E. Muehl.

*

"Give your hands in union
All you free men here,
Serious is this hour,
With a wealth of meaning.
For at stake is all the striving
Towards freedom and light
To courageously press onward,
Till the daylight breaks.

Indeed we are the children
Of a new era,
We dedicate ourselves as messengers
(And that without fear).

---

* This poem and the following is taken from Mühl's *Hermanner Woch-enblatt*, of April 9, 1852.

*"The assembly sang the above mentioned song, supported by a male chorus under the direction of Mr. Kerch."

Of a freer life,
Free from fanatic beliefs,
To a higher striving,
On the path of humanity.

Not what priests have taught
Do we accept as God's word,
Those who deceive the world,
Committed the murder of the spirit.
Where they demanded blind faith,
Scorning all reason
And thereby robbed
The reward of individuality.

What once wise people thought,
Is thankfully recognized,
When they brought to light
That which had lain unknown;
But may their word
Not slavishly bind us
We ourselves must seek,
Inquiringly on and on.

Only so shall we be free,
Children of reason,
The dedication of our faith
Is not wrought by the company of priests,
Our highest striving
Is only morality,
That is divine life,
True piousness.

Indeed let us bid defiance
To every tyranny,
Avoid every injustice,

Without fearing people.
So, to this holy covenant,
Give all your hands
For serious is this hour
Rich in meaning."

The editor of the paper says: „Die Versammlung stimmte obiges Lied an, mit Unterstützung eines Männerchor, unter Leitung des Herrn Kerch."

In opening his address Mühl spoke the following verses:

„Vorwärts! ruft's, wie Klang der Glocken,
In der Ferne liegt das Ziel.
Lasst euch nicht abseite locken,
In dem wirren Weltgewühl:
Blickt in eurem Lebenslauf,
Nach den Sternen kühn hinauf!

Alles ringt, sich zu vollenden,
In der Freiheit Sonnenschein,
Mögt ihr eure Blicke wenden,
Selbst auf's kleinste Gräselein.
Drum ringe Mensch auch du
Höherer Vollendung zu.

Wage nur in deinem Streben
Stets ein *freier Mann* zu sein,
Drücke tief in deinem Leben
Du der Freiheit Bild hinein.
Jeder höhere Gewinn
Stammt aus wahrem Freiheitssinn.

Und so grüss' in solchem Glauben
Ich Euch, „Freie Männer" heut.
Lasset ihn durch nichts Euch rauben,
Wirket für ihn ungescheut!
Ja, dann wird unser Verein
Mehr als blosser Name sein.

"Onward! is the call, like peal of bells,
In the distance lies the goal.
Do not let yourselves be misled
In the confused tumult of the world;
Look on your life's course,
Boldly up to the stars!

Everything strives to perfect itself,
In the sunshine of freedom,
Even when you cast your glance
On the smallest blade of grass.
Therefore, man, you also should
Strive toward higher perfection.

Venture always in your striving
To be continually a free man,
Stamp deeply into your life
The image of freedom.
Every nobler gain
Arises from the spirit of freedom.

And consequently in this faith
I greet you "Free Men" today,
Do not let anything rob you of it,
Work fearlessly for it!
Yes, for then our organization
Will be more than a mere name.

The newspaper continues thus:

„Der Redner fasste nun den Namen dieses Vereins und gab eine
Darlegung des Begriffes, den man nothwendig mit einem „freien
Manne" zu verbinden habe. Ein freier Mann (ward nun ange-
geben):
Verwerfe allen und jeden blinden Glauben. Er bekenne offen
und ungescheut seine gewonnenen Ansichten und Grundsätze. An

dem was eine Zeit bewegt, in der Nähe, wie in der Ferne, nimmt er den thätigsten Antheil, indem er mit aller ihm gegebenen Kraft in die Angelegenheiten einzugreifen und nie nach den Grundsätzen der Aufklärung und Freiheit, zu gestalten ringet."

"Then the speaker referred to the name of this organization and presented an exposition of the concept which must necessarily characterize a "free man". A free man must (it was stated):

Discard all and every blind faith. He must openly and fearlessly confess his acquired opinions and principles. He takes a most active part in that which agitates the times, whether near-by or at a distance, by striving to participate in these circumstances with all his inherited powers according to the principles of enlightenment and freedom."

In closing, the speaker said:

„Der Dienst der Freiheit ist ein strenger Dienst.
Er bringt nicht Gold, nicht allgemeine Gunst,
Er bringt Verleugnung stets, viel Kämpfe, ja oft selbst den Tod.
Und doch ist dieser Dienst ein hehrer Dienst:
Wer sich mit ganzer Treue ihm ergeben,
Den führt er siegreich in ein heil'ges Leben."

The service of freedom is a strict service
It brings not gold, not universal favor
It brings denial always, many struggles,
    indeed often death itself.
And yet this service is a noble service:
Whoever devotes himself to it in complete fidelity
Is led by it victoriously into a holy life."

Before adjournment, the society sang Mühl's verse:

„Kampf sei unser Losungswort,
Für das Wahre, Edle, Gute;
Und der Freiheit, unserm Hort,
Dienen wir mit Männer Muthe.
Freie Männer wahr und treu,
Ewig unser Wahlspruch sei."

"May battle be our choice,
For the true, the noble, the good;
And freedom, our refuge,
We serve with manly courage.
Free men, true and faithful,
Be our eternal motto."

At its very beginning the Verein had 51 names on its membership list. The purpose of the organization, as can be inferred from the aforesaid, was to stimulate independence of thought, to encourage fearless investigation, to hold up as beacon lights liberty, truth and justice; to teach right living by precept and example. It must be lamented that this commendable body could not long exist. Its life-force was centered in its founder, Eduard Mühl. When, on July 7, 1854, this singularly endowed man passed over into another world, there was no one upon whom the mantle of this leader of men should fall, and soon the society disbanded. Freidrich Münch, a strong advocate of such movements, and who had supported Mühl in his endeavors, was too far removed to hold intact the society.

Mühl's last words teem with the thought predominant in him throughout his whole eventful life:

„Der Freiheit war mein ganzes Leben geweiht, und ich sterbe als freier Mann. Ich habe meine Schuldigkeit zu thun gesucht, thut Ihr die Eurige; und möchtet Ihr die Freiheit voller und schöner blühen sehen, als mir leider vergönnt war!"*

"My entire life was dedicated to freedom, and I die as a free man. I have tried to do my duty—you do yours, and may you see freedom flourish more fully and abundantly, which unfortunately was denied to me."

---

* *"Deut. Am. Konversations Lexikon,* Vol. VII., p. 581.

His tomb at Hermann bears this inscription: "Eduard Mühl, Geboren den 4ten August 1800, Gestorben den 7ten Juli 1854. Mit- und Nachwelt! Ehre den muthigen Streiter für Wahrheit und Menschenrecht!"

"Eduard Muehl, born August 4, 1800; died July 7, 1854.

To the present and the future World! Honor the Courageous Fighter for Truth and Human Justice."

He strove not only for mental freedom, but unceasingly advocated the emancipation of the slaves. He was the man who possessed the intrepidity to openly denounce the practice of slavery, notwithstanding the summary vengeance that had been heaped upon other self-appointed opponents of the practice. His love for the sweets of liberty was too strong to be hushed by threats. From the fullness of his heart he spoke, always fearlessly, but without bitterness and without malice. Alas, that it was not permitted him to hear the shouts of freedom that went up ten years after his death! Alas, that he could not live to participate in the meeting of his grateful fellow-townsmen when they assembled to carry out this resolution of the trustees of the town, passed January 12, 1865: "To call a citizens' meeting to take place on the 13th inst., for the purpose of making the necessary preparations for a worthy and general celebration of the deliverance of Missouri from the yoke of slavery."

Mühl was the man who set up the first German printing press on the Missouri. In Cincinnati, Ohio, he had established a paper, which he most fittingly termed *Licht-Freund*. It was fitting because of the principles which the paper defended. It was the organ of a "Freisinniges Deutschtum," which sought to stand on the lofty heights of truth, leaving all superstition far below. In the summer of 1843, Mühl wandered towards the West, taking his printing press with him. He longed for a home close to the bosom of unpolluted nature for a quiet spot where he might better hear the promptings of his real self within. At Hermann he con-

---

*"*Free-Thinking German Culture*"

tinued publishing his paper. His brother-in-law, Strehly, co-operated with him in this work. On the 23d of August, 1843, the first number appeared in Hermann. It was the fourth volume of the publication, three volumes having been issued at Cincinnati. The mottoes which prefaced the first page were these:

„Prüfet aber Alles, und das Gute behaltet." 1 Thess. 5 : 21.*
„Welche Religion ich bekenne? Keine von allen, die Du mir nennst. — Und warum keine? — Aus Religion." — Schiller.
„Es giebt unempfängliche Zeiten, was aber ewig ist findet immer seine Zeit."

"Prove all things, hold fast that which is good. I Thes. 5, 21."

"Which religion I confess? None of all those that you name to me. And why none? On religious grounds.—Schiller"

"There are unimpressionable times, but that which is eternal is acceptable at all times."

Through this paper Mühl hoped to disseminate the light of truth among his countrymen. But, alas, only a few could, or did, appreciate his efforts. The strenuous struggle for an existence absorbed them more than philosophical discourse. In consequence, the publication became unprofitable. The country was yet too young to find time or pleasure in such heavy discussions. In 1845, the same editors abandoned the *Licht-Freund* and in its stead issued the *Hermanner Wochenblatt,* which preserved but few of the characteristics of the old paper, being a carrier of news in the general sense. This paper has survived, under varying fortunes and is now published under the new name of *Hermanner Volksblatt.* Sporadic attempts have been made to launch other publications at Hermann. Such undertakings were always short-lived. An English paper has existed at Hermann for some time, under the title of *Advertiser-Courier.* It is under the same management as the *Volksblatt,* namely, the Graf Brothers.

Other demonstrations of literary activity since the death of Mühl are not worth consideration here.

---

* In the first number of the *"Licht-Freund,"* issued at Hermann, an error exists in the citation of the Bible reference, 1 Corinthians being printed instead of 1 Thessalonians as it later correctly appeared.

CHAPTER III
Then and Now
1836—1986
Dorothy Heckmann Shrader

The reader will wonder about the destiny of this idealistically conceived German colony—about what has happened in the century-and-a-half since the founding in 1836. Have the ideals been met, customs preserved? Where is Hermann today in relation to the dreams of the Germans who committed their lives to this venture in a new and strange land?

Gone is the Harmonie, that wonderful, convivial group of lusty and talented singers, gone is the Männerchor, the men's chorus. Instead the churches boast of great choirs who sing not only at their respective church services but provide annual concerts for the general public. The historic pageants and the Rotunda Show are showcases for local talent.

Gone, too, is the Turnverein, the gymnasts of the early settlers. In its place Hermann provides an ardent following for the high school Bearcats and the Ladycats. The early Keglers have been replaced by a modern bowling alley.

The Schützenverein no longer carries that name but the Rod and Gun Club carries on the tradition of "sharpshooters" with a modern club house and shooting range.

LANGUAGE

The German accent is still heard but few today are bilingual. Fourth generation descendants of the first Germans to arrive are now the elders of the community. For them, German was still their first language. The dream of a totally bilingual community was carefully provided for until World War I. This conflict nearly brought about the death of the dream. No longer could German be taught in the schools. To be bilingual was no longer an asset. By the time of World War II the idea of maintaining the language had died.

Today the interest in German is again on the upswing. Adult conversation classes at the High School are packed. In 1984, Glen Cody, German teacher, took 43 of his High School students to Germany on a language intensive tour to Munich, the Alps, Black Forest, Heidelberg, a cruise on the Rhine and then spent eight days with host families in Ulm. A Sister-City program will be a part of the Sesquicentennial celebration.

ARCHITECTURE

Hermann today has an Old World charm. The architecture is distinctly German, perhaps even more so than Germany itself. The early settlers built houses just like the homes they remembered in Germany. Since many of those homes were already of considerable age, the Hermann copies are just of more recent construction. Thanks to the early foresight of a dedicated group of preservation minded citizens, this architectural heritage has been in large part saved. More than 150 homes are on the National Register of Historic Properties and more are being added each year. Several of the historic homes are open for house tours by prior appointment. The Brush and Palette Club purchased and maintained the Pommer-Gentner house and the Strehly house for years. These properties were donated to the Department of Natural Resources and are now designated as "Deutschheim". Both buildings are open for tours at designated hours.

Historic Hermann, Inc. became the custodian of the German School in 1955. This school, built by local funds, not tax funds, had served the community as the elementary school since 1871. The German School houses the municipal offices and the license bureau, and provides a meeting room for the public—all on the first floor. The second floor houses the museums of Historic Hermann, Inc. The Heritage Room was first established in 1956, the River Room in 1964, the Kinder (Children's) Room in 1969, and the Handwerk (Handwork) Corner in 1971. The museums are open to the public. More than 20,000 visited the museums in 1983.

HISTORIC HERMANN, INC.

Historic Hermann, Inc. established an incentive award in 1979 to promote greater interest in the preservation of historical properties. This annual $1,000 award is based on the owners interest in retaining original architectural features when possible, replacing features with matching design when the original is damaged beyond repair, adding new additions or alterations consistent with the character of the building and finding a practical purpose for the building compatible with the plan, structure and appearance of the building.

A number of historic properties were purchased by Historic Hermann, Inc. to save them from destruction. The Reiff house, on Market Street, was one of these properties. It was resold to the First Missouri Bank. Now completely restored, it is the home of the Drive-In facility for the bank. Other properties were sold to individuals who would restore them.

Historic Hermann was organized in 1954 by a group of public spirited citizens. The objects and purposes of the organization were: to extend appreciation of the area as one of the early German settlements in America through the annual celebrations; to preserve historic sites of Hermann and the vicinity and to encourage preservation and restoration thereof; to promote research and publish findings regarding local history, arts, crafts, culture and education; to foster patriotism and to maintain and extend the institutions of American Freedom, and to provide a museum.

Historic Hermann has faithfully carried out these objectives.

The Cooperage Craft Center, opened in 1980, now displays and sells the work of more than 180 craftsmen and artists. The Craft Center sponsors workshops in painting, weaving and basketry. The director is a local artist. Two resident potters and two assistants make up the staff. The Center is next to the Hermannhof Winery.

In January, 1984, the First Missouri Bank of Gasconade County in Hermann announced the donation of the Showboat Theatre to Historic Hermann Inc., with the agreement that the building be operated as a community theatre. The Showboat project is operated under a separate board but is ultimately responsible to Historic Hermann. The theatre is used for classes, entertainment and for community art's programs. The 400-seat theatre is the first community auditorium.

Historic Hermann's **COOPERAGE** Craft Center

338 East first st.
Hermann, Missouri,
phone 314-486-3313

SELF-GUIDED WALK THROUGH HISTORIC DISTRICT
Maps, compliments of Historic Hermann, Inc.,
available at the German School.

Then and Now

Scharnhorst-Eitzen House, Built in 1855

Harrison-Poeschel House, Built in 1861

Stark Mansion, Built in 1885

Schweighauser-Klenk House, Built in 1841

Graf House, Built in 1892

White House Hotel (Plummer) Built about 1865

City Park Rotunda and Band Stand
1876

Olivo-Bottermiller-Rommel House, Built in 1852

DEUTSCHHEIM

𝕿𝖍𝖊 𝕾𝖙𝖗𝖊𝖍𝖑𝖞 𝕳𝖔𝖚𝖘𝖊

CIRCA 1842

STREHLY HOUSE

In 1842 Carl Strehly and Eduard Muehl came to Hermann and built the Strehly house. They set up their printing press in the basement and published the "LICHTFREUND" and the "HERMANNER WOCHENBLATT" newspapers.

In 1860, Carl Strehly started a wine company. For this he built the two-story addition to the Strehly house with its deep vaulted cellar. The Brush and Palette Club bought the house after the death of Rosa Strehly in 1961.

The Strehly house was donated to the Department of Natural Resources and as a part of Deutschheim, is open to the public.

This history of Hermann must give recognition to Anna Kemper Hesse, local artist and historian. Her research on the architecture of Hermann and vicinity is available in book form from the Historic Hermann Museums and from the Brush and Palette Club. (The Centenarians and Gasconade County Tours). Her historical pageants are also available in book form.   ·

DEUTSCHHEIM

𝕿𝖍𝖊 𝕲𝖊𝖓𝖙𝖓𝖊𝖗 𝕳𝖔𝖚𝖘𝖊

CIRCA 1848

GENTNER HOUSE

G. Henry Gentner and his wife arrived in Hermann with the first 17 people of the "Deutsche Ansiedlungs Gesellschaft zu Philadelphia," on December 6, 1837 on the last boat of the season.

In 1848 Gentner bought the Pommer house for $1,500.

In 1953 the Brush and Palette Club bought the house for the same amount in order to save it from destruction. The club maintained the house until they donated it to the Missouri Department of Parks and Natural Resources.

The Department has restored the house and it is open to the public at scheduled hours as a State Historic Site.

The Brush and Palette Club
"We are dedicated to beauty, perpetuation and wise utilization of our natural heritage; the preservation and the restoration of our cultural past."

HERMANN AREA DISTRICT HOSPITAL

Hermann has had remarkably good medical care. The Hermann Area District Hospital serves a large area.

The Hospital was dedicated in June 1967 and three major buildings have been added since.

The Hospital is a 46-bed facility with 125 employees. There are six physicians on the active medical staff plus two doctors on the dental staff, 10 doctors on the courtesy staff and 25 on the consulting staff. The hospital is equipped with the finest laboratory, radiology, and physical therapy equipment and staff. There is a 3-bed intensive care unit.

Ambulance service for this area is provided by the Hermann Area Ambulance District. Emergency medical technicians are on call 24 hours, day or night.

HERMANN FIRE COMPANY NO. 1, INC.

The Hermann Volunteer Fire Company was organized in 1859 and celebrated its 125th anniversary in 1984. At this time there were 35 active members who all give of their time as a service to the community. No salaries are paid. A $10.00 to $12.00 per household fee is the source of funds for equipment and supplies.

The new Fire House on Highway 100 was built in 1971. Financing was by donations and most of the labor was by volunteers. The equipment consists of 8 trucks, 4 pumpers, 3 brush trucks and 1 tanker.

POPULATION

Population figures have never really boomed in Hermann. In the fall of 1837 the first seventeen persons arrived at the site, then a wilderness. The next spring another 230 arrived and by 1839 the number had grown to 450. The 1850 census showed 860 persons in Hermann and about 1000 in Roark Township just outside of the city limits.

After 1850 growth slowed. The 1980 census shows 2600 inhabitants. The surrounding territory has many suburban homes whose owners consider themselves Hermannites. Hermann today attracts many retirees but few young people.

CHURCHES

The need for spiritual guidance was an early priority.

In 1840 the nucleus of the St. George Catholic church was organized. No resident priest was assigned to the church until 1849. The first church building was finished in 1849. In 1868 the parochial school was started and by 1916 a new church was built.

Looking West on Fourth Street

CHURCHES

In 1841 the beginnings of the St. Paul Evangelical church came about through the organization of two different religious groups. By 1844 the new group adopted the name St. Paul Evangelical Church, now the United Church of Christ. At this time the first church was built, the first in Hermann. A steeple was added after 1884. By 1907 the need for a larger church was evident and the new church was erected on the same site. A parsonage and many renovations and remodelings have followed.

The spiritual needs of the citizens are also met by the First United Pentecostal Church on Washington and the New Life Fellowship on Market.

CHURCHES

The Hermann Methodist Church was organized in 1844 but few regular meetings were held due to the lack of a regular minister. By 1883 a brick church was built, the gift of an old, childless couple. This church was remodeled in 1924. In 1969 a new church was built on Highway 100.

The Baptists in Hermann organized in the early 1950's. In 1981 they dedicated a new church at 14th and Market.

CHURCHES

The "old" Methodist Church building at First and Market is now the home of the Hermann Christian Church.

The Shepherd of the Hills Lutheran Congregation organized in 1982. The new church building is one mile south on Highway 19. The dedication was held in August of 1983.

Hermann R-1 District High School

Hermann R-1 Junior High School

Herman R-1 Elementary School

SCHOOLS

The first item of business of the early colonists was a roof over their heads. The second priority was a school for their children. The matter of education was of prime importance to them.

From Bek's accounts they were also very particular as is witnessed by the rapid change-over in teachers, including George Bayer.

Today the school district has extended out for a radius of 350 square miles and approximately 1100 pupils are enrolled. The district has an Elementary School, Junior High School and Senior High School. The schools are in the Hermann R-1 district.

St. George Catholic Church also has a parochial Elementary School.

St. George Elementary School

EITZEN

Charles Eitzen, often referred to as the town benefactor, became a millionaire through astute business acumen. He hauled iron ore and white pine lumber up to Hermann from the Meramec Iron Furnaces and Ozark forests, a distance of about 65 miles. He engaged in this business from 1840 to 1860. Previous to the establishment of the Chouteau Iron Works in St. Louis, these 100 lb. iron blooms found their way to Cincinnati, Wheeling and Pittsburgh. About two tons was the usual load for a team of from 4 to 8 yoke of oxen. These teams always returned to Meramec loaded down with dry goods and provisions for the men working there. Eitzen owned the local mercantile store in Hermann. The iron ore and the pine lumber was transshipped by steamboat and rail.

As Bek relates, Eitzen willed the county nearly $50,000 with the stipulation that a Gasconade County Courthouse be erected in Hermann with this money. The present courthouse is that building and is the only one erected with private funds in the entire United States. It is open to the public.

𝔜𝔢𝔰𝔱𝔢𝔯𝔡𝔞𝔶   **ON THIRD STREET**   MARY A. STRECK

NEWSPAPERS

Through the years, Hermann's newspapers have been recognized for their contribution to the community's growth and progress through the endorsement and support of city, school and industrial improvement programs. They are further identified with the revival of emphasis on Hermann's German heritage and rich historical background that emerged following the first Maifest in 1952. Much of the community's renown as a tourist center may be traced to the publications' efforts in support of the Maifest through the years.

No recap of the history of Hermann could be complete without the recognition of the Graf family. Although no fewer than 13 newspapers, including seven German-language periodicals, have been published in Hermann's history, only one, the Advertiser Courier, has survived and in 1984 is in its 110th year of publication.

The Advertiser Courier, published by four generations of the Graf family since being launched in 1873, is now owned by James Anderson, who purchased the parent business, Graf Printing Company, in 1981.

Jacob Graf founded the company in 1854 with the establishment of the German-language Hermanner Volksblatt. After the death of the founder the publication of the newspaper continued under the direction of his widow, his sons and his grandsons. Julius J. Graf, great grandson of the founder became editor and publisher in 1950 at the death of Leander Guy Graf and continued in that capacity until the sale of the newspaper in 1981.

The Advertiser -Courier

Licht-Freund.

Prüfet aber Alles, und das Gute behaltet.
[1 Cor. 5, 21.

Welche Religion ich bekenne? Keine von allen, die Du mir nennst.—Und warum keine? Aus Religion. [Schiller.

Es giebt unempfängliche Zeiten, was aber ewig ist findet immer seine Zeit.

Herausgegeben von E. Mühl und Strehly.

Jahrgang 4.   **Hermann, Mo., Mittwoch, August, 23. 1843.**   **No. 1.**

☞ Bedingungen.—Dieses Blatt erscheint monatlich zweimal und kostet 1 Dollar jährlich. Ohne Vorausbezahlung wird kein Blatt ausgegeben. Agenten, welche ein Vorausbezahlung Unterschreiber annehmen, machen wir für die Bezahlung verantwortlich. Alle Briefe und Mittheilungen, so wie Geldsendungen, müssen postfrei eingesandt werden. Alle Herausgeber deutscher Zeitungen welche, mit uns wechseln, sind ersucht, sich der Agentschaft zu unterziehen.

Vorwort
beim Beginne des vierten Jahrganges.

Indem ich die Ufer des Ohio verließ um mich an denen des Missouri anzusiedeln, meine Umgebung aber so eine ganz neue geworden ist, mag es angemessen erscheinen, daß ich in diesem Blatte, mit dem ich den vierten Jahrgang beginne, einige Worte an meine deutschen Genossen richte, mit denen ich, sie freundlich begrüßend, hier in ihre Mitte trete, zugleich bittend, mich mir eben dem Vertrauen aufzunehmen, welches mich unter sie führte.

Wir sind, meine Genossen, die Kinder einer großen und gewaltigen Zeit, die wir erlebten, in unserm Heimathlande jenseits des Meeres. Jene Kämpfe aber, welche wir dort sahen u. an denen wir alle mehr oder weniger Theil nahmen, hatten ihren Grund und ihre Ursache in höherer Bildung, zu welcher die Geschlechter fortgeschritten waren, die so zu höherem Selbstbewußtsein gelangt, ihre Rechte und Pflichten erwogen, und die Mündigkeit aussprachen, nun aber auch verlangten, daß man sie aus einer Vormundschaft lasse, welche wohl für ein Geschlecht der Kindheit getaugt, einem zur Mannbarkeit aber herangereiften entehrend erscheinen mußte. Dies aber eben veranlaßte die vielfachen Bewegungen, welche wir erlebten, das Alte trat mit dem Neuen in Kampf, und ein neuer Zeitraum in der Völkergeschichte hatte begonnen. Das Ende dieses Kampfes, welcher noch fortwährt, wollten wir nicht erwarten, weil es nicht in unser Lebensalter fallen wollte, und wir zogen in dies Land, welches man das der Freiheit nennt, wo jedem Raum gegönnt wird, sich nach seiner Ueberzeugung zu bewegen und auszuleben.

Beziehe sich das jetzt Erwähnte vorzüglich auf das Feld des politischen Lebens, so müssen wir die Bemerkung hinzufügen: daß auch auf dem Gebiete der Religion große Bewegungen stattfanden wurden, und Kämpfe entstanden, welche eine neue Zeit verkündigten. Denn wenn die an Bildung fortgeschrittenen und sich freier fühlenden Geister die politische Dogmatik zu bekämpfen wagten, und sich von keinem Machtworte der Aristokratie in ihrer Untersuchung und Prüfung stören ließen, so erhielt es mir ganz consequent und natürlich, daß man auch auf das Gebiet der Religion und Kirche hinübertrat, und eben auch dasselbe Recht der Prüfung und Forschung geltend machte, wenn man den Völkern eine Dogmatik des religiösen Glaubens als unumstößlich und unwandelbar hingestellt hatte. Zu dieser Prüfung auf religiösem Gebiete gab vorzüglich die Reformation des 16ten Jahrhunderts in Deutschland Veranlaßung. Denn nachdem die Hierarchie der römischen Kirche bis zu der unglaublichsten Ausschweifung gekommen war, daß sie die Gewißen nicht nur sich ganz zu Sclaven gemacht, und selbst den unverschämtesten und ruchlosesten Handel mit den Sünden der Welt getrieben hatte, die sie für Geld sich abkaufen ließ, um es von der Priester- und Pfaffenwelt in Wollüsten aller Art vergeuden zu laßen, so war doch diese Sünde so thierisch und teuflisch raffinirt, als daß sie nicht hätte sollen bei den denkenden Zeitgenoßen Unwillen und Entrüstung erregen. Die Reformation ging von dem Grundsatze der Prüfung und Forschung auf dem Gebiete der Religion aus, worauf die Reformatoren ganz natürlich geleitet werden mußten, um einen sichern Halt zu gewinnen, und Rom wurde auch jetzt in kirchlicher Beziehung in seinen Grundfesten erschüttert und gedemüthigt, wie dies früher ihm schon in politischer ergangen war.

Der Grundsatz des Reformationszeitalters, nämlich der Prüfung und Forschung auf religiösem Gebiete, wurde von da an eine neue Zeitidee, die sich in das Leben eindrängte und sich mit Macht suchte geltend zu machen. Diese Idee, damals hingeworfen gleichsam nur, und beschränkt aufgefaßt von den Reformatoren, ist im Verlauf von drei Jahrhunderten weiter u. freier aufgefaßt worden, als man sagen. Die Reformatoren nämlich nahmen die christlichen Schriften des alten und neuen Testamentes als den einzigen Glaubensgrund an, und opponirten so der römischen Kirche, welche sich auf Tradition berief, durch welche sie allerdings in so vielen Dingen, den Aussprüche des Stifters der christlichen Religion und seinen Jüngern stracks entgegentrat. Aber das todte Wort der Bibel blieb doch noch ihr leitender Stern in Sachen des Glaubens gleichsam nur, und beweist die Dogmatik oder die Glaubenslehre, welche wir noch in den protestantischen Kirche antreffen, welche aber der gesunden Vernunft oft eben so widerspricht, als die der römischen Kirche, und des Unsinnes und Widerspruches so viel enthält, daß man sich nicht erwehren kann, ein tiefes Bedauern auszusprechen.

Jedoch auch diese Dogmatik mußte sich überleben, nachdem man durch Hülfe der Wissenschaften, welche nicht mehr die Magd der Kirche, wie früher, waren, sondern sich frei entfalten und bewegen konnten, auf ganz andere Ansichten geleitet wurde, als die waren, welche man bisher mit den Worten und Aussprüchen in den christlichen Schriften verbunden hatte. Auch gelang man zu der Ueberzeugung, daß jene religiösen Schriftsteller, gleich andern Menschen, den Einflüssen ihrer Zeit und ihres Volkes unterworfen waren, und somit auch so manchen Vorurtheilen, welche die Bildung jener Zeit bezeichneten. So Vieles aber, was uns als Wunder aus jener Zeit erzählt wird, vermögen wir als ganz natürliche Erscheinung jetzt darzulegen. Wo aber dies uns nicht möglich ist, glauben wir doch alles übernatürlich Wundervolle leugnen zu müßen, weil uns ein Blick in die große Hausordnung der Welt lehrt, daß eine ewige Weisheit, welche waltet und regiert, nach stets gleichbleibenden Gesetzen, die sie in die Ordnung der Dinge legte, verfährt, und ein Wunder zugleich ein Aufheben dieser Ordnung sein würde, was der Weisheit des Schöpfers widersprechen müßte, weil sie dadurch zu erkennen geben würde, sie habe etwas Unvollkommenes gethan, darum müßte sie die Lücke nur b ein Wunder ausfüllen. Soll ich aber den leitenden Grundsatz heraußstellen, nach dem man sich bei dem Annehmen oder Verwerfen des religiösen Glaubens richtete, so ist es der: „Man kann nur das glauben, was durchaus den Anforderungen der Vernunft entspricht und dem höchsten Zweck der Religion entspricht, nämlich Moralität, d. h. Sittlichkeit, welche sich in unserm Leben durch Wort und That abdrücken, spiegeln muß. Was aber diesen Anforderungen nicht entspricht, kann nicht Zweck der religiösen Glaubens sein, sondern ist zu verwerfen. Diejenigen aber, welche sich von solchem hier angeführten Grundsatz leiten und bestimmen laßen, hat man mit einem aus der lateinischen Sprache abgeleiteten Worte, Rationalisten oder Vernunftgläubige genannt.

Mit Freuden nimmt nun der Vernunftgläubige in der christlichen Lehre das an, was den Anforderungen der Vernunft entspricht, und bekennt un-

Hermanner Volksblatt.

Graf Printing Co., Herausgeber.   Preis: $2.00 per Jahr. $1.50 bei Vorausbezahlung.   Office: Ecke der Vierten und Schiller Straße.

Jahrgang 51   Hermann, Mo., Freitag, den 4. Januar 1907.   Nummer 10

Ein Brief

Harriman und der Vermeßlichung seine gigantischen Plane.

Einstweilen konzentriert Roosevelt sein Feuer auf Harriman's größtes Eisenbahn Unternehmen. Letzterer gibt übrigens in Regierungskreisen als der anerkannte Vertreter der Standard Oil-Cie. Sie strebt nach nichts Geringerem, als die Beherrschung aller Bahntransportationen in dem Lande.

Es braucht bloß somit die Frage auf, ob letztere unter die Botmäßigkeit der Harriman Kombination kommen sollen, falls es der Regierung nicht gelingt, dieses Schach zu thun bevor sie gänzlich aufzulösen.

Das Schicksal der männlichen Braut.

Nahrungsmittel-Gesetze.

Daß Gesetz gegen Verfälschung von Nahrungsmitteln, das nach Neujahr in Kraft tritt, bietet eine Garantie gegen absolut gesundheitschädliche Substanzen...

Deutschland im Bann des Winters.

Die Prosperität Deutschlands.

Sein Glaube.

„Ich glaube an reines Wasser reich Luft und an Mäßigkeit in allen Dingen...

Whisky als Nahrungsmittel fest.

Begnadigung verweigert.

Gouverneur Folk weigert sich in dem Falle von William E. Church...

Entsprungene Zuchthäusler eingefangen.

Die drei Neger, Sam Thompson und Henry Grimm aus St. Louis und Jefferson Eagan...

Neuigkeiten aus Missouri.

— In der Postoffice zu Moberli fiel am Sonntag die 55 Jahre alte Frau des Toldord C. Adams...

— Aus Rom weil seine Frau seit einigen Monaten getrennt von ihm lebte...

— In Poplar Bluff, Butler County, wurde am Samstag während eines Strauhengankes John McCall von John Chenault erschossen...

— In einem Anfall von eifersucht brachte am Donnerstag in St. Louis der 42 Jahre alte Albert Davidson...

— Am Weihnachtstag hat Gouverneur Folk den ein menschlich Modern gefällt und einen Zuchthäusler begnadigt...

— In Creßtal City, Jefferson County, wurde der Hülfssheriff Bert Edwards von Dave Morgan...

— Um J Anderson, der ungetreue Cassirer der National Bank von Kansas City...

— In Cape Girardeau, Bei. Otto Helpart, am Samstag im Alter von 56 Jahren gestorben...

— Der Neujahrssonntag wird diesmal ein 4. Januar stattfinden...

— Der 80jährige Thomas Fanning, ein reicher Grundeigenthümer...

Stellte sich todt

New York, 31 Dez. Als der treunten Väterreich Namens John...

Große Ackerbau-Ausstellung geplant

Der Chicager Handelsverband plant die Abhaltung einer großen Ackerbau-Ausstellung in Chicago...

WINERIES

Hermann was devastated by the enactment of the Volstead Act in 1920. (Prohibition) The wine industry had been a major factor in the community, the hills were covered with grape vines. Very suddenly this was all gone.

In 1847 Michael Poeschel began the production of wine at the Stone Hill Winery. This winery reached a production of 1,250,000 gallons per year and became the third largest wine producer in the world and the second largest in the United States. By 1900 Hermann was exporting more wine than any other town in the United States.

Located on a prominent hill within the town, the Stone Hill cellars themselves are extraordinary. It took over 20 years of digging into the hill to create the labyrinth of underground vaulted cellars, the largest in America.

The cellars were later converted into the production of mushrooms by William Harrison. As the mushroom business was being phased out, Harrison and his wife saw the potential in restoring the cellars so that the production of wine could begin again. The Volstead Act had now been repealed. In 1965 the Harrisons turned the cellars over to Jim and Betty Held and thus started the old industry anew in Hermann. Today the cellars are living museums that produce wine.

Der Weinkeller
[Wine Cellar]

WINERIES

The Hermannhoff Winery is also in full production of fine wines. Ten vaulted cellars provide constant temperature for the aging of the wines. Located at the mouth of Frene Creek, this winery occupies the cellars of the former Kropp Brewery (1852). The Hermannhof also has a smoke-haus where sausages are made daily. Hermann can again boast the best of the wurst makers specialty: bock, blut, brat, knack, leber and sommer—plus baloney, wieners and hams. A wide variety of cheeses is available, some made especially for the Hermannhof. Jim Dierberg is the owner.

Hermann, Missouri **Hermannhof Winery** Founded 1852

Hermann wines were famous for the many gold medals they won both at home and abroad. Today the Hermann wines are again winning medals and production increases every year.

Both wineries are designated as National Historic Properties.

WINERIES

Stone Hill Winery

Old engraving used to advertise Stone Hill Winery

WINERIES

Hermannhof Winery

Old Heckmann Vineyards—as seen from the St. Pauls church parsonage, looking west. The house at the end of the vineyard is the Haney House on Second Street.

RIVER

The setting of Hermann is reminiscent of the Rhine, with the town nestled within an amphitheatre of hills, the foothills of the Ozarks, and the Missouri river at the base. The river brought the first colonists to the shore of the new settlement in 1837 and was to provide a living for many. In the heyday of the steamboat era more than 30 steamboats were either built at the Hermann wharf or purchased and brought in to enter into the freight business. Weekend excursions were family affairs and many a trip was made up the Gasconade river. A clubhouse at Heckmann's Mill provided a sportsman's paradise and the little steamers carried not only local hunters and fishermen, but also from St. Louis and other cities.

By 1920 the railroads were making inroads into the profits the steamboats could expect and finally brought about the total demise of the boats and river traffic.

The Hermann Ferry and Packet Company was a factor in the river business for 50 years. This company was dominated by the Wohlt and Heckmann families, fathers, sons and grandsons. Many a family was supported by the father's work on the steamboats, in the construction of the boats and in the handling of the river freight. The River Memorial at the Missouri river bridge is a memorial to these river men who contributed their skills to the opening of the farm areas along the Gasconade and Missouri rivers. The bronze plaques around the base record their names: Wohlt, Heckmann, Kirchner, Galatas, Baecker, Scharnhorst, Staude, German, Smith and Ruediger. John Bohlken, while not a river man himself, was the designer and builder of several of these local steamboats. The 9-foot pilot wheel of the str. John Heckmann is all that remains of the largest steamboat ever built at Hermann. The str. John Heckmann, built in 1920 was lost in an ice breakup in 1929. The six illustrated narrative panels inside the memorial tell the history of this period in Hermann's history.

Today the Missouri river flows quietly along most of the
year, rampaging during flood times. Occasional tows go by and
commercial fishermen bring in a few fish, but the golden days of
the steamboats were lost to the railroads.

A Sunday excursion on the Steamer Peerless, 1894

The Steamer August Wohlt loaded with wheat, at the Hermann landing 1909

PORT OF HERMANN

The Port of Hermann at high water—down at Kallmeyers Bluff. Shown are, left to right: Government boat, the str. John Heckmann, the str. Hermann and the mv. Loutre Island leaving shore.

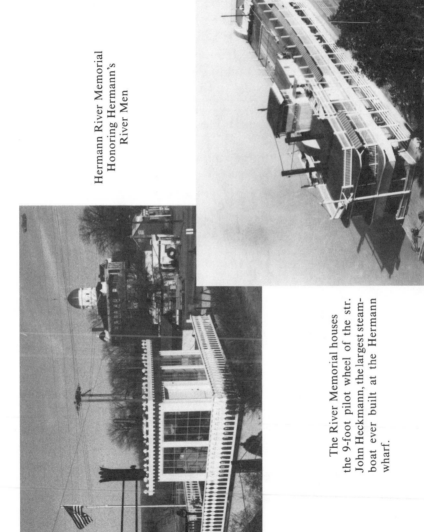

Hermann River Memorial
Honoring Hermann's
River Men

The River Memorial houses the 9-foot pilot wheel of the str. John Heckmann, the largest steamboat ever built at the Hermann wharf.

SCENIC REGIONAL LIBRARY

One of the very first projects of the new settlement was the establishment of a school and shortly thereafter, the beginning of a school library. By the mid-1940's the members of The Guild, a service organization, decided that a public library was needed. Books were collected and the first library was established in an upstairs room of the old Fire House on Market Street. Later a move was made to the little building diagonally across from the German School and ultimately to the German School itself. By 1972 the Hermann Library became a part of the Scenic Regional Library. This added the circulation of a much larger quantity of books by making all books available for the tri-county area, Gasconade, Franklin and Warren. The Scenic Regional also provides a Bookmobile for service to outlying areas.

**Historic
Reiff House**

**1st Missouri Bank
Drive-In**

INDUSTRY

The most stable industry employing a large number of people is the Florsheim Shoe Company. The shoe factory has been a dependable source of income for the longest period of time for the citizens of Hermann. Different brand names have appeared over the years (Peter's, International). The new shoe factory building is on West 16th Street.

The "old" shoe factory building now houses Handi-Pac Inc. a toy manufacturing plant that produces Stevens toys and allied products.

Hermann has an industrial park at the eastern city limits. The first company to build a factory there was Hawthorne, Inc. Hawthorne manufactures canvas products.

A number of smaller factories produce a variety of products. The House of Metal Enclosures and Home, Inc., on West 9th both manufacture metal products and Blanke Plastics, Inc., produces a line of plastic items. Bevco Company, Inc., on Jefferson manufactures Coca Cola distributing machines for export.

Riverbluff Industries, Inc. at 133 E. 9th, is the sheltered workshop for the area. Riverbluff contracts for various hand manufacturing and finishing products.

**Historic Schlender House
Clayton Federal Savings**

MAIFEST

Maifest
Hostesses

Below:
The Hungry Five
at
German School

MAIFEST

The
Loehnig
Family

Below:
The
Wurstjaegers

TOURISM

Little did the early colonists dream that the setting of their instant town would prove to be of commercial value. The street grid laid down in Philadelphia was hardly appropriate to an area of steep hills and streams. yet, that very grid resulted in the pattern of houses clinging to the hills. Curvilinear streets had not been heard of at that time.

Today, the "Little Germany" or "Rhineland" aspect is a tourist drawing card. Nostalgia is a salable product. Hermann provides a bit of yesterday, a bit of European atmosphere, ethnic foods, wines, entertainment and museums to jog memories. The determination to preserve a culture and a way of life, the ability to find ways to enjoy life was always an attraction to those outside of the community—and often the subject of criticism as was evidenced in the local defiance of the Sunday "blue" laws.

The "Maifest" was originally a celebration of spring, a celebration of the close of school, and largely for the children. When revived by the Brush and Palette Club in 1952 it was an instant tourist attraction. The first "Maifest" weekend with 40,000 visitors strained the facilities to the extreme. Hermann today is better prepared for this annual influx of people. While not up to that first overwhelming number, it is usual for 25,000 to 30,000 visitors to attend. The "Oktoberfest" is a celebration of the end of the wine making and is a somewhat lower key event. The "Oktoberfest" draws approximately the same number of visitors as the "Maifest" but distributed throughout the weekends of the entire month.

The "Maifest" and the "Oktoberfest" are showcases for the talents of local craftsmen and musicians, folk music and folk dancing. Today, Hermann is a place to visit at any time.

The "Bed and Breakfast" idea has caught on in Hermann and along with three motels and numerous restaurants provide for the tourists. During the big events the churches help by serving meals.

When Bek wrote his history in 1907 he made a statement that may be a profound truth and account for the preservation of a way of life. Bek said, "This unwavering adherence to existing conditions, this hesitancy to accept new things, though they be well tried, is a characteristic of Hermann."

On December 12, 1839, Wilhelm Schmoele, president of the Pennsylvania Settlement Society of Philadelphia, dissolved the Society with the words, "Mögen unsere Nachkommen Ursache haben, das Unternehmen ihrer Väter zu segnen!"—"May our descendents have reason to bless the undertaking of their ancestors!"

This simple universal wish deserves to be repeated in both German and English. It is as true in 1984, as this is written, as it was in 1839.

We, the descendents, gratefully extend that blessing to them. May our descendents have cause to do the same in the years to come.

EAST APPROACH

STAEHLY HOUSE

COOPERAG

GERMANN SCHOOL

MENU

ST. PAULS

raft Center

Hermann. Missouri **Hermannhof Winery** Founded 1852